Handbook
for Mortals

Joanne Lynn, MD
Joan Harrold, MD
Janice Lynch Schuster, MFA

SECOND EDITION

Handbook for Mortals

GUIDANCE

FOR PEOPLE

FACING SERIOUS

ILLNESS

OXFORD
UNIVERSITY PRESS

Oxford University Press, Inc., publishes works that further
Oxford University's objective of excellence
in research, scholarship, and education.

Oxford   New York
Auckland   Cape Town   Dar es Salaam   Hong Kong   Karachi
Kuala Lumpur   Madrid   Melbourne   Mexico City   Nairobi
New Delhi   Shanghai   Taipei   Toronto

With offices in
Argentina   Austria   Brazil   Chile   Czech Republic   France   Greece
Guatemala   Hungary   Italy   Japan   Poland   Portugal   Singapore
South Korea   Switzerland   Thailand   Turkey   Ukraine   Vietnam

Published by Oxford University Press, Inc.
198 Madison Avenue, New York, New York 10016
www.oup.com

Oxford is a registered trademark of Oxford University Press

Library of Congress Cataloging-in-Publication Data
Lynn, Joanne, 1951-
Handbook for mortals : guidance for people facing serious illness / Joanne Lynn, Joan Harrold,
Janice Lynch Schuster. — 2nd ed.
p. ; cm.
Rev. ed. of: Handbook for mortals / Joanne Lynn, Joan Harrold, and the Center to Improve
Care of the Dying, George Washington University. 1999.
Includes bibliographical references and index.
ISBN 978-0-19-974456-5 (paper : alk. paper) 1. Catastrophic illness—Popular works.
2. Terminally ill—Popular works. 3. Death—Popular works. 4. Terminal care—Popular works.
I. Harrold, Joan K. II. Schuster, Janice Lynch. III. Handbook for mortals. IV. Title.
[DNLM: 1. Terminal Care—Popular Works. 2. Advance Care Planning—Popular Works.
3. Attitude to Death—Popular Works. 4. Patient Education as Topic—Popular Works.
5. Terminally Ill—psychology—Popular Works. WB 310 L989h 2011]
R726.8.H353 2011
362.17'5—dc22
2010025271

9 8 7 6 5 4 3 2 1
Printed in the United States of America
on acid-free paper

About This Book

Many people have been involved in the writing and editing of this second edition of *Handbook for Mortals*, the original version of which resulted from an extraordinary collaboration of professional caregivers, scholars, and ordinary citizens. The original edition benefited from the insights and comments of more than two hundred people. We remain grateful to them for their contribution. Among us, we have cared for thousands of people who died. Among us also are some well-known scholars in art, literature, and health care research.

This edition owes much to the generosity and support of Altarum Institute, a nonprofit health systems research and consulting institute, which is launching a major initiative to improve care for people living with serious chronic illness associated with aging. The original edition was made possible with funding from the Alfred P. Sloan Foundation of New York City. The Retirement Research Foundation of Chicago, Illinois, supported development of a companion book for health care managers and policymakers, and that simultaneous work enriched this book. The Oxford University Press and especially our editors, Joan Bossert and Abby Gross, have been most supportive, flexible, and efficient. We note with gratitude the guidance and commitment of James Levine, our literary agent. We appreciate the dedication of Les Morgan, who has been instrumental in posting this book on the Web. Thanks also to Larry Beresford for research support. We thank Conor Fowler and Joanna Ng for serving as editorial assistants to this project.

Many colleagues and readers have sent us stories and insights for this book. We are grateful to you for opening your hearts and for reminding us why this work is essential. We invite readers to share by emailing info@medicaring.org. We thank you.

FOR THE FIRST AND SECOND EDITIONS

BASED ON THE COMBINED CONTRIBUTION OF THE FOLLOWING INDIVIDUALS:
Joanne Lynn, M.D., Center to Improve Care of the Dying
Joan K. Harrold, M.D., Hospice of Lancaster County (Lancaster, PA)
Sandra Bertman, Ph.D., University of Massachusetts Medical Center (Worcester, MA)
Gwen Glesmann, Pensaré Design Group, Ltd.
Janice Lynch Schuster, Altarum Institute
Joel D. Smith, Center to Improve Care of the Dying
Mary Ellen Vehlow, Pensaré Design Group, Ltd.
Conor Fowler, University of Maryland, Baltimore County

DRAFTING AND RESEARCH AT GEORGE WASHINGTON UNIVERSITY

Anne Boling	Brian Green	Katalin Roth
Felicia Cohn	Phil Higgins	Mary Ryan
Rachel Duvack	Jill Joseph	Phyllis Schmitz
Janet Heald Forlini	Nicole Makosky	Lisa Spear
Nancy Freeborne	Kristen McNiff	Anne Wilkinson

DRAFTING AND RESEARCH CONTRIBUTORS
Larry Beresford, San Francisco, CA
Rev. Timothy Cherry, Coppell, TX
Rabbi Kenneth L. Cohen, Bethesda, MD
Rev. Hank Dunn, Hospice of Northern Virginia
Marcia Levetown, M.D., Galveston, TX
Cherri McKenzie, McLean, VA
Casey Milne, Resource Connectors, Ltd., Portland, OR
Debra Nichols, M.D., Pittsburgh, PA

LITERARY AND VISUAL IMAGES
Lois LaCivita Nixon, Ph.D., Tampa, FL
Marilyn Field, Ph.D., Washington, DC
Michael Lipson, Ph.D., New York, NY
Ronald Carson, Ph.D., Galveston, TX
Digital CLAY Interactive, Ltd.

FOCUS GROUPS
Barbara Kreling, George Washington University Medical Center
Kyle Anne Kenney, George Washington University Medical Center
Susan W. Morris, Global Exchange, Bethesda, MD

WRITTEN CRITIQUES AND SUGGESTIONS

Janet Abrahm	Harlan Krumholz	Marian Secundy
Robert Arnold	Kristie Martin	Mary Sklencar
Marshall Chin	Kyle Nash	Harold Sox
Ann Armstrong-Dailey	Michael Rich	William Steinberg
Myron Ebersole	Walter Robinson	James Tulsky
Ted Greenwood	Ellen Rooney	Marilyn Webb
Patti Homan	Diane Rule	Doron Weber
Hana Janjigian	Greg Sachs	

ADDITIONAL INFORMATION AND INSIGHT

Susan A. Berger	Patricia Bomba	Denise Brown	Beverly Cummings
Deborah L. Grassman	Karl Lorenz	Christina Puchalski	Charlie Sabatino

Contents

Contents

Foreword

Our ancestors were all too familiar with serious illness and death. Few lived to old age, and death often came suddenly from infections or accidents. Today, science and modern medical technology have given us different expectations. Most of us can look forward to being healthy longer, and we have hope for defeating some of humankind's most terrible diseases. We are fortunate to live in an age of tremendous advances in medicine, but when the inevitable end of life nears, sadly, we usually die of slowly worsening illness, and treatment is complex and intimidating. Often, people who suffer and those who care about them do not know what to expect or how to act.

The time near death can be fruitful and worthwhile, but it is a time when we especially need others. I know from our own family experiences that we can all find meaning by caring for one another, even when illness is severe. I always remember my mother's care of my father and grandfather, memories that have continued to inspire me and my family when we have had to face serious illness and death. And when Jimmy's mother, Miss Lillian, was ill, helping her brought our far-flung family together in ways that still endure.

We often put off what is important in life, and it sometimes takes the shadow of death to make us appreciate that love, family, and faith are things that really matter. The *Handbook for Mortals* will help you explore some deep truths about relationships and values—things we often take for granted until death threatens. If you have not been able to find the words for your anguish, you will find them here. If you feel overwhelmed, you will find support and resources. If you are grieving, you will find comfort. Here, too, you will find many moving and insightful stories and poems.

The *Handbook's* practical information will make you confident in your ability to deal with specific issues such as pain management and decision making. It will give you information and strategies that let you control the things you can manage—and help you recognize those things that you just have to endure. The *Handbook* gives you facts. Just as every new parent welcomes a friendly and authoritative book on baby care, everyone facing serious illness and death will welcome this guide to end-of-life care.

Serious illness and dying now occupy many years of the lives of most of us. Unfortunately, these years are often a time of fear and suffering. But they need not be. Here is the help you need to be sure that these years, whether your own or those of someone you love, are full and rewarding. Here, too, is help to make sure that the time near death is peaceful and comforted. This, indeed, is the *Handbook* that all of us mortals need.

Rosalynn Carter

Introduction

I've always looked to the Bible for stories to guide my life. But no one in the Bible lived like this!
Eighty-two-year-old blind woman with heart and lung failure

If you have picked up this book, you may be trying to find help to live with a chronic illness that may end your life or that of a loved one. You may have just received news about how serious your case is, and you may be feeling anxious and worried, at a loss about what to do next or what to expect, where to turn for help, or how to live with—and despite—illness. You may be trying to figure out how to keep track of many medications and physicians; you may wonder what the future holds or whether you can plan for any of it; you may feel frightened by the uncertainty. You may be seeking answers to questions that range from the practical—such as how to get a wheelchair into your house—to the spiritual—such as why this has happened to you or someone close to you.

Answers to these questions can be hard to find. Unlike the information so readily available to help new parents manage pregnancy and prepare for childbirth, our society has few tools or guideposts to help manage chronic illness and prepare for the end of life. In fact, because modern health care and medicine can keep many of us alive and well for a very long time, most of us have very little firsthand experience with dying. Our parents' and our

It is difficult
to get the news from poems
yet men die miserably every day
for lack
of what is found there.
Hear me out
for I too am concerned
and every man
who wants to die at peace in his bed
besides.

WILLIAM CARLOS WILLIAMS
from "Asphodel, That Greeny Flower"

own generation will likely live for many years with chronic illnesses before eventually dying from them or their complications.

The extraordinary ability of modern medicine to treat so many people successfully, increasing their lifespan dramatically, has sometimes given us a false sense of immortality: We assume that there will always be something to fix what ails us. After all, people with serious chronic illnesses live and work everywhere in our communities. We may not realize that they are, in fact, living with diseases that will eventually kill them, and we certainly don't talk about what it means to be living with such illnesses. Because we often do not notice or acknowledge the presence of serious illness, we have not developed a widely understood and expected set of patterns for living with—and dying from—those illnesses. Indeed, our health care system, our family expectations, our news stories and popular programs, and even our language, have not made sense of the fact that so many of us will live for so long, often for years, with diseases that once killed people quickly.

This book is meant to help you find answers to your questions and to reassure you as you try to map a course through to the end of life. We aim to help you as you face serious illness or death, your own or that of someone you love. By providing practical information for some of the challenges and questions you face, we can help you to feel better prepared for whatever comes next. In many situations, you are likely to discover that your instincts are right and that you are doing exactly what needs to be done. In other situations, you may find new approaches to a problem or resources that can help you through whatever you are experiencing.

The living and the dying

When we talk about people who are "dying," who do we mean? We often speak of the dying as if they were a separate sort of person, in stark contrast to those who are living. Once someone has been labeled as dying, we expect him or her to do certain things—to say good-bye, to make peace with God, to take strong painkillers, to sign up for hospice, to give up the routines and activities of ordinary daily life. Often, talk about the dying makes it seem as though they are a distinct group with different interests, roles, and abilities than everyone else has.

> Death is different from what anyone knows, and luckier.
>
> WALT WHITMAN
> from "Song of Myself"

Characterizing people as living or dying can be misleading. As we age, most of us will experience several serious illnesses. One person might have a heart attack at age sixty, followed by years of progressive heart failure. After later developing diabetes or hypertension, the person may have a stroke and die at age eighty. Is that twenty years of "living with" or "dying from"? Another person might live for two decades with breast cancer. Another might die after two months of pancreatic cancer. Yet another might be slowly disabled by Alzheimer's disease. It is less than clear, isn't it, who is "dying" and who is not? Most of us will live with serious chronic illness, slowly worsening for years before eventually causing death. The timing of death may be quite unpredictable, even when the illness is quite advanced.

Perhaps the classification as "dying" is more like height: Some people are clearly tall and others short, but many more are "in between." Likewise, some people are clearly dying, whereas others appear to be fully healthy, but many are somewhere along that spectrum, in between, living with *and* dying of.

In fact, most of us will die without

experiencing any substantial period of time in which we are seen as "dying" or "terminally ill." Most of us will die after having lived for years with a disease whose complications kill us in the end. We may never sense a change from "living with" to "dying from."

Most of us would not want to have such a clearly marked transition, anyway. People living with serious illness often want to maintain their usual habits and routines for as long as possible. Because they are among the living, they want to be with family and friends, pursue hobbies and interests, go to work (or retire), participate in community life, and generally keep their normal routine. Although illness disrupts our daily lives, it rarely eliminates our desires to live well, to find meaning, and to seek happiness. People living with serious illness usually find that some aspects of daily life continue to bring them pleasure and meaning. Other aspects may assume heightened importance or significance; other things that once seemed important will fall away or seem less urgent. No matter what the experience, how we live with eventually fatal conditions matters.

What you will find here

Recognizing the importance of living with a disease, this book aims to help those who are doing so by offering practical advice, guidance, and information. In writing this book, we have tried to give you straightforward information that will help you understand issues and manage your care. We have focused on giving you the words and questions that will help you talk about issues that trouble you. Perhaps most important, we have tried to share pictures, stories, and quotes that we hope you find helpful, reassuring, comforting, even funny.

Our first few chapters give a general framework about how one might think about the last phase of life. We describe how people might talk to one another during this phase of life about what is important and what isn't, about decisions to be made and postponed. In our work, we have found that the last phase of life can be a time of meaning and growth; it is not time wasted or lost to illness, but time to reflect on one's life, to nurture and appreciate relationships with others, and to seek meaning and purpose. And we discuss the uncertainty and unpredictability of the last phase of life.

Later chapters guide you through practical issues such as having effective conversations with your doctor and other health care professionals, making plans, handling symptoms, stopping treatments, and dealing with the time just before death. The book is designed to be helpful to people living with advanced stages of any illness, but we have included a chapter with advice specific to particular diseases. We also discuss issues surrounding suicide, both because many patients think about suicide and because it is such a widely discussed topic in the news.

We have included two chapters on less common experiences: the dying of children and dying suddenly. Although many people say they would rather die suddenly or die in their sleep, it is a mercy that traumatic and unexpected deaths are less common than they once were. In general, we address the person who is living with serious illness. Throughout the book, the word *you* refers to the reader, the person a doctor would call the "patient," except in later chapters where we speak to survivors. Family members and caregivers will be able to translate much of this information so that

> We got back last night after a wonderful trip. We sang; we cried; we ate and drank some damn good champagne. Best of all, we were able to live outside our lives for a while. Now I'm exhausted and need to rest.
>
> RAUL MUSTELIER, Cancer patient, a few months before his death

it applies to their roles and concerns. We expect that each reader might focus on the sections of the book that are relevant to particular situations, that the reader might skip around from chapter to chapter and skim information. We have tried to include chapter headings, boxes, and quotes that will help you quickly locate information.

Handbook
for Mortals

1

Living with Serious Illness

Trust yourself. You know more than you think you do.
BENJAMIN SPOCK, from Baby and Child Care

Over and over, as they realize that they are facing serious and incurable illness, patients and their families ask doctors and nurses: "What do I do now?" and "What's next?" Often, we really do mean that we have no idea what comes next or what we should—and could—do. What *does* come next? Now that we can live for months or years with diseases that once killed in weeks, we often do not know what to expect—how to live and what to do. What will happen to us? How will our families cope? How can we best prepare? Unless and until we have cared for a person going through this last phase of life, we generally have little practical understanding of the dying process and, other than what we've seen in the movies, very few images of how things could—or should—turn out.

The first thing to tell yourself is that you really *do* know more than you might think—you may not know what to do at this precise moment, but you do know how to cope with and respond to challenges. Living with serious illness and the fact of your own mortality *is* a difficult thing to do, and yet you will manage. Trust yourself; more often than not, you will know what is best for you and what direction you will need to follow. Throughout your life, you have made major decisions, confronted challenges, and figured out what is important to you and how to achieve it. You will now, too.

"I don't want to die in my sleep," you declared. And I said, "Why?" (I'm sure I sounded quite exasperated.) "Well, if I die in my sleep I might miss something."

SARAH L. DELANEY
from *On My Own at 107: Reflections on Life Without Bessie*

This book aims to help. It builds on the belief that people, even very sick or very burdened people, have remarkable spirits, inspiring creativity, the capacity to cope with illness and mortality, and the wonderfully human drive to find experiences that give life its meaning. Despite the fear and anxiety you may feel, you may also find that living with a serious illness can open up an unexpected variety of new possibilities. Although your activities may be constricted by the unpredictability of good and bad days, you may feel free to do those things you put off until *someday*. You may find happiness in the simplest activities—in finishing a woodworking project or playing with a grandchild, in an especially beautiful sunset, or in the changing of the seasons. You may open yourself up to the love and care of those around you, even as you try not to overwhelm them with your needs. You may find deep meaning in the smallest of things, even if you question your faith in the greater powers of the universe.

You may feel overwhelmed. You may feel fearful about what is to come next, what will happen to you, or what will become of your family and friends. No matter your beliefs about what is to come, you will have to face the certainty of your earthly mortality. You will probably find yourself living with much uncertainty. What should you expect as your disease progresses? How and when might you die? What will it be like? How will your family come through this?

Even with this uncertainty, people often find that living with a serious illness proves to be a time of growth, meaning, and healing. Many find, often to their surprise, that the period of time when life may be short is a very precious time. You may be surprised to discover how much you want family and friends to stay near—and how much they want to be with you and to talk. They may want to hear your old stories one more time and to share with you their hopes and dreams and worries. They may look to you for blessings and advice. You and those you love will often look to a shared faith in God, nature, and each other to make some sense of life and death. You may find the opportunity to heal relationships that were torn apart long ago.

Like other times of transition and profound change, this time will not always be comfortable or rewarding. But it can be meaningful to you and to those around you. You may not think that you have taken on a "search for meaning," but that is one thing that most people actually do when dying (though you may say it differently). For some, the search reassures them that they have lived life as well as they could. Others find new insights and make commitments to live the rest of life a little differently. Some want to complete an important life task. Some focus on each day as it comes and work to live as well and as happily as they can.

No matter how you approach the end of your life, your loved ones will remember your experience and use it to shape their own when their time comes. Just as you have modeled other important roles for your family and loved ones—being a parent, or a sibling, being a good citizen or a responsible employee—you are modeling what it is like to die. Others will long remember your experience and may use it to shape how they live near the end of their own lives. It is not a role that anyone would volunteer to play, yet it is very important and often satisfying.

To give you some examples of how the end of life might be, this book is full of people, stories, ideas, and advice to help you find what is meaningful in the final phase of your life. At the same time, this book recognizes that dying can be a time of frustration, fear, poor communication, and physical discomfort. This book offers stories and practical advice on getting through these problems, too. You will find help with managing pain and other symptoms, with talking with your doctor, and with wrestling with some of the difficult issues that may arise.

Am I "living with" or "dying of"?

Those things that people do while dying have a special meaning. Deathbed requests and confessions are particularly powerful. Getting one's affairs in order, taking one last trip, and saying good-byes are especially poignant—and

Things To Do When Time May Be Short

Very Important

- Spend time with people who are important to you.
- Create a legacy for those who care about you. Letters, a tape recording, or a video can be a special gift for your children and grandchildren.
- Call or visit an old friend.
- Tell your story to those who will live on.
- Accept some compliments and gratitude. (Don't make people wait until the funeral!)
- Forgive yourself, and seek to make things right within your own faith.
- Say "I love you," "I'm sorry," "forgive me," and "I forgive you."
- Right old wrongs.
- Take a "last trip" or two (and do it again if time allows).
- Make time for spiritual issues and struggles.
- Say good-bye (or "until we meet again").
- Eventually, be at peace with the end to come, and the uncertainty of when you will die.

Important

- Make plans so that care and treatment will be as close as possible to what you want (see Chapter 10).
- Specifically decide about resuscitation, hospitalization, and, if it might be important, artificial feeding (see Chapter 11).
- Choose someone to make decisions for you if you are too sick to make them for yourself (see Chapter 10).
- Write a will that directs your heirs in what to do with your possessions and how to manage your finances.

ADAPTED WITH PERMISSION FROM IRA BYOCK, *DYING WELL: THE PROSPECT OF GROWTH AT THE END OF LIFE*.

are to be encouraged, even if very difficult to do. Yet, if you don't know when you are "dying," you might miss the opportunity to do these things. And doing them before you are *really* "dying" might seem out of place, premature, even irresponsible!

If our dying is to be meaningful, spiritual, or even just peaceful, it does seem that we should know *when* we are dying. But how will we know? In the

movies, the last minutes are so obvious. Whether hero or villain, profound words and meaningful glances are offered before the eyes close and the last breath escapes from the lips. But if we wait for the obvious in real life, we are likely to miss the chance for any meaningful expressions.

Most of us will die of chronic diseases such as heart disease, cancer, stroke, or dementia. Many will live with these diseases for years before dying of them. Often, your diseases and their related symptoms are treated with medicines and procedures, and all the while you feel mostly well. So when do you stop seeing yourself as "living with" these diseases and start seeing yourself as "dying of" them?

How we die—then and now

A hundred years ago, most adults died quickly from infections or accidents. Although there was not a lot of time for good-byes, there was little doubt when good-byes were appropriate. Now death may not come quickly, but the time for good-byes can pass by without notice. Often, missing this opportunity doesn't arise from the lack of time but from lack of certainty that the time has come. You probably expect that you will either die suddenly (from a heart attack, for example), or be sicker and sicker before you die. With chronic diseases, however, you often experience episodes of being really sick, but in between those episodes, you get along rather well. During any of the really sick times, you could be sick enough to die. But, if you survive several of these episodes, then you hardly know when you are really going to die. Is dying going to be just the end of those really sick times? Will it be something altogether different? If you die during one of the otherwise "well" times, your loved ones may feel as if you died "suddenly," even though you had been "living with" a fatal disease for a long time.

Think of people that you have known who were said to be "dying." Nearly everyone knows someone who has outlived the time a doctor said was left. And nearly everyone knows of someone who believed she had much more time left than she did. Just as we have no guarantee that we can sense when time is short, our doctors cannot be certain, either. In fact, there is no medical definition of what "dying" or "terminal" is or how long before death someone should be considered to be "dying."

> "Am I dead yet?" he asked the nurse.
> "No," she replied.
> He thought for a moment, "How will I know?"
>
> Patient with a serious illness

In one study of nearly ten thousand seriously ill patients in hospitals across the United States, nearly half of the patients died within six months of their enrollment in the study. But the best medical predictions by statistical methods and by the patients' doctors had trouble sorting out who was "dying." One week before death, the average patient still had a 40% chance of living six months. Even on the day before death, the average patient still had a 10% chance of living six months.

Many people have a tough time saying that someone is "dying" if he has a 10% chance of living for a year or more. (We so easily ignore the 90%

chance of "not living.") Being in a group that will have 40% still alive in six months is not even close to being sure that a person is "dying." In general, we do not want to say that someone is "dying" until we are almost 100% certain of death within days or weeks. To do so sounds like giving up on someone we love. We might even feel guilty if we give up on them and they get better.

This leaves us in an awkward position. If we want the end of our lives to be a time of growth, meaning, or even merely comfort, how do we know when that time is? How can you say "good-bye" if you might be living longer? If you have been pursuing all kinds of treatments and technologies that are uncomfortable, how do you know when to let go of these and make different plans for how to spend the end of your life? An old saying calls on us to "live every day as if it were your last." Although this may sound rather grim, especially if you are seriously ill, there is some useful wisdom here. Even though you usually will not know exactly when you will die, you can try to be prepared. Planning is helpful, and practice may make it better. The planning and practice have to be realistic about just how uncertain the timing of death is likely to be.

Practice, practice, practice

If you have episodes of being quite sick, you and your loved ones might look on them as rehearsals. If you had died, what would have been left undone? What good-byes would not have been said? What business would have been left unfinished? What goals would not have been met? You do not have to begin every day anxiously wondering whether it will be your last. But you can take advantage of these rehearsals to be sure that you have done what you most want to do in the time you have.

Planning for uncertainty

If no one can know when you will die, that doesn't really get you "off the hook" in dealing with dying. It just makes the job a little complicated. What would you do if you knew that the army was going to draft you with only a few days' warning, but you did not know when the notice would come? You would probably try to visit family and friends, wrap up business affairs, and write some long letters to leave for loved ones in case you were gone for a long time or were killed. You might also find that you were especially sensitive to the joys of nature and family and especially eager to heal old rifts and wrongs. You can approach your uncertainty about dying in this way.

No one can tell you whether this spring is going to be your last one, but why not rejoice in it anyway? Just because you might live another few years is no excuse not to tape-record (or video-record) some stories and advice for grandchildren or great-grandchildren. Everyone has some rift among family or friends. Just having a serious illness is enough reason to re-establish contact. You don't have to wait until later.

"Wait," you may say, "it will be embarrassing to do all this and then hang on! What if I find my brother and we hug and forgive one another, and then I am still here, weighing on him some years later? Or what if I tell my granddaughter that my mother's silver pin is hers when I die, but I don't die?"

Surely you will see that it is a fine thing to have reconnected as a family and that the heirlooms can wait. The profound sense of impropriety that demands that you die on a schedule and do things in just the right order is really silly. Do things that are important just because you are a mortal who will die someday,

and you know it. You probably cannot put your affairs in order and then live for a few years without some affairs becoming disorderly. Don't worry; this job can be redone periodically.

When you have a serious illness, you may not be able to count on having a short time when you are "dying," when friends and family can gather and say farewells. You may have to take the opportunities that you create to do what is important, despite the uncertainty. It is, after all, better to have told people that you love them more than once than to have missed the opportunity while waiting for just the right moment.

> It's not what you look at that matters, it's what you see.
>
> HENRY DAVID THOREAU

The power of words

The words we use to talk about death and dying make it very hard to talk about death and dying at all. If you try to plan for your death, you are urged not to "talk that way." If you are considering stopping certain treatments, you

---

Talking with a Sick Person

When a family member or friend wants to say:	Try this instead:
Dad, you are going to be just fine.	Dad, are there some things that worry you?
Don't talk like that! You can beat this.	It must be hard to come to terms with all this.
I can't see how anyone can help.	We will be there for you, always.
I just can't talk about this.	I am feeling a little overwhelmed right now. Can we take this up later tonight?
What do the doctors know? You might live forever.	Do you think the doctors are right? How does it seem to you?
Please don't give up. I need you here.	I need you here. I will miss you terribly. But we will get through somehow.
There has to be something more to do.	Let's be sure we get the best of medical treatments, but let's be together when we have done all we can.
Don't be glum. You will get well.	It must be hard. Can I just sit with you for a while?

> We encounter each other in words, words
> spiny or smooth, whispered or declaimed,
> words to consider, reconsider.
>
> We cross dirt roads and highways that mark
> the will of someone and then others, who
>   said,
> "I need to see what's on the other side.
>
> I know there's something better down the
>   road."
> We need to find a place where we are safe.
> We walk into that which we cannot yet see.
>
> ELIZABETH ALEXANDER
> from "Praise Song for the Day"

may be urged not to "give up" or "give in." If you are thinking about whether or not to have resuscitation attempted when your heart stops, you may be asked why you don't want "everything done." In our society, it is more common to hear that someone "is gone," "was lost," "did not make it," "passed away," or "expired" than that he "died."

From all of these phrases, it is obvious that even talking about death is to be avoided, as if the words themselves might somehow steal life and bring death quicker. Words will not hurry death, but they can cast a different light on life. If you are told not to "talk that way" when you are making plans or saying good-byes, remember that you are making plans for very good reasons. Your plans or actions help you to live well, not to die more quickly. If you decide not to use a particular treatment and others tell you not to give up or give in, suggest that you are only giving up one course of action so that you can follow another one. If someone asks if you want "everything done," remind them that you want everything done to treat pain, minimize suffering for you and your family, and enjoy life to its fullest. Certain high-tech, aggressive or burdensome interventions may not be worthwhile if they get in the way of a full life and a peaceful death.

Not particularly interested in dying...

People who are said to be dying often have a lot of living left to do. There is no requirement that someone with a serious illness spend all of his time thinking about how close he may be to death. Although some observers may think that this behavior is some kind of "denial," it is actually healthy to continue to focus on living.

Lynn, Harrold, Lynch Schuster

Feel free to refuse to dwell on the nearness of death. You do not have to talk about dying when you have better things to do. After all, most of us have many roles to fill, dying or not. As husbands and wives, parents and children, friends and colleagues, we work, play, love, and argue. Your interests and concerns do not suddenly disappear because you are ill. In fact, some issues may become much more important to get resolved while you still can. Often you will appreciate ordinary daily life and its stresses and troubles even more.

Patients with fatal illnesses may pursue medical treatments for a variety of conditions. These conditions may or may not be related to their fatal diseases. As one nurse noted, even hospice patients do not usually want to die early from a treatable problem. Prolonging living can go hand-in-hand with accepting the inevitability of dying.

Decisions to make, decisions to wait

In the course of a serious illness, there may be lots of possible pathways. Treatment choices—tube feeding, cardiopulmonary resuscitation, diagnostic tests—are likely to be brought up for discussion and decisions. Almost none of the decisions that you might be called on to make have to be made immediately. Sometimes you need time, experience, and advice to choose a plan.

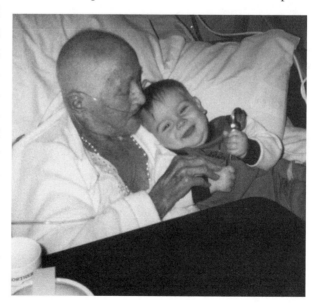

Sometimes the actual plan is less important than what you talk about and who you talk with when you discuss alternatives. Usually the important decisions are not the ones that show up in legal forms. However, one key decision to make involves choosing who should speak for you if you are too sick to let the doctor know what you want for yourself. Often, there is time to make most other decisions. Issues need decisions only if and when certain situations arise, and often only then will you know all the details that could influence your choice.

No one "right way"

There is no one right way to live with or die of a serious illness. It may be more important that you are comfortable with your situation and your choices than that you have made perfect plans. Most of the really wonderful things that happen as time gets short could not have been planned. If you have a trustworthy nurse or doctor and some friends and family who will miss you, all the rest can be quite manageable.

2

Enduring and Changing

Every day something else changes. It's like being on a roller-coaster,
sometimes riding high and then all of a sudden, plunging to the bottom.
Knowing I'm going to die is not as terrifying as the getting there and
wondering how it will happen.
N O R M A, *facing serious illness*

It is little wonder that those who are dying, like Norma, dread the process of dying as much as death itself. At the same time, most people who are dying are struck by the wonder of life: *For everything there is a season, and a time for every matter under heaven: a time to be born, and a time to die* (Ecclesiastes 3:1–2). You may want to fight your illness, or deny it, or do both at different times. You may feel as though you should accept your illness without complaining and simply take whatever comes your way. Or you may be too confused, frightened, or sick to deal with anything for a while. This chapter offers ideas on how to cope and describes how other people came to terms with their illnesses and their fears.

From the time that you learn that you have an illness that is expected to take your life some day, the rhythm of your life changes. When you face a

> Hold fast to time! Guard it, watch over it, every hour, every minute! Unregarded, it slips away, like a lizard, smooth, slippery, faithless. . . . Hold every moment sacred. Give each clarity and meaning, each the weight of your awareness, each its true and due fulfillment.
>
> THOMAS MANN
> from *The Magic Mountain*

serious illness, you also face the challenges, uncertainties, and worries that go along with it. You, and those who care for you, may wonder how you will cope with your life as it changes in so many ways.

One place to start—and, from there, to cope—is to look at your particular situation: What is the nature of the disease? How old are you? What are your relationships with others? How have you dealt with illness in the past? What do you know of dying? Have you cared for someone else who was sick or lost someone you loved? Your experiences are likely to shape your experience at the end of life.

Knowing that your life will have an end brings lots of concerns and questions that may have seemed to be far in the future before. You are not alone in wanting answers to questions such as these:

- How long do I have?
- Where can I find joy in this phase of life?
- How sick will I be?
- Will I be mostly comfortable?
- What will happen to my children? My spouse?
- How long can I keep on working? Do I want to?
- How will I pay for everything?
- Who will help me care for myself?
- Can I stay in my own home?
- Will I be a burden?
- Can I finish the projects that are important to me?

You may feel very troubled, worried, and afraid. You may not know how to express your concerns, what to do, or what to say. The uncertainty and the distress can be just as troubling as other symptoms of your illness. In fact, your emotional state—the stress you are under—can profoundly affect how you feel physically.

At eighty years of age, Norma had lived with congestive heart failure for several years, and although she was weary of her illness, her primary concern was for her elderly husband, who suffered from advanced Parkinson's disease. "I worry about what will happen to him when I'm gone. The children are close by, but they have their own lives, so I have to hang on as long as possible."

Janie, a twenty-eight-year-old suffering from advanced breast cancer, worried about her six-year-old daughter. "This has all happened so fast, and I don't think Lisa understands what's going on. She gets so upset when I can't do things with her. There doesn't seem to be anything that I can do."

A middle-aged corporate executive, Tom, struggled enormously with his declining physical ability, the result of an aggressive lung tumor. "I once managed hundreds of people and everything ran efficiently. I was never sick and now I need help with everything. This can't be happening to me."

Much of the suffering that comes with life-threatening illness arises from overwhelming feelings of loss on all levels of human experience. These feelings can be complicated by the ambivalence that so commonly directs the ebb and flow of emotions in the course of a long illness. Norma longs to be free of her restricted life but is afraid for her spouse. Janie admits that sometimes death seems preferable to the terrible pain she has at times and yet cannot bear to think of her child as motherless. Tom can't imagine a time of "not being." Your life may be a series of ups and downs. When you feel well, you may feel that a mistake has been made and that life will continue uninterrupted. Then, as if on cue, some change occurs, reminding you of your illness.

As troubling as your situation may seem at times, there is reason to be hopeful. Knowing that changes will occur and that anxiety and ambivalence

Enduring and Changing

Rituals to Mark Transitions

Ritual is one way cultures and individuals give meaning and continuity to their lives. You may want to use rituals to mark your changing body and life.

If you are religious, a prayer service can allow you to acknowledge the gift of your body, thank God for the use of it, and symbolically surrender the part(s) no longer useful. This can be healing for the body, the mind, and the spirit. A member of the clergy or a chaplain can help you plan this service.

Another ritual involves making something that is uniquely yours to leave for your children or their children. In a simple ritual, Janie gathered all the photos of herself and, together with her family, reminisced about old times. Afterward, she placed the photos in a small box, requesting that they be put away and not shown again until after she had died. You might go through photos and label them, especially if others will not readily recognize people from the past.

You might make gifts of items that have been special to you or that are significant to members of your family.

These activities are helpful ways to change focus. Physical decline is often inevitable with fatal illness, so dealing with the changes is crucial. By trying to keep a positive view of yourself, you may be better able to endure the changes you experience.

---

will sometimes disrupt your life can also free you to make choices about how you will respond. You may not be able to change the outcome of your illness, but you can decide how you want to react to the emotional and spiritual pain, the anger, the frustration, the losses—the emotional roller-coaster ride you may sometimes experience.

Mourning your losses

The downward spiral of emotion and the roller-coaster feelings are the natural consequence of loss. Like most, you have undoubtedly experienced loss in the past. Perhaps you lost a pet as a child. You might remember the loss of a "first love," or friends left behind when your family moved away.

You will often have lost important relationships through separation, divorce, and death. Now you are confronting the loss of your life, as well as your dreams for the future.

Norma summed it up well. "Death is the least of my worries. I always knew it would happen someday. But it's watching part of me die each day that is so terrifying." She is referring to her succession of physical losses. Your losses may be different. You may not have the energy or spirit to function well as a parent, spouse, or friend. You may not have the strength to work or pursue activities you once enjoyed. You may often want to be alone. Medications may make you very tired. You may be alone because family and friends begin to distance themselves, in part as a way to cope with their own loss. It is then that you will realize that life is propelling you to the finish line over some rough terrain. Can you recover from the changes and disappointments? It is possible to survive the "little deaths" if you are able to mourn your losses as they occur.

> It's terrible to die if you're angry with someone, or if you have a misunderstanding. The person left alive feels guilty, and it's hard for them to grieve for the dead person. Grief is necessary. You have to be able to mourn.
>
> REBECCA BROWN
> from *The Gifts of the Body*

In spite of what our society suggests or well-intentioned friends offer, sadness and mourning are normal, healthy responses to loss. These help us to survive all kinds of troubles so that we can make the necessary adjustments to respond to changes. It's

> When they came to take me
> I wondered – how much
> of a person can be given away
> without being erased?
>
> MYRA SKLAREW
> from "Surgery"

generally easier to mourn for another, and perhaps it feels a bit self-indulgent to mourn for yourself, but letting yourself do so can be healing for your body and your mind. What's especially important is that you find a way to mourn that makes sense to you and ultimately brings you some comfort.

You may find that crying provides the best release, especially when sadness overwhelms you. Far from being a sign of weakness, crying is often an effective way to soften the emotional pain brought on by the changes in your life. Whether you are able to cry and how often depends on whether crying was acceptable when you were growing up; it will depend, too, on your particular temperament and the significance of the loss. The need to grieve for your losses in this way—or in whatever way you are comfortable with—will recur at different times in your illness. Norma, who referred to "little deaths" happening each day, said, "I find that every time my body lets me down or I see myself getting thinner, I become inconsolable. I wish that I could pull the covers over my head and disappear." Crying can be a good way to mourn the "little deaths." Other ways can be just as effective.

Gloria was in her late forties when she was diagnosed with breast cancer, a disease that had killed her mother when Gloria was seventeen. Now, her own children were in grade school, and she needed ways to reassure them about her health while preparing for just how sick treatment would make her. Because chemotherapy would make her hair fall out, she had tried to prepare herself for that eventuality by cutting her luxurious, long black hair. One day, though, while talking to the children about what it would be like to see Mommy bald, she decided to let them cut her hair. She herself had always wondered how it would look cropped, or cut stylishly short. Her daughter was given one side to trim as she pleased. Gloria's husband asked to do the other. In the end, her hair was a little ragged and uneven, not quite professional or stylish—but, for a while, beautiful to Gloria and her family. The love, and the story, are what matter, and what will be remembered.

Seeing yourself more clearly

Seeing yourself and what is important to you more clearly will mean:

- Being honest with yourself.
- Knowing your limitations, but living fully.
- Being open to the lessons and gifts life continues to offer, despite the difficulties of being ill.

Making adjustments in your life will require that you be honest about what you are feeling and experiencing, in both good times and bad. You don't have to hide or be embarrassed by tears, anger, and frustration. A touch of humor may help you cope. Janie would post a sign on the front door, either "Mom's Having a Good Day" or "Mom's Having a Bad Day," depending on her mood. She said, "I guess folks ought to know what to expect when they come to see me. This gives them an out if they're not up to the challenge." Your own challenge is also to be honest with yourself and to live within your limitations, but to live fully within them.

In addition to determination and honesty, be open to what life has to offer now. Tom said, "You know, I never stop being afraid of dying. But I'm more afraid of not living. I've got just so much time, so I have to make the best of it." He started painting again, a hobby he had long ago put aside. It served as a powerful antidote for the depression that haunted him.

No longer able to participate in her regular activities, Janie learned to knit and taught her daughter some simple stitches. Eventually, their "knitting time" became their special time together. Learning new skills or finding renewed pleasure in interests long forgotten can be a wonderful affirmation of your spirit. Tom and Janie would quickly say that it wasn't easy to find their way through the "shadow of the valley of death." They discovered that they had to turn to others who gently helped them see a different direction, nurturing the determination that lay quietly within.

Coping with changes in appearance

Changes in appearance can be devastating because they are so undeniable. Surgical procedures can disrupt your self-image, and weight loss or gain can be difficult to disguise. The effects of medications and treatment can also take a toll on your appearance. Your skin, for example, might become much more pale than usual or have a yellowish cast to it. The hair loss associated with chemotherapy can be especially disturbing.

These physical changes sometimes have a profound effect on how you feel about yourself. Our culture places so much value on "looking your best!" When your health care providers and everyone else around you focus on your body, assessing the effects of illness and treatment, it's not surprising that you may also be preoccupied with your body. Befriend the new face that you see in the mirror. A necessary first step will be to let go of your "old self," or at least of your image of that self.

"Look Good, Feel Better" is a national public service program in the US designed especially to help women adapt to their appearance as it changes with illness and is available in many communities (www.lookgoodfeelbetter. org). Hospitals or other sponsors bring in professional beauticians, cosmetologists, and stylists to advise people on how to wear makeup, turbans, and wigs, not only to minimize changes but to look truly good.

Many people lessen the effect of physical change by changing their wardrobes. If you have lost a great deal of weight, your old clothes may be uncomfortably baggy. If your skin is fragile, certain fabrics may irritate it. Soft cottons, velour, and chenille may feel better than wool and nylon. Clothing can disguise many changes, and makeup and wigs work wonders. Janie had a number of brightly colored loose-fitting robes that she wore frequently because, she said, the colors lifted her spirits and hid what she described as her "bony body."

Taking care of yourself

While you try to live your life fully, making the most of each day, you will need to focus some attention on taking care of yourself. It may seem as though the effort isn't worth it, that you're "too sick" or there "isn't enough time." Your ability to take care of yourself—your appetite, energy level, and fatigue—can be affected by troubling physical symptoms, so getting good and reliable help from your doctor is crucial. You will need to be honest about how you feel and persist in your requests for whatever medication or therapy will be helpful in alleviating these symptoms. In most situations,

Self-Care: The Basics

Just like any other time in your life, try to:

- Eat as well as you can.
- Exercise, within the limits of your disease.
- Get adequate rest.
- Enjoy the time you have.

adequate relief from troublesome physical symptoms is possible. Even though you may slip into despair from time to time, enjoy what you can and maintain your connections with family, friends, and colleagues for as long as possible. Above all, don't give up hope—not the "wishful thinking" variety, but the kind that looks forward to security, comfort, and meaningful time

Self-Care: Part Two

- Ask for help when you need it. Getting assistance in tough times can reduce your experiences of frustration. Tom fought the idea of getting help with his personal care until he realized that trying to do what needed to be done on his own left him with little energy for anything else.
- Identify sources of strength that you can lean on during moments of despair, when the world looks bleak. For some, strength is in religious faith; for others, in nature, or a special friend.
- Find ways to feel useful and focus on interesting or pleasant activities. Distraction is a wonderful way to reduce stress. Music can be comforting, as can a warm bath or shower.
- Reduce your isolation by finding a support group. Living with an eventually fatal illness can be an isolating experience. Within a support group, you might discover friendship, as well as a sensitivity and understanding that are hard to find among people who haven't shared your frustrations, fears, and losses. Support groups allow you to share your thoughts and fears, providing a chance to hear how others find strength and learn new ways of dealing with the changes in their lives. Others, no doubt, will learn from you. Even if you have never been a "group person," joining such a gathering is worth considering.

for you and those you care about. Pick up the pieces of your life and make something good out of them.

Turn to a family member, a trusted friend, or a member of the clergy for support and guidance. Find a support group or trained counselor who can help you explore your options. If you prefer the Internet, books, or libraries, there are some excellent resources that can further guide you (see Chapter 17). The goal is to find a way for you to *live* with—or despite—your illness and dying. Finding your way will help you live on your terms.

If you are in a support group, listen to what others report to be helpful to them. If you are still able to be physically active, continue to exercise. This can be especially helpful if exercise has been a tension reliever in the past. If solitude has brought you peace of mind, spend some time alone. Meditation, listening to relaxation tapes, and guided imagery can be useful, but their effectiveness may depend on whether you are already familiar with such exercises. If you have the time and inclination, ask your doctor to recommend a relaxation class in your community; often, hospitals offer them as community outreach programs. Your faith community might have programs on how to meditate or pray.

Setting realistic goals

It's important to be clear about what you will be able to achieve. Many a noble venture was sabotaged by overly ambitious goals. Sometimes you try far too much, perhaps due to denial, but more often you just don't consider all that is necessary to achieve your goal. You may find it most helpful to set daily goals. Aim for something each day—something modest that has a good chance for success, such as doing a little exercise, performing specific tasks, or making phone calls. Accomplishing goals will do wonders for your self-esteem and can serve as a way to find meaning for yourself.

You may wish to set a much more complex goal, but you will need to be realistic about how you are going to accomplish your objective. Janie decided that she wanted to have a surprise sixtieth birthday party for her mother. Once she realized that the planning would be an enormous task, well beyond her capability, she engaged others (at the suggestion of members of her support group), and the party was a success.

One man decided he wanted to complete his woodworking projects, which had always given him satisfaction. He no longer had the energy to do everything alone, but his wife was able to follow his directions and help complete the projects.

If you are setting long- or short-term goals, flexibility is a valuable ally. It helps if you expect to encounter unexpected challenges. Plans will have to be altered when your energy level is not up to the task or your illness causes an unexpected problem. You may need to shift gears. The disappointment of letting go of your original plan will be somewhat easier to deal with if you can appreciate the pleasure you had in planning something and imagining it done. Just realize that it was good to have made the plans and imagined the outcomes, but then let it go and make new plans within the new possibilities.

> It's so strange, when we become aware that we're talking about a very short period of time together, how the extraordinary becomes ordinary and vice versa. A good meal or a long walk has never meant so much before.
>
> ALAN MARKS, facing death within a few weeks

About relationships

By nature, we are social beings and define ourselves by our relationships: parent, child, spouse, sibling, friend, and so forth. These relationships remain crucial when you are ill. But your illness can improve them or shatter them. How these relationships emerge from this experience will depend on how healthy they were to begin with and how open all those involved are willing to be. Maintaining connections to those you care about is conducive to a feeling of well-being. The practical support that others are willing to give you, along with their love and concern, can be important sources of strength and comfort.

You will probably discover that many people will feel uncomfortable because of their own fears of dying and because of their awkwardness around the subject of illness. They may distance themselves. If you can be open and share your feelings, including your frustrations and your fears, you may give them a way to deal with their own apprehension. Be prepared, though; some people may never want to deal with your illness, and your only options

will be to adapt or to let them go. Over time, you will know those with whom you can be most comfortable, and you can focus your energy on sustaining those relationships for as long as possible. You can avoid offending those in the distance by offering information or sentiments by note, by phone, or through a mutual friend.

If conflict has strained an important relationship, it is worth the effort to try to mend the differences. If you feel inept at attempting this on your own, or if your illness has depleted necessary physical and mental resources, seek the help of your clergy or another professional. There are counselors trained to facilitate discussions aimed at resolving conflict, but anyone with interpersonal and communication skills can probably be of help. Working toward mending rifts among family or friends can be an important gift to those you love, as long as you recognize as well that some relationships are beyond repair.

Norma was able to benefit from just such an intervention. She had long thought her children were indifferent to her and became resentful of their behavior. A social worker from the hospice gathered the family members together. During that time, they realized that most of what divided them was not so terribly important and often was based on misunderstandings. This left the family much closer and more supportive than they ever could have been if things had never been said and sentiments had never been explored. Although your life is ending, those left behind will have memories to sustain—or overwhelm—them. Those memories can often be freed of bitterness.

Life is changing, but . . .

Consider how you can best meet the challenges that await you. Be compassionate toward yourself. Allow yourself to find a measure of joy in your life, despite the sadness you are sure to feel. Extend the same respect, concern, and affection to yourself that you would offer someone else—that will help you live fully while dying.

> It's horrible to watch my body slowly wilt away to nothing. But it's also wonderful because of all the time I get to say good-bye.
>
> MORRIE SCHWARTZ
> from *Tuesdays with Morrie* by Mitch Albom

3
Finding Meaning

You need to know me and my spirit—that I seek meaning in
suffering . . . some days I am able to make meaning of suffering.
STEVEN A. SCHMIDT, from "When You Come Into My Room"

When you have an illness that will eventually cause your death, a door closes on what had seemed a future of endless possibilities. Everything may seem beyond your reach. Things once taken for granted are now uncertain, and new and unfamiliar issues arise. While others go about their activities and the business of the world continues, the road you travel may suddenly seem unfamiliar, its signposts poorly marked. At this crossroads, you are likely to question issues you once felt were settled or that you hadn't really thought of questioning yet.

Hope may be an essential part of the meaning and purpose that form our spirituality. Although hope for recovery may not be realistic, there is still much for which to hope: time with family and friends, time to finish important tasks, comfort to enjoy what is left of your life. One can hope for

---

Spiritual Issues

- Finding renewed meaning and purpose
- Hoping for acceptance and redemption
- Making meaning out of the life you have
- Sharing memories and stories with family and friends
- Creating a legacy
- Experiencing confidence in the love of family and friends
- Expressing gratitude for the life you have had
- Having a new focus on spirituality or religion
- Exploring a changing relationship with God or the universe
- Seeking and finding forgiveness and resolution

---

small things that are part of daily life. Contemplation, through meditation and prayer, may also be important as you make this spiritual journey. You are likely to find yourself transformed by this experience in ways you could not have expected, seeing yourself and the world in a new or different light.

Religion and relationships

Some have said that all religion is about the same thing: death and trying to make sense of it. Indeed, the connection between spirituality and end of life may seem obvious to people who have strong roots in organized religion. Religion gives believers a pathway with clear road signs and expected activities. If you have faith, you may take comfort in the milestones that mark the way, no matter how troubling the journey. If you have been actively addressing spiritual issues throughout life, with or without formal religion, life's last journey may feel like the natural conclusion to a lifelong journey, not requiring new answers.

> My dad always worried, as he got older, that he had no money to leave his children—and in the end he didn't. We always told him that it didn't matter . . . while my father suffered much illness in the last few years of his life, he died secure in the respect and love of his children.
>
> GARA LAMARCHE

But most of us are caught up in the challenges of daily life and arrive near the end of our life's journey with more questions unanswered than we would like. It is helpful to see the spiritual journey at the end of life—despite its challenges and troubles—as an opportunity to learn and grow.

Serious illness often requires an important redefinition of self, because it lets us get beyond the usual "currency" of being worthy, whether that's making money or being a good citizen. Serious illness, like other significant life challenges, forces us to rethink what it is that really matters. Often, we discover that what matters most are relationships with others, with ourselves, and with the world that surrounds us. These are the relationships that may concern you as you approach death and question God or the universe: "Why me? Why now? Why this?" The way you come to answer those questions or understand what is happening to you also shapes your spiritual life.

How do you handle the urgent need to find meaning for yourself in what is soon to be a completed life? First, it helps to see this search for meaning as an important "task" for the end of life. In a sense, this is the valuable opportunity that dying with some forewarning offers: You have the chance to seek and find your own meaning. The fact that most people find this search to be terribly important and rewarding means that it is worth resisting the temptation to spend all your energy on medical treatments or on relatively

unimportant tasks. It is as important to seek space and time for spiritual concerns as it is to seek the right treatment or therapy.

Second, it helps to seek spiritual companions. Perhaps you can talk to your spouse or someone else who is close to you. He or she may be on a spiritual journey, too, and sharing thoughts can help you both along the way. Often, it helps to seek out others who have more experience—including religious advisors, older persons, or groups of people who have taken on these issues together. Perhaps you will find it especially meaningful to share your journey with someone much younger who is not yet driven by a search for meaning but senses its importance.

Third, it may help to think about "letting go." Some things you will let go because your situation demands it; you will know what those things are. You can choose to let go of other things that are really not important to you right now. Doing that may be frightening and freeing at the same time. It may be frightening to realize that you want to let go of things that you used to consider very important. It may be freeing not to be bound by old thoughts and to embrace those things that are meaningful to you now.

Meaning and loss

You are likely to experience many emotions as you recollect aspects of your life, think about accomplishments or disappointments, contemplate what lies ahead, and consider how illness affects who you are. Among the most powerful of these feelings are grief and anger. People with life-threatening illness have to confront their illnesses, their approaching deaths, and all of the losses they must face.

Grief is a normal human reaction to devastating news. Grief will take its time with you—and you must take time with your grief. Some days, it may feel like a tidal wave of emotion, threatening to overwhelm you and knock you off your feet; on other days, you may feel gently rocked on a calm sea.

> When my mother died, I inherited her needlepoint tapestries. When I was a little boy, I used to sit at her feet as she worked on them. Have you ever seen needlepoint from underneath? All I could see was chaos, strands of threads all over, with no seeming purpose. As I grew, I was able to see her work from above. I came to appreciate the patterns, and the need for dark threads as well as bright and gaily colored ones. Life is like that. From our human perspective, we cannot see the whole picture. But we should not despair or feel that there is no purpose. There is meaning and purpose, even for the dark threads, but we cannot see that right away.
>
> RABBI KENNETH L. COHEN

You are likely sometimes to feel very angry at the universe, at God or fate, at your own body or its illness, and at your family and others whom you love. For people who have been taught to worship and revere God, or trust in His will, feelings of anger can be very upsetting. However, as Rabbi Earl Grollman has reminded us, "Don't worry. God can take it." Feeling angry is also a normal human reaction to a life-threatening illness. You may feel that your spirit is subsumed by anger; like grief, this anger can stay with you for a while, but watch for the ways to let it go.

Remember that the intensity of your grief and anger is not likely to last. It will fade over time, although it may flare up and startle you with its strength. Sometimes, people feel as though they are going crazy with grief, that they will never have their lives back, that life will always be clouded by sadness and loss. Recognizing that these feelings are natural can help even while being aware that they usually come and go. If your grief persists and prevents you from living your life, you might talk to your doctor. Some people experience what is called "complicated grief," and working through it may require professional help and care for symptoms that are very much like depression.

Finding your way to finding meaning

He did not say: You will not be troubled, you will not be belabored, you will not be afflicted; but He said: You will not be overcome.

MOTHER JULIAN OF NORWICH

There are many ways of finding meaning and purpose. Sometimes it helps to think about steps to take and categories of things to do. Other times, it helps to have more guidance, such as answers to a list of questions. Perhaps the material in the boxes here will help you when you need a tool of one kind or another. You can find similar tools on the Internet, in books, and from chaplains and clergy who specialize in helping with spiritual journeys and questions.

Chaplains and others who can help

If you are in a hospital, hospice, or palliative care program, a chaplain will usually be available to offer support, prayer, and spiritual guidance. Chaplains are people who have a special commitment, and frequently specialized

Four R's For The Spirit

REMEMBERING. Take time to reflect on your life and its events. What were your accomplishments? What must be left undone? Who influenced you, for better or worse, and whose lives did you influence? Who did you love? Who do you love? What do those relationships mean to you now?

REASSESSING. Take time to see your life as a whole. You may ask what your life really added up to, or who you really were. You might share your thoughts with those who know and love you. Even if you accomplished much in the worldly sense, you may feel you really came up short on doing well with your life. And if life was really tough, you may feel unfairly denied your chances. This is the time to be honest and thoughtful. You are likely to find that you did pretty well, on the whole, and you will probably find ways to forgive yourself and others. Surprisingly, you may even find ways to see and complete important tasks—instructing a grandchild, affirming the goodness of someone who really needs your support, arranging your finances to protect your spouse, or creating something, perhaps needlepoint, woodworking, or fine art.

RECONCILING. Try to be at peace with yourself. You may need to reconcile yourself to not having done the things you always wanted to do. You may need to forgive yourself for your shortcomings or transgressions or to forgive those who hurt or disappointed you. You may need to ask others to forgive you. Reconciliation with your imperfections can help you find peace.

REUNITING. Try to be at peace with those you love. Most of us have had various relationships disrupted over our lifetimes due to death, anger, relocation, and the many forces that push people apart. As serious illness threatens, you may find that it is important to come together with family and friends, when you can, and to have the chance to say farewells. Don't wait too long to try to see that long-estranged sister or son, or even to sit awhile with a friend from long ago. If you believe in a life beyond death, that afterlife might also be where our souls will be reunited with those who have died before us.

There are many ways to find and give meaning to your experience. These are offered as examples of things others have done to heal and grow.

MEDITATING: Meditation is a way to center yourself and your thoughts, to quiet your mind and connect with the Infinite. Recordings can help you learn to meditate; you might also ask the hospice or hospital chaplain or a social worker to help you find ways to meditate.

GATHERING: Gathering with people you love and who are important to you can be enriching to you and to them. One man, told he had but four weeks to live, organized a party and invited his many friends to come. Family and friends made tributes and shared memories and stories. Such gatherings can be surprisingly happy and can give you a chance to say good-bye to people you have enjoyed and loved.

CREATING: Making recordings of stories or memories, sharing your experience with family members and friends, is a wonderful gift to you and your family. By making a tape, a special photo album, or a scrapbook for those you will leave behind, you can help create memories of times you shared. Some people, especially parents, write letters to the children who will survive them.

GIVING: Some cultures and traditions emphasize gift-giving. Native Americans, for instance, give valuable keepsakes to signify the end of life. This ritual allows the giver to show appreciation for the relationship shared.

LEAVING A LEGACY: You can give more than your material treasures to those you love through an "ethical will." Leave a letter or recording sharing your values, hopes, insights, beliefs, and wisdom. Even just tell your story. Your bequest becomes both a cherished memento and a way to continue your good ways.

training, to work with people who are seriously ill. They come from various religious backgrounds but provide care regardless of religious affiliation. They can join you, your family, and your friends for prayer or worship services or for other rites and rituals that honor your faith. They can also help you wrestle with some of the spiritual questions and concerns that you may have. If you would like assistance from a religious leader of your own tradition, a chaplain will work to make that possible. You also may want to invite health care professionals to join you in prayer or ritual; often, they are willing and even happy to do so.

Life Review: How You See Your Life

Take a few minutes, alone and with a piece of paper, to fill in the blanks in the following sentences. Then ask your loved one to take a look at what you've written and perhaps to complete a similar review.

- One of my favorite childhood memories is:
- Words that describe me include:
- One event that had a big effect on my life was:
- One of the most difficult things for me to deal with in my lifetime has been:
- The reason this was so difficult was because:
- What I have learned because of the burdens I have endured is:
- One of the things I am most proud of is:
- One of the things I like best about myself is:
- If I were to live my life over again, something I would change is:
- If I were to live my life over again, something I would *not* change is:
- One of the ways I think I have touched other peoples' lives is:
- One of the things I most want to be remembered for is:
- If I could give one piece of advice to someone it would be:
- Something that would bring me peace right now is:
- Something I want to say to my family/friends is:

Then ask someone else to complete a review of your life again, filling in the blanks.

- My favorite story about my loved one is:
- A memory that always makes me laugh is:
- A favorite story from my childhood about my loved one is:
- A meaningful story my loved one told me about his/her childhood is:
- One of the things I most appreciate about my loved one is:
- One way in which my loved one has touched my life is:
- The difference this has made for my life is:
- A virtue that my loved one has that I want to carry on in my own life is:
- Something I think would bring my loved one peace right now is:
- A hope I have for my loved one right now is:
- Something I want to say to my loved one is:

ADAPTED WITH PERMISSION FROM *PEACE AT LAST: STORIES OF HOPE AND HEALING FOR VETERANS AND THEIR FAMILIES* BY DEBORAH L. GRASSMAN

If you are seeking spiritual help, ask your care team a few questions:

- Do you offer chaplaincy for spiritual care?
- How are chaplains affiliated with you? Are they full-time staff members, contractual employees, or local clergy? Are they board-certified?
- How does the chaplain approach care for people from religious traditions other than his or her own?
- If I have fears, doubts of faith, and other concerns, is the chaplain able to help me talk about them?
- Where does my own religious advisor fit in?
- Can you visit me in my own home?

Some people feel reluctant to talk to chaplains for fear that the chaplain will preach at them or attempt to convert them. This situation should not occur. Chaplains participate in rigorous clinical pastoral education programs, many have board certification, and their desire will be to help you and to offer you comfort and care that is centered in what you believe and value—not to persuade you toward any particular religious faith. Because chaplains have been trained to listen to your concerns, you may find that they are easy to talk to and that you can lean on them to help work out problems or issues that trouble you. Board-certified chaplains must complete at

---

What You Can—And Should—Expect From The Chaplain

You deserve to:

- Tell your story and your concerns to a chaplain who listens to you and hears your concerns.
- Meet with a chaplain who is affiliated with an established religious denomination.
- Understand the person's credentials.
- Maintain control over your care. If a chaplain makes you feel pressured to take a particular direction for medical care, you are probably not working with the right person.
- Work with someone who respects and values you as you are.

- Talk to a chaplain who understands the dynamics of disease and knows how to talk about your illness.
- Be comfortable with the chaplain who listens to you and is not judgmental.

PATRICK MCCOY AND TOM SMITH

least one year of training and also pass a rigorous peer review process. As is true in any profession, credentials are no guarantee of quality. However, people can ask questions of chaplains, such as the level of formal training they have received and their focus on interfaith care. Chaplains will work with people from a variety of religious or spiritual beliefs, including those who are atheists or agnostics.

A religious leader in your own faith is also someone you might turn to for help. Your own community's ministry may have recommendations on how to seek spiritual support and care for end-of-life issues. When you leave the hospital, you may want continued professional support and guidance. Pastoral counselors are well suited to help. Pastoral counselors are individuals who have training in theology or ministry, as well as formal training in counseling and psychology. They can help you and your family work through spiritual concerns, fears, and problems and can counsel those who may be depressed, overwhelmed, and under a great deal of stress. They can help you put issues in perspective. If you are uncomfortable discussing your spirituality with your family, pastoral counselors offer the security and privacy you may need. If you want to bring up spiritual concerns but don't know how, pastoral counselors can help with this, too. Most pastoral counselors accept payments according to a sliding fee scale, so the cost should not be a barrier for you.

> The nearer she came to death, the more, by some perversity of nature, did she enjoy living.
>
> ELLEN GLASGOW
> from *Barren Ground*

Your worship or faith community (meaning your church, synagogue, temple, mosque, or other site) may have prayer support groups and lay ministers. One widespread lay group is called the Stephen Ministry. People from

Finding Meaning

Religious Practices: A Sampler

PRAYER: Most denominations include prayer. Prayer can be formal, that is, recited or read by an individual such as a member of the clergy or congregation, or informal, created spontaneously to give thanks or praise or for specific needs. For some people, meditation and silence are forms of prayer.

READING SACRED TEXTS: Reading sacred texts can be comforting, especially because they can help people to see their experience in the context of their faith and to see that experience as part of a normal relationship with the Divine. For Christians and Jews, this might involve reading the Book of Psalms; for Muslims, it might include the Koran.

CONFESSION: Many religions, including Christianity, Judaism, and Islam, have a form of confession. Catholics often make private confessions to a clergy member, and some other Christians confess directly to God; Jews and Muslims may confess sins to family or in ritual prayers. All who confess do so with the expectation of forgiveness.

ANOINTING: Priests and ministers in many faiths bless the sick by anointing them with sacred oils, often touching them on the forehead, hands, or diseased part of the body. Once called "the last rites," Roman Catholics now receive "the sacrament of the sick," in which communion, confession, and anointing occur. This sacrament, which is considered to be a healing one for the soul, can be received several times during an illness.

RELIGIOUS ARTICLES AND ICONS: For many people, items such as statues, rosaries, medallions, prayer beads, and prayer wheels offer a comforting connection to their beliefs.

your church or congregation may visit you at home or in the hospital, pray and offer sacraments, and provide practical support, such as grocery shopping or respite care for your family. Some communities have prayer support groups that meet to pray together or pray on behalf of specific people facing challenges. People who participate in these groups find them supportive and comforting. In fact, such groups can even be found on the Internet.

You may also find support and comfort through practices such as yoga, relaxation therapy, meditation, healing rituals from other cultures, writing and journal exercises, or spirituality courses offered by local colleges and adult education programs. Ritual and tradition give form and focus to faith and offer strength and support for many people and families. You may find that praying alone or with your family or other caregivers (even if this is not something you have ordinarily done) is comforting. When you have died, shared prayers and rituals will offer a way for people to reconnect with you and the love you shared. In fact, you might think of creating some more family rituals while you are very sick. How do you say good night, how do you say good-bye on a daily basis? Sometimes it makes time seem much more meaningful and orderly if there is some little prayer or another action that marks important times each day.

When I was a preschooler and afraid of the dark, my grandmother—whose house my family lived in—would leave an M&M trail through the house from my bed to hers. I would set forth through the dark house to the night-light of her room. Once I'd eaten one M&M, I could find the courage to search for all of them. My presence in her room always woke her. She would say, "Hello, doll. Dark getting to you?" Then she'd turn back the blankets to make room for me.

It was many years before I believed, as my grandmother often said, that there was nothing in the dark that did not exist in the light. Thirty years later, when a doctor told my grandmother she had widespread kidney cancer, we found ourselves in a different dark.

My mind played with the terrible anticipation of her absence, the way your tongue cannot avoid exploring the pain of a fever sore. I wanted to become some sort of light for Grandmom, to blaze a trail from the dark room of her illness, fear, and pain to the light of my love and the love of our family. But as the days wore on and cancer

took her life piecemeal, I clung to what little we could still share. I held her hand and stroked her head. In those last weeks, I sang for her: hymns, spirituals, Irish drinking songs, sea chanteys, "Amazing Grace," and "Lord of the Dance." When I tired of singing, I read aloud: trashy novels, magazine articles, newspaper stories, reports I was writing. The content was meaningless, but my voice calmed her.

During the last two weeks of her life, she taught me to pray the rosary, a ritual I had somehow missed, despite years of Sunday school and church. To her, the rosary was a daily obligation. To me, it was an odd and time-consuming task from an archaic world. She could no longer recite the entire litany aloud and could not keep count of the prayers she had said. She wanted someone to pray it for her. I volunteered.

The rosary connected her to her faith and to the past, her parents, her brothers and sisters. Praying with her as she lay dying became a way to connect and comfort us. I had to concentrate to say each of the prayers on each of the beads, moving them through my grandmother's sore fingers. I could think of nothing else. When we began to pray, it was usually in the midst of her pain and my fear. But by the time we had come full circle, she would be asleep and peaceful, and I would have forgotten, for a while at least, how awful things were.

On the last day of my grandmother's life, she lay in pain in a hospital bed. I could not see the world without her in it, yet I could not bear the world that kept her now. I wanted to say something to release her, and so began to whisper names. I named my sisters and brother, my cousins, my grandmother's siblings; I named streets we had lived on, countries where she had traveled. I whispered and prayed that her tight grip on this life could be loosened by memories of how much she had loved this life and how well she was loved.

She began to grow calmer later that evening. A priest suggested we play a tape of Gregorian chants for her, and the music stilled her. I went home. My mother and sister were just falling to sleep in her room when she stirred for a moment, sighed, and was gone.

As I drove back to the hospital that night, my loss was as overwhelming as the darkness had been

> When we walk to the edge of all the light we have and take a step into the darkness of the unknown, we must believe one of two things will happen—there will be something solid for us to stand upon, or we will be taught to fly.
>
> ANONYMOUS

thirty years earlier, on my M&M trail to safety. I made that late-night drive to the hospital because I so desperately needed to see my grandmother at peace; it was her turn, again, to guide me through the night, to teach me to walk without fear into the hard moments of this life. I held her rosary beads in my hand and let them rattle against the steering wheel.—Janice Lynch Schuster

4
Helping Family Make Decisions and Give Care

[This story] is worth telling because it reminds us that successful dying, like successful child-rearing, depends on family.

ROBERT J. SAMUELSON

The person dying is almost never the only person who is affected by illness and death—family and dear friends are, too. Often, entire families and even whole communities become involved in caring for a very sick person—and mourn for that person's suffering and death. Many of the people you love, and who love you, will feel your losses and their own. While experiencing these powerful and difficult emotions, families and loved ones will have to make practical decisions and support one another while they support you. They will have to make arrangements to help you. Some employers, for example, recognize the stresses you and your family face as illness progresses and offer time off or flexible scheduling for patient and caregivers to manage doctors' visits and other appointments. Your faith community might recognize what your family is going through and offer help, support, and comfort.

However, not everyone will recognize that families and close friends are really "going through it" with a seriously ill or dying person.

Caregivers may experience quite a range of emotions, from deep joy and gratitude to profound frustration. Denise Brown has structured the evolution of a caregiver in six stages, starting with the point at which someone is just thinking about caring for another adult and concluding with the death of that person and the end of the caregiving relationship. You and your caregivers may not pass through all stages, or follow them in exact order, but you may find that the categories give you some useful language and structure. The main thing is that specific actions match each stage to make caregiving a little easier for everyone. This chapter focuses on stories and advice about family togetherness, caregiving, and the roles caregivers play.

Six Stages of Caregiving

Thinking about these stages of caregiving often helps caregivers to see where they are in the process—and what the future might hold. Not everyone experiences each of these steps, and the steps may not be in order or clear-cut.

Stage 1. "I may need to help." A person realizes that a family member or dear friend is likely to need help and begins to wonder about his or her role in providing such help. This is the time to look up services, such as those offered in the United States by your local Office on Aging, as well as Internet resources and advice from the clinical care providers, to get an idea of what might be needed and what services might help.

Stage 2: "I am beginning to help." The caregiver's help is needed only a few hours each week to manage intermittent chores or activities. Ask about services that are available to help the patient and family, especially if the caregiver has to be unavailable for a time.

Stage 3: "I am helping." Now the patient needs more intensive help. Sometimes, the patient is enrolled in a hospice, home care, or palliative care program. The primary caregiver needs to learn many skills, including how to protect his or her own time and agenda. Anticipating the likelihood of substantial time and effort being needed, the primary caregiver also needs to learn to encourage offers of help. This may mean recruiting other family members and friends to provide regular and reliable help. It also means scheduling others to provide respite care when the primary caregiver needs to be elsewhere or take a break.

Stage 4: "I am still helping!" Caregivers are often surprised to find that they are still at work for many years and through many challenges. The commitment is often surprising to the caregiver and to others in the family and the circle of friends. Endurance and a positive outlook are highly valued character traits when caregiving goes on for years. Many states or localities have at least some provision for respite care to give the caregiver a little time off, and often other family and friends are willing to help in order to give the main caregiver a break.

Stage 5: "My role is changing." The patient's health may be declining, and the caregiver may have to provide substantial hands-on care, ranging from bed baths to assisting with toileting. The patient may be in the final phase of life and, more than anything else, may really need a family member or close friend to be present. The caregiver often needs to allow himself or herself to mourn and grieve losses—including the loss of the patient's health and former abilities.

Stage 6: "My caregiving has ended." The patient has died, and the caregivers are left to treasure their memories, find comfort in the time shared, and continue with their own lives. Or the patient has entered a nursing home or another setting that relieves the caregiver of much of the work. This may be a confusing time, because often the caregiver expects relief and simply to pick up life where it left off, but instead caregivers may find themselves adrift without the demanding work that structured their lives. Even going back to work or other important activities may not make life feel "back to normal." Long-term caregivers who were close to the patient are often quite bereft when the patient dies and merit special attention from loved ones and professionals.

—ADAPTED WITH PERMISSION FROM DENISE BROWN, WWW.CAREGIVING.COM

In addition, people who have been caregivers often have learned skills and gained wisdom that are valuable to their families and communities, and they may also have important insights that can help guide improvement in the services that clinicians provide and for which the government pays. Seasoned caregivers can find important work in reforming care or guiding friends and family.

Families deciding together

Serious illness can suddenly make families come together more closely than they have been for years. Adult brothers and sisters, for example, may have to understand what is happening to their parents and to make decisions, not only with parents in terms of illness but also with each other. In some situations, it is clear who will decide and how. In others, many people are involved, available options generate much friction, and those involved have too little practice in making decisions together.

> Even the kids say they wouldn't have missed being there, caring for Pops, for the world.
>
> —DAUGHTER OF A CANCER PATIENT

Think about how your family operates. Could you make a decision about a business matter without one of you being in charge? Are you still arguing about what to have for lunch when it's time for supper? Do you tolerate one another's shortcomings and habits or annoy one another endlessly?

You, your family, and your closest friends can plan for how all will work together. Perhaps it will be best for you to make many decisions in advance, or to name one person who has final authority. Perhaps it will be fine to let things go, trusting loved ones to work it out. However, checking out understandings with one another is usually a useful thing to do ahead of time. Let your family learn what it is to pull together on some early issues that really don't matter too much. Rather than letting the first family decision be something really shattering, such as selling a family home or stopping a ventilator, start by figuring out how to make decisions on which doctor to stay with or whether to take a trip.

Reflect a bit on how the family is working and how it will do without you. Encourage family to think about who will fill some of your roles. If you are the one who always remembers birthdays or hosts the celebrations, encourage others to start doing these things. Offer advice, or share your address book or calendar. If they say that this is uncomfortable while you are still alive, be glad to keep the role while you can, but be gently forceful about passing it along, too. Remember, in many situations, these are the same children who were so eager to learn to drive, to get a place of their own, or to

> I kept thinking she was somewhere in between the world of the living and the world of the dead. I watched. I am trying to remember if I was any help to her. I think I just had to be there.
>
> —DEBRA FOULKS, Caregiver to her dying mother

stop calling if they were going to be late. They *can* take on some of your responsibilities now, when you are ready for them to do so.

Sometimes families really are too distant—emotionally or geographically—to work together. Then the best you can hope for is some camaraderie and contact. Of course, some people have no family or friends at all and rely on volunteers and health care providers. At times, families get into fierce disagreements over the treatment of a seriously ill family member. All too often, a caregiving family member ends up pitted against a distant family member who may feel guilty for not "being there."

If there has been a history of feeling left out, arguing, or providing an unfair share of caregiving, there can be deep resentment, too. Often, family members need some perspective. Starting a conversation with a prayer, if that is in your tradition, may set the right tone of humility, service, and working together for something important. Turning to a professional for help is also worthwhile. A chaplain, social worker, nurse, or doctor may be able to listen and advise. It is not as important to be "right" as much as it is to be dedicated, helpful, and forgiving.

Family caregiving

> One after the other they came bounding up the steps to lean and kiss her. I saw her hand, the half-clenched one, fold over each bent back in turn, pressing, and it struck me in a way it had never struck me before (why not? why ever not?) how touching and attractive the gestures of human affection are.
>
> —WALLACE STEGNER
> from *Crossing to Safety*

Watch for serious, long-term illness on television, in the newspapers, in the movies—it is almost never there. One would think that America is made up of vigorous young people who never grow old and never get sick (except for emergencies and short hospital stays). Very few people realize that almost all of us will have a substantial period of our adult lives in which we are responsible for the care of an older relative who cannot live independently any more. At any one time, one in four American households is providing unpaid care to an older relative for a substantial period of time. The family that does not have this experience is rare.

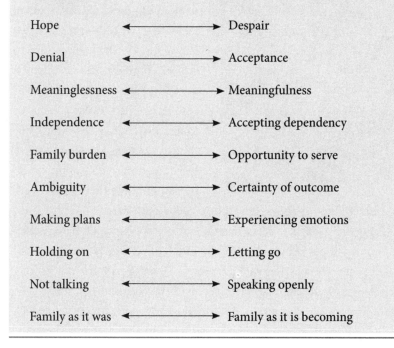

Tensions for Families

You will often find your family torn by emotions. People deal with tension in all sorts of ways, but it often helps just to be able to name the problem. Note that the best "place" to be is not usually at one end or the other, but somewhere in between.

Hope	⟷	Despair
Denial	⟷	Acceptance
Meaninglessness	⟷	Meaningfulness
Independence	⟷	Accepting dependency
Family burden	⟷	Opportunity to serve
Ambiguity	⟷	Certainty of outcome
Making plans	⟷	Experiencing emotions
Holding on	⟷	Letting go
Not talking	⟷	Speaking openly
Family as it was	⟷	Family as it is becoming

Caring for children is expected and fairly predictable in onset and in completion. However, the need to care for a sick elderly relative often happens unexpectedly and is ordinarily an unpredictable way of life. Caring for one another, though, is probably the defining trait of families. How families provide this care challenges creativity, commitment, and virtue. In some families, taking care of one's relatives is absolutely expected, and people can take on extraordinary burdens to honor that expectation. Other families, however, find it to be sufficient just to keep in touch with one another and to oversee paid caregivers.

Eight of every ten family caregivers (of a person with an illness) are women, and most will be caregivers for more than ten years. No matter what

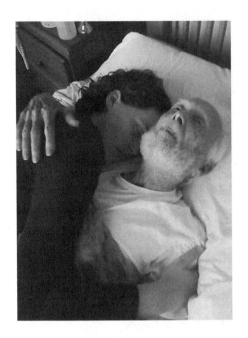

her social class or her status in the workplace, it is the woman who will most often be expected (in her own eyes as well as by others) to take physical care of family members who are sick or dependent. Even now, having a lot of daughters and daughters-in-law still gives one the best chance to stay in a family home when one is dying. In the past, having sons (unless married) did not help one much. This may be changing, though, as men are living longer, learning more skills in homemaking, and finding themselves in situations in which they are the best people to provide the care.

Caregiving often starts rather abruptly—after a stroke or a fall, for example. After an initial period of adjustment, which often comes with no guidance or help, caregiving settles into a pattern of coping with the day-to-day. It can become easier to arrange for breaks and support in this stable phase, but only if the caregiver is encouraged to do so. Caregiving for someone who is seriously ill often ends with death, though it might also change if the dying person is admitted to a nursing home, hospital, or inpatient hospice. Although the caregiver may feel relief when this work is done, the end of hands-on caregiving is another major life transition that is often quite uncomfortable and disorienting.

Caregiving for a dependent adult is often most difficult for the person needing the care. If the person is mentally sharp, he or she is often quite offended by dependency and troubled to impose a burden on younger relatives or a spouse. Needing help with private matters such as using the toilet and dressing can feel terribly humiliating. If the person is not mentally sharp, he or she may be upset by needing help but may be unable even to understand why there is no choice.

Caregivers have problems of their own. They can wear themselves out, cut themselves off from most of the world, and sidetrack their own

> ### Rest and Renewal for Caregivers
>
> - Hire a sitter or an aide for occasional events or on a regular basis.
> - Arrange for other family members to provide care.
> - Use a nursing home or assisted living facility for planned vacations of a week or more.
> - Use a day hospital or adult day care.
> - Get a family member to take on some responsibility regularly—paying bills, taking your loved one for a daily walk, giving a bath and shampoo.
> - Adjust expectations—let the housework go a bit, for example.
> - Meditate or pray.
> - For some people, nursing homes or assisted living facilities are the best option.

career prospects. They can lose their jobs, their health insurance, and their economic security. So why do they do it? Because it is such an essential part of what it is to be a caring person—to take care of those who are part of your family or those you love.

If the person facing dying is likely to have only a few months and the caregiver works for a large employer (or an understanding one), caregivers can often arrange to return to their jobs when caregiving ends. However, if the caregiver had a job with a small employer or needs to take a longer and more uncertain amount of time off, it can be very hard to be sure of having a job waiting. Likewise, caregivers may have health problems and have problems getting insurance if they leave their jobs. In the United States, the federal Family and Medical Leave Act may ensure that a caregiver has some unpaid leave to care for a sick family member—be sure to ask. Often, other workers are willing to pool some extra leave, or an employer will make some accommodation if you ask.

Because most caregivers have had little experience with friends or family who have provided similar care, many feel they need a "road map," some sense of what it is to do this job well. This guidance is made even more difficult by the fact that many of these caregivers also must keep working in conventional employment. Juggling multiple obligations becomes the routine for most.

How can a caregiver know whether things are out of control?

Having some perspective is one of the hardest things for caregivers to do. Caregiving is often stressful, yet people do it and do it well. On the other hand, some caregivers really do stay in situations in which they cannot possibly give good care, in which the needs are overwhelming. When the caregiver notes that the patient is suffering from some inattention, such as having skin problems or being overmedicated, the caregiver should be concerned. A trouble sign is the caregiver becoming more and more exhausted, depressed, angry, and unable to sleep or eat well. Another is the caregiver's feeling that there is no other person to call on for help. The terrible isolation that many caregivers feel is both a symptom of an overwhelmed caregiver and a sign of a community that does not know how to care for one another.

What to do when the caregiver is overwhelmed

Few caregivers maintain their connections with the rest of the community. Often, just re-establishing some relationships helps. If the caregiver was active in a church or social organization or has a fairly stable neighborhood, these friends will often be eager to help if someone just gives them permission and encouragement. Isolation can really sap caregivers' self-esteem and their ability to reach out for help. If at all possible, join some sort of support group and get together with people who are "in the same boat." Even if it is necessary to hire a sitter for a few hours or bargain with a neighbor for help, caregivers should try hard to get a break and get out in the world.

Help for the Caregivers

- Ask the doctors and nurses: What will the patient need? Who can help? How does one become a good caregiver?
- Consult a social worker or case manager, especially to understand Medicare and Medicaid rules and what facilities and services might be available.
- Use a support group. Even if a caregiver is a little uncertain about meeting with others, she or he should try it a few times. Most people find it enormously helpful to hear how others have met challenges and to share stories with others who have really "been there."
- Get information from the relevant national organizations. All kinds of good information is posted on the Internet, and a librarian can help you get it if you don't have access. Some groups also have toll-free phone numbers (see Chapter 17).
- Contact a local hospital or hospice to locate support groups and special services that they might have for people who face similar challenges.
- Do some research—in the library or on the Internet—in getting second opinions. Try to become something of an expert on the particular illnesses affecting your family.
- Call on family and friends—don't do it all alone.

ADAPTED FROM ROSALYNN CARTER WITH SUSAN K. GOLANT, *HELPING YOURSELF HELP OTHERS*

How does a caregiver find support groups?

Ask around. Check listings in the local newspaper. Try the patient's doctor, nurse, and social worker. Try hospitals, hospices, and nursing homes in the area. Call national organizations to ask how to contact a local chapter. In the United States, check with the local Area Agency on Aging, which may have a list of a variety of services for the elderly; those services are often available to younger persons, also. Call the patient's church or other religious institution or others that are nearby even if they are not associated with your religious tradition. A support group at any church or synagogue is usually quite welcoming to persons of all faiths. Then try it out a few times. If you don't find it supportive, move along and try something else. Some people find a great deal of support by joining Internet chats or participating in online blogs. If you do this, be cautious—it is hard to know whether the information being given is honest or accurate or to know exactly whom are you are talking to. You might want to check with some of the organizations listed in Chapter 17; many sponsor reputable interactive online programs.

Is it possible to help from a distance?

If your family does not live nearby, they may be unable to help with day-to-day caregiving tasks—but they will still want to help and be present for you. Long-distance caregivers find that they can offer different kinds of support and help, from making visits to relieve the primary caregiver to helping with financial management and bill paying. On a visit, a long-distance caregiver may want to accompany you to a doctor's appointment, giving him or her a chance to learn more about your condition, how it is changing, and what your wishes and preferences are. Because long-distance caregivers do not see the day-to-day reality of your situation, they may notice changes—and pick up on needs—that a daily caregiver does not. Depending on the long-distance caregiver's strengths, she might be able to help in managing routine tasks that have just come to be too much, such as hiring home health aides or doing the shopping. Although a long-distance caregiver cannot be physically present, you may appreciate the support and help she has to offer—and she may appreciate being able to help you in some way. As with direct caregiving, long-distance caregiving is a way to show support, concern, and compassion.

Is there anything good about caregiving?

Yes! Many family caregivers say it is the toughest job they ever had and the most rewarding. Dedicating oneself to an elderly relative or spouse certainly affirms your virtue and good character. Family caregiving usually saves the family money, too. Round-the-clock service by an aide in the US would cost upward of $100,000 per year. Even more important, caregiving often helps reorient a household around matters of enduring value, such as faith, prayer, and love, rather than the material issues that often dominate home life. Once the dependent person dies, caregivers generally are more confident that they have "done well." They have "been there" and know what the person went through, and they know that they, the caregivers, were loyal and trustworthy and kind.

5

Getting the Help You Need

And that's just the point: we will have another month like this—and then how many more? . . . How many hundreds, how many thousands this month; how many "next months" will there be? How much of that is our "copay"? I know I'm not supposed to be thinking about money in a crisis like this, but where will we get the money?

ROBERT STINSON, from *The Long Dying of Baby Andrew*

Most people want to be well informed about things that are important in their lives, but it is very difficult to know everything you need to know about the kinds of health care you might need. Coping with a serious illness, our own or a loved one's, causes a lot of anxiety and confusion. This can be made worse by a health care system that is really a mix of disconnected groups, plans, services, and professionals. If what you need is a little help for a short amount of time, you might have difficulty finding such a program. At another time, when you need extensive care for a long time, that may be hard to find, too. Paying for those services can be confusing, especially if you are eligible for multiple kinds of benefits—from the government, your private insurance company, and others. It is important that you understand enough to obtain the most appropriate services. Here are some strategies you can use to help the system work better for you.

How to find help and advice

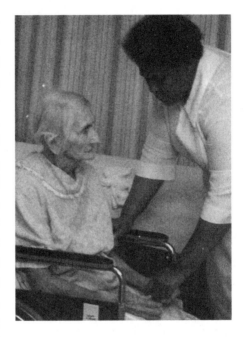

Ask a lot of questions—of everyone! The art of getting the information you need is to ask questions of different people who have a variety of expertise and experience. Here are some examples. Talk to doctors, nurses, social workers, friends, neighbors, priests, pastors, and rabbis. Call your local churches, hospitals, hospices, and civic or volunteer service organizations. Call your city, county, or state government officials. Talk to people who have gone through similar experiences. Join a support group. Tell them your story. Ask your questions, but also be willing to listen to thoughts, ideas, and suggestions that may not have occurred to you.

The Internet may prove to be a treasure trove for you, with information on everything from online support groups for family caregivers to programs that help you coordinate care from a distance. With websites, remember that many are run by groups that are looking for new business or by people with little interest in medical facts or clinical evidence. Be sure you check out the reputation of anyone running a website before divulging anything about yourself on the site. One good way to access reputable and useful sites is to go through Growth House (www.growthhouse.org), a California-based organization that reviews the organizations which it recommends to visitors. You can also find reliable and accurate information on the many websites run by the United States government and on sites managed by major charities; some important ones are listed in the resources section beginning on page 244.

Getting the help of a care manager

In the United States, Area Agencies on Aging or various individual professionals or companies may be able to provide you with a care manager (sometimes called a "case manager" or a "navigator"). Sometimes your health care system or insurance company provides this service. You may want to consult a care manager early on to make plans and coordinate care. This person is usually a nurse or social worker who helps to coordinate services in your home. For example, if your family members live far away, you may choose to hire a care manager to help hire persons to provide care in your home. The care manager will visit your home, or at least interview you at length, and find out what your specific needs are. A care manager, for instance, could arrange for you to hire one aide to help with laundry and cooking and another aide to help you with personal care, including bathing, dressing, and eating. She could assess whether you might need special equipment in your home, such as a shower chair or a raised toilet seat.

> Without outside help, our attempt at caring for our parents would have been misguided and poor but wrapped in the best of intentions.
>
> A FAMILY MEMBER

A good care manager will also help you adjust to having a paid household worker. Many people find having a household employee to be anxiety-provoking, and you may need someone experienced to talk it over with. The cost of a care manager varies, sometimes depending on your income. You may need to consult a care manager only once or twice, and some good advice at the beginning may well save anxiety and money in the long run.

Getting your wishes followed at home

Most doctors, nurses, and others in the medical world are focused on curing disease, or at least trying to stop it in its tracks. Although cure is a worthy goal when it can be achieved, the high-tech treatments that are commonly used may not be what is most helpful or desirable at this stage in your life, and they may take energy and effort that you would rather use on other things. There are some steps you can take to be sure that your caregivers follow your directions (see also Chapter 10).

- Whenever possible, decide in advance when you would call emergency services (911 or other number for an ambulance).
- If there are times not to call emergency services, know what to do instead.
- Talk with your doctor about what kinds of symptoms or sudden changes you might expect with your illness.
- Get the medications you might need for a sudden problem in advance, and keep them in a place that's easy to find (but safe from children).
- Have important phone numbers by the telephone with instructions about who to call and when.
- Keep an up-to-date list of your medications (name, dose, route, and timing), illnesses, and symptoms in a designated place.
- Review your instructions with caregivers and your medications with your doctor often.

When you have help in your home

If family or friends are distant or not available to help, you may find that you rely on paid caregivers, such as home health aides or chore aides, to help around your house or apartment. You may find that their schedules vary and that you cannot count on seeing the same person every day or even every week. You need to think through what it is that really matters to you in their work and their relationship with you and be prepared to choose agencies or personnel on that basis. You can't spend your energies on frustrations with hired workers!

Sometimes, a hired home caregiver comes to be your close friend, but often they will never know you well enough to understand what you hope for in life and in dying. It is important to place a simple set of instructions near all phones and review them with all caregivers. Here are two contrasting examples:

Instructions About Jane Smith

DO NOT CALL 911!
If I die, I do not wish to have CPR (resuscitation) or go to the hospital (see my bracelet).
I do want a comfortable, natural death.
Call John Smith at 555-1212.
Call my physician at 555-1010.
The funeral home number is 555-1111.

OR

Instructions About Mary Doe

I expect to live a long time, despite age and illness.
If I collapse, call 911.
Call my physician at 555-0101.
Call my friend Jane Smith at 555-2121.
They will know what to do.

Whether your caregiver is paid or is a friend or family member, there is information that he or she will need to know. Once again, ask nurses and support group members who have cared for others as to what will make it easier to give good care. In the United States, call the National Caregiving Foundation for information, support, and a caregiver's support kit (www.caregivingfoundation.org or call 1-800-930-1357).

What to do when things don't go well

When things seem out of control, try to find a sympathetic person who knows the care system well and who can help you see new perspectives and creative solutions. If you feel that you or someone you love is being treated poorly, you will probably have to find the energy and thoughtfulness to complain effectively. Hospitals and health care providers are not unfeeling or unwilling to honor your wishes—although it may sometimes seem that they are. It may help you to recognize that problems are often the result of systems and procedures designed to cure disease or, at the very least, prolong life. If you can imagine yourself in the doctor or nurse's place, you might be better able to state your concerns constructively, without creating tension and hard feelings.

When you complain, try not to just "take it out" on whoever is closest. Probably the person who has to be persuaded that something is wrong is not nearby. Find out who supervises the services you find troubling. Then set a time to talk with that person. Write down the key facts to remind you of the things that will make the person see just how important the problem is. If you don't find a satisfying response, call the government agency that licenses the provider.

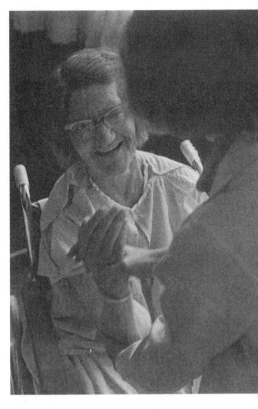

Mistreatment: what to do if anyone suspects mistreatment or neglect

Caring for another adult, especially someone with whom the caregiver has long had a difficult relationship or whose care is particularly overwhelming and stressful, can be more difficult than most people imagine or anticipate. In some cases, caregivers may—inadvertently or intentionally—wind up mistreating a loved one. In some cases, older adults may not realize that they have become unable to care for themselves. In both cases, mistreatment or neglect can take many forms, including emotional, psychological, physical, and financial. By being alert to signs of mistreatment or neglect, anyone can recognize when a person who is elderly or ill is in harm's way, perhaps at the hands of a paid caregiver or because a friend or family member needs respite

Getting the Help You Need

and relief from caregiving. Signs that the situation may be deteriorating include the following.

- Bruises, pressure marks, broken bones, abrasions, and burns, especially if repeated, may indicate physical mistreatment.
- Unexplained withdrawal from normal activities, a sudden change in alertness, and unusual depression may indicate emotional abuse.
- Sudden impoverishment may be the result of financial exploitation.
- Bedsores, unattended medical needs, poor hygiene, and unusual, unexplained weight loss may indicate neglect.
- Caregiver behavior such as belittling, threats, and lies may reflect verbal or emotional abuse.
- Strained and tense relationships and frequent arguments between the caregiver and the patient may indicate mistreatment.

Medical problems can also cause these situations. So any observer, including the patient, should raise their concerns immediately with the patient's physician, who should respond in a way that safeguards the patient without inappropriately disrupting the relationship with the caregiver. In addition, any observer can and should report potential mistreatment to the patient's local office of adult protective services or the equivalent.

Self-neglect describes situations in which people put themselves at risk, often because they have a disorder that impairs memory or judgment. They may be struggling with a chronic disease. Deciding where to draw the line between a person's freedom to live as he or she chooses and self-neglect can be hard. Signs that it may be time to intervene include:

- Hoarding (e.g., food, newspapers)
- Failure to take essential medications or failure to seek medical treatment when necessary
- Leaving a burning stove unattended
- Poor hygiene
- Not wearing clothing that is suitable to the weather
- Inability to attend to housekeeping
- Easily persuaded to trust strangers and vulnerable to their suggestions

When no one helps, the individual is at risk for further harm. In these cases, again, talk to the patient's doctor or the adult protective services in your area for instructions on what to do next.

A guide to settings and services

Hospitals

What is a hospital? The traditional hospital is a health care institution that has an organized staff, inpatient care, surgery and diagnostic testing equipment, and nursing services. Generally, hospitals are designed to provide aggressive and curative medical services. Because we are most familiar with hospitals, they might be the first place that we would turn to in an emergency. But a hospital might not be the appropriate place for particular situations. Although the hospital usually provides good emergency and rescue care and life-prolonging treatments, hospitals may not be the best place to get good symptom relief and care planning. As with any important decision, the first thing is to think about what matters to you now and to discuss your choices with your family and doctor. Many people find that there comes a time when the patient is "too sick" to benefit from hospital care. At that point, if there are alternatives, it is better not to take on the risks of infection, falls, and confusion that occur in hospitals.

The ways that doctors and hospitals are paid for the services that they provide create gaps when you need care over an extended period or at the end of life. Most often, doctors are trained to treat illness within a medical services system that generally pays well for definite treatments such as surgery but does not pay well for counseling or adjusting medications. If the questions you have are medical, such as about medication for pain, calling your doctor is the best option. If the questions are about how to pay for services or plan for care, asking advice from a social worker or a care manager from a home care agency or another setting may be the better choice.

Intensive Care

Critical care units for heart disease, surgery, brain injuries, or just overwhelming illness are very special settings. Most patients are so sick that they

> ... we need to find hope in other ways, more realistic ways, than in the pursuit of elusive and danger-filled cures. . . . Hope should be redefined. Some of my sickest patients have taught me of the varieties of hope that can come when death is certain.
>
> SHERWIN B. NULAND

require all manner of tubes and treatments. It can be quite intimidating. Try to find a few identifiable people—your nurse, for example—and have one of them tell you how the system works. You will usually find that the processes around you make sense, once you have a "translator."

Hospice and Palliative Care

Many organizations have the words "hospice" and "palliative care" in their titles, but what does that mean? Unlike a hospital, which is an actual building in which medical services are provided, "hospice" is more of a concept or a description of a type of care. Some communities do have hospices that care for patients in designated facilities, but the majority of hospice care in the United States is provided to patients and families in their own homes, whether that be a private residence or a nursing home. Hospice care emphasizes physical comfort, pain relief, and symptom management and addresses the patient's spiritual, psychological, social, and financial needs. Bereavement care for the family is also an integral part of hospice care.

Palliative medicine is a medical discipline that, like hospice, focuses on caring for the entire person: physical, emotional, spiritual, and psychological. Some doctors may be "board certified" in palliative medicine, which means that they have received additional training in how to provide it. Like hospice, palliative care can be provided in many different settings. Some palliative care units, for example, are based in hospitals and have beds set aside for palliative care patients. Other hospitals have what is called a consult program. Your doctor (or you) can ask for a palliative medicine consultation. Then the palliative care team will review your diagnosis and care and make recommendations on how to change or improve any elements of that care that do not seem to be working for you. Through the consult, you might be referred to a hospice program, or you might be referred to the hospital's own palliative care unit or program, or you might just have the benefit of better medication or care plan suggestions.

Palliative and hospice care require an interdisciplinary approach. This means that the doctor works with a team of other professionals, including nurses, social workers, chaplains, respiratory and physical therapists, nutritionists, and anyone else who can ease the symptoms associated with chronic illness and the end of life. The team suggests and negotiates a treatment plan that works for you and your family.

Although many large hospitals and Veterans Affairs hospitals have palliative care programs, most smaller hospitals do not. Palliative medicine is a rapidly growing field, and the availability of palliative care programs is likely to increase. For now, you can check with your hospital to find out if it offers such a program or, if not, whether there are hospice programs or palliative care physicians in the area whom you might consult to help address problems and formulate a care plan.

Hospice programs in the United States care for about a million patients each year, most of whom use the services for less than a month. Most patients suffering from chronic conditions cannot use hospice services except for a consultation. Under current rules, a patient must be expected to have less than six months to live before most insurance, including Medicare, will cover hospice care. Patients who might want hospice service and who believe they qualify should not assume that a doctor will automatically refer them to hospice at the right time. It is often up to patients and families to ask questions and take an active role in defining what kind of care fits them best. Doctors usually cannot reliably predict who will die within a six-month period. (See Chapter 1, Living with Serious Illness.) Hospice programs often admit patients, such as those with heart disease or dementia, whose prognosis is less clear or certain but who can benefit from the kinds of services hospice and palliative care can offer. Hospice services vary substantially among different programs in the same area, so you or your family may need to interview more than one hospice program to negotiate the services you need.

Long-Term Care

Long-term care often means a nursing home or other facility. But long-term care can also describe a type of care, rather than an actual place. Long-term care is the range of health, personal care, social, and housing services provided to people who are unable to care for themselves independently for many

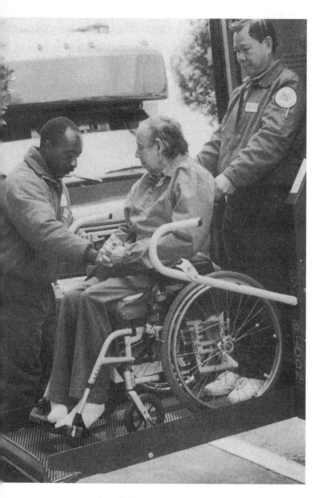

months as a result of chronic illness or mental or physical disability. Not all individuals will require the highly skilled, intensive care that some nursing homes provide. Many can remain fairly independent and may only need assistance with a few activities of daily living. These activities could include a range of things, such as help bathing, getting in and out of bed, or with other daily functions, such as grocery shopping, housekeeping, and balancing a checkbook. Some may prefer to remain in their homes and receive services there. With the advances made in technology, this option is becoming more available, even to individuals who may require intravenous or nutritional therapies. A care manager, home care nurse, or, in the United States, the Area Agency on Aging, can help answer any other questions that you might have about the different kinds of facilities and services in your area.

Finding the services that fit your needs can be difficult. Information will be your best tool. Start with asking your doctor. Although many doctors don't really have much experience working with nursing homes and home care, they at least know the organization's reputation. Doctors can also help work out a description of what services you probably need now and in the near future.

Home Health Services

Home health care can help for a short time during recovery from an illness or a procedure, or it can be a long-term arrangement that provides an alternative to institutional care. These services aim at allowing individuals to remain at home and be independent. Advances in technology have also directly expanded the capabilities of home health care services, which now can provide intravenous medications and devices that can circumvent disabilities. Home health agencies provide skilled home care services through physicians, nurses, therapists, social workers, and homemakers whom they recruit and supervise. Home care aide

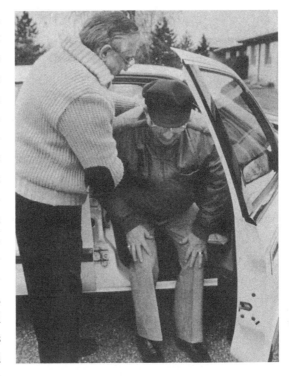

agencies provide more informal assistance, such as meal preparation, bathing, dressing, and housekeeping. Many other types of organizations and agencies provide home care services to clients and their families.

Ask your physician or social worker what kinds of services would benefit you and your family. Be aware that some services are licensed and regulated and others are not.

In the United States, Medicare will cover some home health services. To qualify, the person must be confined to the home (with a few exceptions), require part-time intermittent nursing care or physical or speech therapy, and have specific services ordered by a physician. The rules and coverage for other home-based services are complex, and you and your caregiver may need to expect some variation in answers to your questions.

Adult Day Services

Adult day care programs combine personal services and light medical and nursing care in a "center" that is used daily or a few days each week. Such centers are typically open long hours during the day so that family members can work and raise children. Adult day care centers can provide important support to family caregivers and enrichment to patients.

Generally there are two types of adult day services. One is more informal, with no legal requirements, required activities for the clients, or staff qualifications. These "social day care centers" are funded through private payments.

"Medical adult day care," in contrast, is regulated, licensed, and often paid for by government insurance. The center can be freestanding or affiliated with a nursing home or a hospital. Participants are similar to those usually found in a nursing home. This service allows people with mild to moderate dementia, chronic physical problems, or other conditions requiring daytime care to live at home because the daily burden of care is reduced for their family caregivers. Licensure is mandated, along with requirements for certain services, including transportation to and from the facility, medical monitoring, group activities, and medication administration. In the United States, one program offering these services is PACE, the Program of All-Inclusive Care of the Elderly.

Providers sometimes specialize in specific conditions. For example, there are day programs for people with AIDS or multiple sclerosis. Others offer special rehabilitation services, such as occupational therapy, intravenous therapy, speech therapy, and wound care. Clients may need these services for just a month or two, and day care can be a good alternative to the more expensive and restrictive care one could receive in a nursing home.

Subacute Care

Subacute care focuses on care right after a serious illness in a hospital, when you still need complicated medications or physical therapy while recovering. Nursing facilities provide hospital-like medical services to seriously ill patients of all ages. Generally, the individual's condition is such that the treatment does not depend heavily on high-technology monitoring or complex diagnostic procedures.

In the United States, subacute care facilities are usually reimbursed by Medicare or other insurance. Subacute facilities are usually licensed as nursing homes or rehabilitation centers, not hospitals.

Based on a Scandinavian and Dutch model for senior living, assisted living first emerged in America during the mid-1980s. Assisted living combines housing, personal services, and light medical or nursing care in an environment that promotes maximum individual independence, privacy, and choice. Clients can receive help with personal activities, including eating, dressing, and bathing, as well as meal preparation, laundry, housekeeping, recreation, and transportation. Although assisted living customers may be too frail to live alone, they are too healthy to need most of the nursing services provided in a nursing facility. Assisted living residences typically do not provide twenty-four-hour skilled nursing services but do help with daily tasks. The "typical" assisted living customer is an eighty-six-year-old woman who is mobile but needs assistance with bathing and housekeeping. Whether proprietary or nonprofit, assisted living residences in the United States serve mostly a private-pay clientele.

Between forty thousand and sixty-five thousand assisted living residences house up to one million people in the United States. Customers stay in assisted living residences an average of thirty-four months. Elderly people leave assisted living residences mostly because they need more extensive services.

Getting the help you need

When you are living with a serious, chronic condition, there are days when just getting through your usual routine can seem overwhelming. You and your family need to remember that help can be found, although you may have to do some legwork to find resources in your own community that you can afford or that your insurance will cover. Look to friends, neighbors, civic and faith organizations, and your local hospital for resources. Many organizations have support groups around the country (and online), and you or your family might find comfort and guidance by participating in one of these.

In some countries the "district nurse" or the locality's aging services are reliable and effective. In the United States, the Area Agency on Aging is always present and at least keeps lists of services. But the situations in different localities and in each family vary so much that you often really can't avoid having to do some exploration to figure out what will work best for you. The experience of living with a serious illness can be very isolating, yet if you are able to connect with others in similar situations, you may find the friendship and support you need during this time.

6

Talking with Your Doctor

When the doctor asks, "How are you?" and you say, "Fine," the doctor thinks he has gathered clinical facts, while you think you have been polite.
MOTHER OF A CHILD WITH CANCER

It isn't easy to talk about disease and dying. Talking specifically about your own dying is harder and more important to do. Sometimes talking about it is hard because you don't know the words to use. That isn't your failure—our society doesn't have the words and shared stories that would make it natural to talk of death and dying. Sometimes it is hard to talk about your own dying because you are afraid to learn what might happen next. You might fear that if you talk about something bad, you will cause it to happen. Even if you know this "magical thinking" is illogical, it can still keep you from talking and asking important questions.

When you put something into words, sometimes it feels more "real" than if you hadn't mentioned it. However, the future may seem less threatening when you name and describe it. Until then, your thoughts and feelings may be too vague to confront and manage.

Found

It is the long, slow unwrapping
of the last great package
the unraveling, the uncovering, the
understanding that the package is us,
all of the artifice, all of the conceit, all
of the painstakingly built-up
resistance to the world
undone, unhealed, until we remain at last
unmasked, pure, the essence of who
we are in that one eternal moment of passage.

For you, Perdita, whose very name means
"lost"
they gather here, in your house, mindful
of your presence after-the-fact;
your children and grandchildren
mourn their own loss of you, but
I smile at the photographs which,
in death, you have returned
to many of us, your friends and confidants,
and wonder if the universe isn't better off
for your presence, now, in it.

JAMIE BROWN

Of course, you might be afraid of what kind of response you will get when you speak of dying, pain, and fear of what is likely to happen to you. Although doctors are supposed to take care of sick and dying patients, you might be afraid your doctor will think you are "giving up" and give up on you, too. But it is not "giving up" or being overly anxious to ask questions. "What is likely to happen to me?" "What treatments are available, and how might they help me?" "What do I do if my pain gets worse?" "What will happen to me as I die?" You can talk with your doctor and get information that will help you live more comfortably day to day. You can also improve the care you get by talking to your doctor about the issues that affect you.

There is no "right" way to talk with your doctor—there are only ways that work for you. And they don't always work perfectly, either. When the lines of communication get crossed, despite your best efforts, it's okay to try something different. You can also shrug and say "oh, well" and see if the next conversation is better, especially if you and your doctor have usually had a good rapport. However, you can do some things that increase the likelihood that your conversations will be successful.

Know what you should expect from your doctor (or physician's assistant or nurse practitioner)

When you are living with a serious illness, your relationship with your doctor becomes especially important. You should feel confident about that relationship, and you should know what you can expect. If you have many doctors, then you should identify one as your *primary doctor*. This is the doctor you call for emergencies, medication changes, new or changing symptoms, and even to clarify what other doctors may have told you. This doctor may be any of the doctors that you have. If you expect one of your specialists to fill this role, you should explicitly ask the doctor if he or she will do so. Many specialists expect to limit themselves to advising family practitioners, general practitioners, and internists. Other specialists, however, are prepared

to be the primary doctor who will provide treatment and see you through the frequent changes, complications, and treatments of a chronic, severe disease. Sometimes a nurse, nurse practitioner, or physician's assistant will be your "primary doctor." Throughout this book—and throughout health care—these professionals function very much like doctors, and we use the term *doctor* for all.

Only you can decide whether a doctor has a sufficiently pleasing personality, comforting bedside manner, and respect for you and your time to have a good relationship. In fact, writing down what characteristics are important to you can help you choose a doctor (see p. 74). Other expectations are universal; your doctor should be competent, dependable, and have a professional demeanor. Your doctor should also have reliable coverage "after hours." It is a real advantage if the covering doctor knows you, also, or has your record.

Competence can be judged in several ways. You can ask if the doctor is board certified in her specialty or look for her in medical specialty directories found on many websites. Doctors who are board certified have had additional training and passed an examination in their fields of medicine. You can ask how much experience your doctor has in caring for patients who lived and died with your disease, and you can ask how those deaths went. You want a doctor who is proud of service to dying patients. In addition, you should consider your previous experiences with

Questions Worth Asking: What Can We Expect

Although it is hard to talk about what to expect, knowing what comes next can reassure you about the future. During early visits with the doctor, you may want to ask specific questions about what to expect, based on your situation. These questions might be useful:

What usually happens to people who have this disease? What kinds of complications do they face?

How long do people usually live with this illness? What kinds of treatment do they need along the way?

How do people with this illness die?

What is the best that I can reasonably hope for?

What is the worst that I am likely to face?

What kinds of medical problems might come up suddenly? How can I plan to manage them?

How does this illness and its treatment usually affect family members?

When something new arises, ask, "Does this change what I can expect?"

---

the doctor, as well as opinions of friends or other doctors who referred you to her.

Dependability includes many different things. Your phone calls should be returned in a timely fashion by someone who can reasonably be expected to answer your questions. Dependability also means that getting information about yourself and your situation should be easy. Test results should be relayed to you promptly and in a professional manner. That may mean a phone call or a mailed note, but not an uncertain wait. Ask your doctor how you can expect to get this kind of information and how long it usually takes for different tests to be completed. If you are told, "We only call you if the results are abnormal," then you may be in for days of uncertainty that fades but doesn't completely disappear. If the "no news is good news" approach does not satisfy you, ask how arrangements can be made to notify you when results become available, or ask when you should call for the results. Some practices now communicate at least routine results, appointments, and answers to questions by e-mail.

Your doctor should be professional in all aspects of your relationship. That doesn't preclude a genuine friendship. It does mean that your medical information and personal concerns are kept confidential by the doctor and staff. It means that your care is not shaped by the doctor's self-interest. Your doctor should have a way to handle emergencies at any hour, and the doctors providing services when your doctor is unavailable should know something about you and be able to get to your records quickly. Your doctor should know a great deal about the capabilities of the hospitals, hospices, home care agencies, nursing homes, and other services in your community. If your doctor provides services only in the hospital or only out of the hospital, she should be familiar with the "other part" and share records promptly.

You may want to have a family member or friend come with you for doctor's visits. Sometimes the doctor will have you sign a form that authorizes a family member or friend to learn details about your medical situation that would otherwise be kept private. Having a caregiver accompany you may be a good idea in some situations, especially if you feel overwhelmed or too sick to be able to process all of the information the doctor is likely to give you. Your companion can take notes as the doctor answers your questions. If you need some private time with the doctor, mention this to your companion, and ask him to wait in the waiting room for a few minutes.

The person accompanying a patient on a doctor's visit needs to understand the role he is to play. The patient may not want that person to ask or answer questions for her, for example. However, the person accompanying someone who has Alzheimer's disease or dementia may have to be the patient's spokesperson. In that case, the caregiver role may also be to gather information and make decisions about care and treatment.

Your doctor should also accommodate reasonable requests to stay in touch with your family. For example, a particular family member could be called before the patient leaves after an examination or consultation.

Choosing a Doctor

If you are looking for a new doctor, decide which qualities are important to you. Ask family members, friends, and other health care professionals for the names of doctors they recommend. Then find out the answers to some important questions.

- Is the doctor accepting new patients?
- Is the doctor in a group practice?
- What days and times does the doctor see patients?
- How far in advance do I have to make appointments?
- How fast can I be seen if something happens that scares me? Who will likely see me then?
- Can the office do simple urine and blood tests?
- Who takes care of patients after hours or when my doctor is away?
- Does the covering doctor have access to my records?
- Is the office located close enough to be a comfortable trip?
- Which hospital does the doctor admit patients to?
- Does the doctor see patients at home? In nursing homes? Assisted living? Hospice?
- Does the doctor see patients in the hospital, or does a "hospitalist" take over? If a hospitalist, do they share records and consult together?
- Does the doctor accept my insurance or health plan?

Call the office of each doctor you are considering, tell them that you are looking for a new doctor, and ask the relevant questions. Also, ask if the doctor has introductory visits available for people who want to meet before deciding on a doctor. If so, ask what you should bring with you to such a meeting and what the fee will be. When you know you have a serious illness, mention it and be sure that the practice has substantial familiarity with that illness.

When you visit a doctor's office for the first time, don't wait until you meet the doctor to begin forming your impressions. Take note of how attentive the office staff is to patients, how long you and other patients wait, how long the phone rings before it is answered, how organized everyone seems to be, and how easy it appears to be to arrange payment and follow-up appointments.

Also, pay attention to see whether other patients' personal information is handled quietly or is discussed loudly enough for everyone to know why they called. A beautiful waiting room is nice, but it can't substitute for polite, professional care from the staff.

ADAPTED FROM *TALKING WITH YOUR DOCTOR: A GUIDE FOR OLDER PEOPLE* BY THE NATIONAL INSTITUTE ON AGING

Getting the most out of each visit with your doctor

You can prepare for your visit in a way that helps you get the information you need—and manage the information you get.

Prepare a List of Questions and Concerns That You Want to Discuss

This should include any new or changed symptoms that you have experienced since your last visit. It should also include any major changes or stresses in your life, such as changes in your living arrangements, difficulties getting your medicines, or the death of a loved one. Number the items on the list so you know which are the most important to talk about.

Consider Bringing a Family Member or Friend to Help You

You may need only moral support or company in the waiting room. You may forget to ask something important (especially if you didn't put it on your list!). You may wait longer than usual and feel too tired to drive yourself home. If you get test results or treatment recommendations, it is helpful to have someone there to help you remember or write down many of the details of what was said.

Bring All of Your Medicines or a List of All of Your Medicines and Symptoms

Although you may think your doctor knows everything you are taking, sometimes things get left out of the record. This happens often when a patient is being seen by more than one doctor and information about test results or new medications hasn't gotten from one doctor to the other yet. Bring any vitamins, nutritional supplements, or herbal medicines you are taking, too. Although these usually do not require a prescription, they can still interact with other medicines. You may also want to write down a list of symptoms you have been experiencing. If you have a pain diary, bring it along.

Set Your Priorities for the Doctor's Time

At the beginning of the visit ask, "How much time do you have for me today?" Then address the issues on your list, beginning with the most important one. If you are not going to cover everything on the list in the time available, ask, "Next time, how can I get 30 minutes (or whatever you need) to talk about the concerns I have that we don't have time for today?" This lets the doctor know that you have more concerns and that you are aware of the time constraints he may be facing.

Be Honest

Telling the doctor what you think he wants to hear will not help him to help you. It is natural to want to seem to be improving, sometimes for your own well-being and other times to feel like a "good" patient. But misleading information will result in less than the best therapy and support for you.

Be Honest About Your Priorities

It is often easier for doctors and patients to talk about medicines and treatments than it is to talk about what else is happening in the course of an eventually fatal illness. Do not be afraid to say, "We have talked a lot about the side effects and the schedule for the next round of chemotherapy. I really want to know what it means that there is almost no change in the tumor."

Ask Questions

If you have questions about anything your doctor says, ask! Ask what unfamiliar words mean, why you need a certain test, or what to expect from a new medicine. Ask what new treatments and medicines are supposed to do to help you and how likely it is that they will do what they are supposed to do. Ask whether the therapy being recommended is supposed to treat symptoms or prolong life or both. Ask what side effects you might experience. Ask what is likely to happen to you if you do not try the therapy. Do not hesitate to ask about the cost if that is of concern to you.

Take Notes

Be sure to bring pencil or pen and paper to record the doctor's answers to your questions. You can assign this task to whomever comes with you if note taking is hard for you or if you want to concentrate on talking to the doctor.

Repeat What the Doctor Tells You—In Your Own Words

Nothing tells you or your doctor what you think he said better than to repeat it in your own words. "If I understood what you just said, then I should increase my pain medicine from two pills to three every 12 hours, and I should call back day after tomorrow if that doesn't help." This allows you to uncover and correct any misunderstandings.

Make Contingency Plans

Doctors can't predict every symptom or complication that you might experience, but they should be able to tell you the major ones. And the ones you already have may change over time. Ask the doctor what to expect and what to do if you have a problem. Do you take more medicine? Do you call the office? What if it is 3 A.M.? Asking these questions and planning in advance can save you frantic trips to the emergency room when you have a problem.

Talking with your doctor—special situations

At different times during your illness, you are likely to have different kinds of conversations with your doctor. Some might fall into the category of

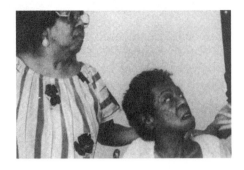

"social pleasantries," the equivalent of "how do you do?" Other conversations might be more difficult and full of decisions for you and for your doctor, such as a conversation in which you don't really want to know the answer, or times when you just don't know what to do. Still other conversations might put you in the position of asking your doctor about the latest research in a particular field. Knowing how to approach these conversations can help you to make the most of them. Following are several examples of how to have these conversations with your doctor. One of these approaches may fit you perfectly all the time. Some might fit at different times. Maybe you have your own method of talking to your doctor, asking questions, or investigating new ideas. The most important thing is that you feel that your doctor supports you so you can explore your options and stay as involved as you want in choosing treatment or care options.

"The Social Pleasantry"

Doctor: *How are you doing?*
Patient: *Pretty good, thanks.*
Doctor: *Good, good. We'll see what the tests today show.* (Leaves)

Have you had this conversation with your doctor? Was the doctor insensitive to your need to talk or ask questions? Did you feel you were not assertive enough in demanding some of the doctor's time? Did you think you were exchanging a social pleasantry while the doctor thought he was gathering clinical information? Or was nothing wrong with this exchange? Maybe each of the above, depending on your circumstances.

If you needed to talk to your doctor about something important to you, then you probably felt slighted, hurt, even angry at the doctor's lack of concern for your needs. He should have known better. You were sick and obviously needed his attention. Of course you weren't "pretty good." That was a polite response, a prelude to real conversation. On the other hand, you might have blamed yourself for not speaking up and demanding that the doctor stay and listen to you or, at least, schedule a definite time to come back and talk with you. Both of these reactions are natural, but neither helps you get what you really want—more time and consideration for something causing you distress.

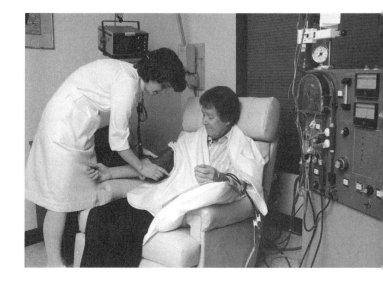

If that was the case, there are several ways to avoid the feeling that your doctor is insensitive or that you are suddenly incapable of speaking up for yourself.

"The Useful Conversation"

First, consider that what sounds like a variation on "hello" may be a real question and answer it accordingly. It may feel awkward or impolite, but it will get your point across.

Second, offer an answer that suggests there is more to come. In a hospital or home setting, you can even combine this with a little old-fashioned hospitality that will encourage the doctor to hear you out.

Finally, ask a question to gauge whether your expectations of a lengthy conversation are realistic. This is very important to do if you have scheduled a "routine" or "follow-up" appointment or if you are in the hospital, but you want to discuss a new problem or an especially troubling issue.

Doctor: *How are you doing?*
Patient: *Not so good today. The nausea's worse, although my breathing is a bit better.*

Doctor: *How are you doing?*
Patient: *I'm glad to see you. I have some questions about my breathing getting more difficult. Won't you have a seat?*

Doctor: *How are you doing?*

Patient: *Pretty good, but I really want to talk about what I should expect if my cancer keeps spreading. How much time do you have for me today?*

Even if the doctor doesn't have time to sit for a long conversation, you have put him on notice that you expect to talk further. If he offers to return to your hospital room later, ask: "When should I expect you back?" If you are at his office, and you have the time and energy, you can offer to wait. If that is not a good option, ask: "What should I say to let the nurse or receptionist know that I need more time with you next visit?"

But maybe you see nothing wrong with the question, answer, or doctor's response. You might have been in the hospital or office specifically for tests, and the greeting was meant to be social. You might have been feeling "pretty good" with no pressing needs to discuss. Maybe you choose to discuss your medical problems with your doctor but your feelings, fears, or other concerns with someone else. As long as your questions are being answered by someone knowledgeable about your condition and your plan of care—and your needs are being met—that is okay.

"I read somewhere..."

Doctor: *Do you have any questions?*

Patient: *Doc, I know you said nothing will cure this disease, but last week I read in a magazine about something new…*

Some people like to be very involved in researching their illnesses, diagnostic tests, and treatment options. This may mean asking other people how they've managed the same disease or doing research on the Internet or in a medical library. Your involvement may vary depending on how well you feel and how far along you may be in the course of your disease. The reception you get from your doctor may also vary.

She might listen intently, offer to take the information, and research it further. She might listen briefly and then tell you why such an idea is experimental or why it is not likely to help you. Or she might cut you off, telling you that such articles are nonsense and that she would have told you if there was something else to try. You are the only one who can decide which of these responses is acceptable to you on any given day.

If you are bothered that your doctor is not taking your concerns or ideas seriously (and you do not want to change doctors), you have several choices. You can try the direct approach: "I want to know more about this treatment that I was reading about." Be careful not to take an aggressively direct approach: "I'm the one who's sick, and I want you to listen to this!" Although it gets your point across, it is more likely to encourage your doctor to hide from you than to listen to what you are saying.

Doctor: *That's nonsense. I'll tell you about anything that will help you.*
Patient: *Well, I'd still appreciate hearing what you know about it.*

You might try the curiosity approach. "I was just wondering about this treatment that I recently read about...." It is still an honest question. If this feels like a weak approach to you, you might be concerned that your doctor will not take your question seriously. If you feel that you or your question is dismissed, you can have an insistent follow-up ready.

Being insistent is not being rude. It does not make you a "bad patient." Some doctors do become abrupt when questioned about new treatments. They may feel that their knowledge or judgment is being questioned. On the other hand, they may be worried that you are denying your illness by grasping at "treatments" that will not help you (and may harm you in some way).

Still, you should be comfortable asking your questions, even if you do not like the answers. If your doctor is exasperated or abrupt when you ask questions, you can be direct without being apologetic. "I hope it doesn't bother you to talk about other treatments, even if you don't think they will help. After all, it is important to me to feel that I've made the best choices

I could." If you find your doctor to be frankly hostile, it may be time to save your energy and consider changing doctors.

"Tell me what to do!"

Even if you are very assertive about knowing all there is to know about your illness and making your own decisions, there may be times when you just

---

Set The Stage for a Successful Conversation

Although you probably can't rearrange medical office space (or even many hospital rooms), you can control some of your surroundings to maintain a feeling of being more in control of your medical care.

- When you are brought into an examination room, sit in a chair, not on the exam table.
- If you are asked to sit on the exam table for a blood pressure reading or other measurements, move to a chair when the measurements are finished.
- If you have a choice, choose the chair that is closest to the doctor's chair.
- If you are too weak to sit in a chair, have the head of the examination table raised to a sitting or half-sitting position.
- In a hospital room, if you are in bed, offer your doctor a chair. "Do have a seat here, doctor." The one nearest the head of the bed will allow the easiest conversation between you and your doctor. You can also offer a spot on the foot of the bed if that is comfortable for you to do.
- If your encounter is in the hall, say, "Let's go back to my room," then walk in that direction. This not only encourages privacy but also allows you to choose the most comfortable place to sit and feel in control.
- Extend your hand when the doctor walks into the examination room to begin the visit on a more equal level. This can even be done if you are lying flat on your back in a hospital bed.

---

want someone else to make the decision. It may be a relief to have someone just tell you what you should do. And that's okay.

Having a serious illness, especially one that you are likely to die from, can be overwhelming in at least two important ways. First, the very thought of dying can be overwhelming. Second, the multitude of decisions that must be made throughout the course of the illness can be overwhelming. These decisions can tax the healthiest of people, not to mention those feeling ill from side effects of medication, lack of sleep, or just being sick and tired.

Doctor: *Have you thought about the different treatments that we talked about?*
Patient: *Yes, but I don't know what to do.*
Doctor: *Well, do you have more questions?*
Patient: *No, I just want to do what you think is best.*

Some people are very comfortable having others make decisions for them, or at least weighing others' opinions before making their own decisions. If that's you, then it is important to identify family members, doctors, and other people whose opinions you trust.

Some people fear that if they ask other people to make decisions for them, they are "giving up" control or letting go of the will to live. Neither of those is a bad thing if it is what you need to do. In fact, it can be a relief.

But if the need to let someone else take control, even for a while, distresses you, it may help to tell yourself a few important things.

Remember that you've made a lot of decisions up to this point. Choosing to let one pass is really a choice, not a loss of your ability, adulthood, or right to make future decisions. If you are truly unhappy with the decision, it is likely to be flexible; few decisions are one-chance-only opportunities. If you are relying on a family member or friend to make a decision for you, then you probably picked that person (and this decision for him

or her to make) because you are comfortable with his or her judgment. If you are asking your doctor to decide for you, then you are relying on someone whose knowledge and judgment you trust.

"I don't want to know"

Patient: *If it's bad news, I don't want to hear it. I especially don't want to know if my heart was worse on that last test. Tell my daughter, not me.*
Doctor: *Okay. I'm giving you this medicine to treat your pain. Take two pills every day, first thing in the morning and again about twelve hours later, and come back in two weeks.*

The "don't ask–don't tell" policy is not much in vogue these days because it seems too paternalistic for our modern society. Patients are encouraged to take control of their care, and doctors are taught to tell their patients the "truth." But some people really don't want to hear their diagnoses—or at least not just yet. Sometimes people guess what is going on, but they don't want to hear the words or talk about their illness in specific terms. Still others don't want to be told for other personal or cultural reasons.

Although this form of communication is not for everyone, it can be very important for some. If you are one of those folks, you might focus on the effects that your illness is having on your life (too tired to go shopping, lack of appetite, etc.) without discussing the effects of the illness on your organs and body chemistry. You can ask your doctor what you can expect in terms of daily life without listening to a list of medical facts. You can certainly change your mind and ask questions later if you want to talk about specifics. You should know that most doctors and many family members are uncomfortable with this method of living with illness,

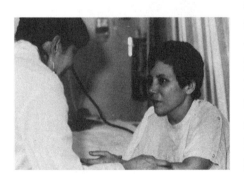

even if you prefer it. You may have to insist that this is the way you want to handle things. You may have to insist more than once. Family, friends, and doctors may be uncomfortable, but not totally surprised. Your choice, then, may be a source of puzzlement without being a source of friction.

When you are hesitant to ask questions

Some people are shy about asking "too many" questions. Many people are hesitant about asking some questions, but not others. Usually, your doctor has heard your questions before, no matter how silly, embarrassing, or far-fetched they sound to you. At some point, however, you may want to ask a question but just can't get the words out. At times like those, try the "surrogate approach." Have your spouse, parent, child, or whoever is close to you ask about the information while you look on tolerantly. This may seem rather devious, but it works well if you are uncomfortable with any sign of irritation, real or perceived, from your doctor. Such irritation is often easier for someone else to bear if they are very protective of you or don't feel as dependent on the doctor. Furthermore, your family member may welcome the opportunity to have his or her own questions answered. The surrogate approach works just as well for gathering other medical information. Although you may be just as interested in the details of your care, you may be expending most or all of your energy on get-

Patient: *I'd like to do the best I can in the life I have left. What do you know about whether I'm likely to be able to walk again? Am I going to need someone to help me for the rest of my life? How long might that be?*

Doctor: *That's a lot of questions. Let's just take it a day at a time.*

Patient: *That may work for some people, but not for me. My family and I have to make some plans. We need the information.*

Doctor: *Sometimes it's better not to know.*

Patient: *Not for me. Not in my situation. I need to reshape my life.*

Doctor: *OK. Here's what I can see…*

ting treatments or managing day-to-day activities. Someone else may have more energy for gathering information, asking questions, keeping track of answers and other details, and running down hard-to-find people. They may also be less troubled or discouraged by brusque replies, impatience, or evasions.

Doctors and hope

Many doctors are very worried that telling patients the truth about what they face will rob them of hope and make life bleak and lead them to "give up." They feel they are being kind to wait and let the future unfold. Some don't really follow patients across time and don't know much about what families and patients face as illness worsens. If you want honest information upon which to base realistic hopes, you may need to ask quite clearly.

7
Controlling Pain

Oh, oh, oh! she cried
as the ambulance men lifted
her to the stretcher—
Is this what you call
making me comfortable?
W. C. WILLIAMS, from *"The Last Words of My English Grandmother"*

Many people fear being in terrible pain at the end of life. This fear is understandable: Pain, after all, is a symptom of many illnesses. Even so, you—and the people caring for you—should know that there are effective pain management strategies that can bring even the most severe pain under control. Although treatment might not eliminate all pain, most pain can be reduced to a tolerable level without serious side effects.

Pain management strategies include a variety of medications and alternative or complementary therapies—but for them to work, you may need to rethink some of your ideas about pain and treatments for it. The goal of pain management is to do just that: to manage your pain so that it doesn't get in the way of what you want to do.

Too often, people feel that admitting to pain is a sign of weakness, or believe that suffering is somehow part of their illness. Some think that pain is just an inevitable part of illness and aging. Many others are reluctant to take pain medications. Some people hesitate to take medications because they fear becoming dependent on—or even addicted to—pain relievers. Others are worried that, if they take medicine "too soon" in the course of their illness, then there will be no medication strong enough later if the pain gets really bad. Still others are afraid that side effects will interfere with their thinking, concentration, or energy level. The fact is that good pain management can usually control your pain throughout the course of your illness without lots of side effects, without addiction, and without keeping you too tired to enjoy the things you want to do. In addition to taking prescribed pain medications, some people find relief by using alternative or complementary therapies, such as breathing exercises, meditation, visualization, or acupuncture.

If your doctor is not able to help get your pain under control, he or she may request a consultation from an expert in pain management. Palliative

---

Pain Does More Than Just Hurt

Pain is more than "just" hurting. Pain decreases your physical, emotional, social, and spiritual well-being in a variety of ways. It affects you physically, mentally, and emotionally. With pain, you may:

- Be less able to function
- Feel tired and lethargic
- Lose your appetite or have nausea
- Not be able to sleep, or have your sleep interrupted by pain
- Experience less enjoyment and more anxiety
- Become depressed, anxious, or unable to concentrate on anything except pain
- Feel a loss of control
- Have less interaction with friends
- Be less able to enjoy sex or affection
- Experience a change in appearance
- Feel that you are more of a burden on family or other caregivers
- Suffer more

ADAPTED FROM *MANAGEMENT OF CANCER PAIN* BY THE AGENCY FOR HEALTHCARE RESEARCH AND QUALITY medicine doctors or pain specialists, physicians who are specially trained to care for people with a variety of serious illnesses and conditions, can help your doctor develop a pain treatment plan that works for you. Your doctor may also suggest hospice care or a hospice consultation so that a team of experts can offer several approaches to relieving and controlling your pain.

Types of pain

The best way for your doctors to know about your pain is for you to tell them. In some cases, especially if people are unable to communicate, doctors may look at behaviors, such as grimacing or changes in how a patient moves; they may also ask family members to describe whether the patient appears to be in pain. How you describe your pain will guide your doctors' plans to relieve it. Understanding and using these descriptions may help you get the relief you need more quickly. There are different types of pain, and you may experience none, one, or several of them, depending on the diseases you have. Pain is associated with many diseases, including cancer, heart disease, diabetes, osteoporosis, and HIV/AIDS.

To choose the best treatment for pain, doctors usually classify pain according to *duration, cause, location, pattern*, and *severity*.

Your Doctor Will Ask about the Duration of Your Pain

Acute pain is usually sudden or caused by a specific event, such as surgery or injury. It lasts for hours or days and may cause increased heart rate, increased blood pressure, and anxiety.

Chronic or persistent pain may exist for months or years, often from diseases such as arthritis and cancer. Chronic pain rarely causes changes in heart rate or blood pressure but can cause loss of appetite, sleep disturbances, and depression. Many patients have trouble labeling this kind of pain as "pain" at all. Instead, they use terms such as "discomfort," "ache," or "troubles." This is fine, as long as patient, family, and caregivers all understand one another. Many people with chronic pain don't "look" as though they are in pain. They are not crying out, writhing, or moving about as if they have an injury. But they may look tired, depressed, unwell or uncomfortable. They may not be able to enjoy or participate in activities that once gave them pleasure.

You can locate pain that occurs in bones and muscles. It is usually described as sharp, aching, throbbing, or pressure.

Some pain comes from internal organs. It is usually spread out and not easy to locate in one place. Internal pain may be gnawing or cramping, or it may be sharp, aching, or throbbing, depending on what internal organ is the cause of the pain.

Pain sometimes comes from diseases affecting the nerves. These are the same nerves that help us know when things are hot, cold, sharp, or dull. Neuropathic pain is really a variation of these sensations—burning, tingling, shooting, and stabbing.

Some pain does not have an easily identified source. Such pain is very real; the fact that you can't quite describe it doesn't mean it is "all in your head." In fact, if you have had moderate to severe pain for a long period of time, it may be harder to say exactly where the pain is. It may feel diffuse or spread out over a larger area than it did when it first started. Do not feel embarrassed if that is the case. It is a common way in which long-standing pain affects people.

All pain is part *physical* and part *psychological.* The physical part comes from the irritated tissues and nerves. The psychological part involves how pain affects the rest of your life. And, just as pain affects your appetite, sleep, mood, social activities, and sense of well-being, these things affect your pain.

Words for Pain

Sharp
Aching
Throbbing
Pressure
Burning
Tingling
Shooting
Stabbing

Your Doctor Will Ask about the Pattern of the Pain You Feel

Try to recognize the pattern of your pain. It will help the physician decide which types of pain medicine are right for you: long-acting, short-acting, or a combination of the two. Do you have pain all the time? That is **chronic** pain. Even if your pain relief is good most of the time, does pain occasionally come unpredictably and intermittently? If so, you have what doctors would call **breakthrough** pain. Does it occur predictably when you do certain activities, such as taking a bath, changing wound dressings, getting out of bed, or traveling? If so, you have what doctors would call **incident** pain. Does the pain increase just before the next dose of medication is due? Doctors call this pattern **end-of-dose** pain. The pattern of your pain may be like one or more of these, or it may have its own pattern. It is important to describe all your pains for your doctor.

Your Doctor Will Ask You to Describe the Pain

Pain is often described as **none, mild, moderate, severe,** or **excruciating.** The doctor or nurse may want to know how the pain feels—for example, achy, stabbing, raw, sharp, dull, or burning. They may want to know what makes the pain better or worse. YOU are the only one who can determine the severity of your pain. How much pain anyone else has in similar circumstances is not important in figuring out what you need. However, you might feel comfort knowing that others have been through similar experiences and have found ways to cope. You might find some people to talk with about severity of pain, medications, or activities that affect pain in order to share experiences. Just don't expect that things will be the same for you.

During the course of your treatment, a doctor or nurse is likely to ask you to rate your pain on a scale of 0 to 10, with 0 being no pain and 10 being the worst pain you can imagine. Scales using drawings of faces help measure pain for children or people who cannot talk. In addition to using the 0–10 scale, you might also want to describe how the pain affects your daily life. Are you in so much pain that you can't talk to friends and family? Is the pain sufficiently under control that you are able to go to work? Also be sure to note which pain

Controlling Pain

medications you are taking or alternative therapies you are trying and whether they are effective in reducing your pain.

People experience pain differently and need different doses of medicine to relieve pain. Using more or less medicine than someone else doesn't reflect on your character or ability to tolerate pain. Some people will require larger doses of medication to achieve pain relief; pain management experts recognize that this is perfectly normal. However, some people, including doctors, may express surprise at your medications or dose; the reason is usually that they do not understand one of the most important rules of pain control: **The right dose of pain medicine is the dose that relieves the pain.**

Choosing the right pain medicine

You may have already taken nonprescription, over-the-counter medicines: aspirin, acetaminophen (Tylenol™), ibuprofen (Advil™, Motrin™, etc.), and other nonsteroidal, anti-inflammatory drugs (NSAIDS). These are the same medications your doctor is likely to suggest for mild pain. Check with your doctor before starting any new medication, and don't take more than the recommended dose without clear instruction from your doctor.

Keep A Pain Diary

You might try using a pain diary to track your pain for a week or so. Keep a notebook at your bedside or next to your favorite chair and make notes throughout the day (and night) as your pain increases or decreases. You might use a pain scale to rate your pain so that you have a consistent frame of reference. Using the same standard every day will make it easier for you, your doctor, and other caregivers to recognize patterns. Notice what is going on around you at the time: Have you just changed positions? Bathed? Visited with family? Experienced something stressful? Even daily activities can sometimes trigger pain. Take your pain diary with you to doctors' appointments. If you are unable to keep such a diary, perhaps a family member can keep one for you. Doctors and the Internet can provide blank tables that you might find to be helpful.

"What if over-the-counter medicines aren't helping anymore?"

If these medications are not relieving your pain, tell your doctor. The doctor needs to know that you are in pain, where the pain is located and how it feels, and what medications you have tried and in what doses. Your doctor will probably add a medication called an **opioid** (sometimes called a "narcotic"). In some cases, your doctor might recommend medications that are usually used to treat conditions other than pain but that have been shown to relieve some painful conditions. For example, certain antidepressant medications and antiseizure medications are effective in helping to relieve certain types of nerve pain.

Common Opioids

Codeine
Oxycodone
Hydrocodone
Morphine
Hydromorphone
Fentanyl
(but avoid meperidine)

These medications are often given in pills that also contain aspirin or acetaminophen. Such combinations of medicines have a **synergistic effect**— that is, they work together to relieve pain better than either medication could do alone.

Your doctor may prescribe different types of opioids, either short- or long-acting, depending on the kind of pain you are experiencing. For occasional or moderate pain, you will likely receive medications that last three or four hours. For ongoing or more severe pain, longer acting medications, which can last up to twelve hours, may be prescribed.

For example, people with cancer that has spread to their bones (bone metastases) might try a nonsteroidal anti-inflammatory drug (NSAID) such as ibuprofen, naproxen, or similar medications in addition to an opioid; however, these NSAIDs have side effects. Patients should always check with their doctors before taking them. People with a history of stomach ulcers, internal bleeding, or heart, liver, or kidney disease are especially prone to side effects.

If these opioids or combination medications do not relieve your pain, or if you are having severe pain, other opioids should be prescribed. Although there are many such medications, one older opioid called meperidine (Demerol™) has too many side effects and should not be used for pain relief. If your doctor prescribes any opioid, ask if you should add or continue any over-the-counter medicines as well.

Pain management guidelines from the American Geriatrics Society suggest that doctors should rely more on opioids and less on NSAIDs to treat pain in older adults, especially those over the age of seventy-five. The harm of even over-the-counter NSAIDs may be greater than their benefits when using them to treat pain in older patients. The guidelines recommend that physicians consider using opioids to manage ongoing moderate to severe pain in older adults.

> *"I've read about problems with people stealing Oxycontin and that some drug addicts are using it. What if people think I'm an addict?"*

It is always important to safeguard opioids in your home, just as you would any other medication. People who use pain medications under a doctor's care and direction rarely become addicted to them. Needing the medication to manage pain is not addiction. One government study found that only four out of twelve thousand acute pain patients became addicted to opioids. In fact, most patients will take only as much medicine as they need to control their pain. Drug addicts, on the other hand, abuse drugs, including OxyContin, for other reasons.

Sometimes the patient or someone close to the patient has abused drugs in the past—or even in the present. A patient who is used to using opioids will often require increasing doses to maintain pain control. Patients who have abused drugs in the past do not generally abuse pain medications when they are prescribed and adjusted to control pain at the end of life. But if that is a concern, your doctor can work with you to treat your pain safely. If it is a family member who has a drug abuse history, again work with your doctor to implement a safe plan.

The problem of diversion of legal drugs into illegal sales can also be a serious problem. If the physician or clinical team cannot be sure that prescribed drugs are being used as directed—by the patient—then they may insist on special arrangements and precautions. In extreme situations, a patient may need to move to a safer living situation in order to get reliable pain relief.

"My mother has advanced dementia. How will I know that she is in pain?"

Pain management is an important part of caring for someone with dementia or confusion of any type. In fact, pain can be a cause of increased confusion and unusual behaviors in people who cannot otherwise express their pain. Health care professionals rely on nonverbal cues to determine whether such a patient is in pain. For instance, a patient who is smiling and calm is not likely to be in pain. A patient who appears to be anxious, irritable, or crying may be in pain. A patient who is immobile or afraid to move may be in pain. It is important to know how a patient usually acts or behaves to have some context for determining whether or not he or she she is in pain. Facial expressions, body placement or movement, vocalizations, and changes in vital signs are all cues to consider when assessing pain in a patient who cannot report or describe pain well. There are even some pain assessment tools that have been developed to help assess pain in people who have dementia.

Sadly, pain is often not assessed or treated in older patients, even if they do not have dementia. You may need to advocate for your loved one and insist that professional caregivers listen to your reports that your loved one appears to be in pain, and that they try a trial of treatment.

"I am taking opioids. Should I keep taking the medicine I used to take, too?"

If your doctor writes a prescription for a pain medication, ask if you should continue to take your over-the-counter medications. Do not continue to take over-the-counter medications unless your doctor tells you that it is safe to do so.

Different ways to take pain medicine

Pain medicine can be taken in a number of ways. Most of the time, you will take pain medicine orally, by mouth, as pills or liquids. In other cases, pain medication may be given via a small tube in a vein (intravenous, or IV) or just under the skin (subcutaneous, or SubQ). Most pain medications need to be taken on a regular, around-the-clock schedule to prevent the pain from reoccurring and to achieve adequate pain control. It is very important to take the medication exactly as it is prescribed.

People sometimes wait until their pain reaches an intolerable level before they decide to take something for it or do something about it. Although it is possible to deal with any level of pain, it is best to try to get it under control before it becomes excruciating. If you wait to take the medication until you are already in severe pain, it may be less effective and require more medication to regain control.

Over-the-counter medicines are usually taken regularly every 4 to 8 hours, depending on the medication. Opioids are usually taken regularly by mouth every 4 to 12 hours. Morphine, hydromorphone, and oxycodone are available in long-acting forms that may be taken every 8 to 24 hours. Doses of opioids for breakthrough pain may be taken as often as every 30 minutes, depending on the dose and the specific medicine.

> I knew I was free in a way I'd never felt before…. The pain was still unquestionably in me; but…it seemed contained and watched from a distance.
>
> REYNOLDS PRICE
> from A Whole New Life

Be sure you know your schedule for taking medications. Write it down and review it with your doctor.

Once your pain is controlled, you should continue to take your medication. Sometimes your doctor may reduce your dose somewhat if you were treating a particularly painful episode. But usually lack of pain will mean that you are taking the right amount of medication, not that you are taking too much.

"My mother is in severe pain and cannot swallow the pills we have for her."

For pain that is difficult to control or for patients who are having trouble swallowing, various options are available. Pain medicine can be given subcutaneously, through a thin catheter attached to a very small needle placed just under the skin. A small battery-operated pump can deliver injections continuously or on a regular schedule and allow patients to take extra doses for breakthrough pain.

Patients having trouble swallowing for a short period of time may be given rectal medications. This is especially useful if swallowing becomes difficult or if a pump malfunctions in the middle of the night. Most oral pain medications, but not all, can be given rectally with good results. However, many people would not want to use suppositories for a long period of time. Rectal medications are not useful for patients having diarrhea.

Some people treat their pain with a transdermal ("across the skin") patch. Fentanyl is the only opioid currently available in a patch in the United States. The patch is placed on the chest or back and usually changed every three days. The patch is an effective method of controlling pain that stays fairly constant because it keeps the dosage at a fairly even level. But, because it

Controlling Pain

97

takes medicine in the patch 12 to 18 hours to reach a useful level in the bloodstream, a quicker acting (oral, sublingual, or injectable) medication must be used during the first few days of wearing a patch and should be available to treat breakthrough pain.

Finally, many medications can be administered intravenously (IV) through a catheter in a vein. This often works in a hospital setting when an IV may be placed for other reasons, but it may also be used at home. Some people will have had "permanent" catheters placed in order to give other medications. These are easy to use for pain medications, but patient and family have to learn some routines to care for the catheter safely.

Pain medications can also be given by the intramuscular route through injections into muscle or even into the space around the spinal cord, by a special procedure.

Doses of pain medicine

Over-the-counter medications are taken in the same doses as recommended on the label. When medications such as aspirin, acetaminophen, or ibuprofen are included in prescription medications, the total dose of these

should still not exceed the maximum recommended daily dose on the over-the-counter labels. In some cases, even that amount is too much. Be sure to ask your doctor or pharmacist what the maximum dose would be.

"What is the usual dose of morphine? How do I know if mine is too high?"

The right amount of opioid medication is the amount that relieves your pain with minimal or tolerable side effects. There is **no usual** or **normal dose**. Some people need small doses of opioids, whereas others need much larger doses. The amount of medicine that you need for pain relief is not related to how well you tolerate pain or how well you are coping with your disease. It is not a weakness to take higher doses of medicine if that is what you need to relieve your pain.

> "That's just pain," she said. "It goes eventually. And when it's gone, there's no lasting memory. Not the worst of it, anyway. It fades. Our minds aren't made to hold on to the particulars of pain the way we do bliss. It's a gift God gives us, a sign of His care for us."
>
> CHARLES FRAZIER
> from *Cold Mountain*

Just as there is no usual dose, there is **no maximum dose** of opioids. This is unlike over-the-counter medications, which DO have a maximum dose (and have serious side effects if you take too much). With opioids, you increase the dose if your pain increases. Also, there is no ceiling effect; there is no point at which increasing the dose won't work anymore to reduce the pain. Some people worry that they will get so used to the medication that it will not relieve their pain anymore. There is always a dose that will overcome any tendency of the body to be "used to" opioid drugs.

> "My husband says he won't take more pain medication—he feels as if he's giving in to his disease."

Some people do not want to take medication for pain because they feel that doing so is giving in or giving up. Trying to ignore your pain will not make your disease go away. Ignoring pain will only make you even more aware of your disease and will detract from the time you have left. Treating your pain will keep your disease from controlling your life any more than it already does.

Some people look at the amount of pain they are in as a measuring stick. They judge whether their disease is getting worse by how much pain they are having. Although pain may worsen as some diseases worsen, it is not a reliable indicator of disease activity. Sometimes a small injury or change hurts a great deal. Some people have a lot of pain with less disease; others have little pain with advanced disease.

A few rules about pain management

There are some general rules that are helpful to know.

If you have more pain after having had no pain on a stable dose of an opioid, your regular dose will generally need to be increased by one-quarter (25%) to one-half (50%). For example, if you are taking 10 milligrams (mg) of morphine every four hours, your doctor will usually need to increase your dose to about 15 mg every 4 hours to get pain relief again. This is just as true if you were taking 100 mg every 12 hours; the new dose is likely to be at least 120–150 mg.

The dose of medication needed to treat breakthrough pain—severe and sudden pain that "breaks through" your usual pain medication—is determined by the dose of pain medicine that you take regularly. The breakthrough dose is usually equivalent to two to four hours' worth of your regular dose. So your breakthrough dose should increase as your regularly scheduled dose increases. The reason is **NOT** that you are taking too much medicine. It is that the breakthrough dose has to be calculated as a percentage of the regular dose. Again, the person taking 10 mg every 12 hours will need 5–10 mg for breakthrough pain. The person taking 100 mg every 12 hours will need at least 20–30 mg. These larger doses often cause some anxiety for professionals who are not used to using them. Talk to your doctor about the dose of medicine you should take for breakthrough pain and have your doctor talk with people in your family or care team who need to understand how the dosing works.

Because incident pain is more predictable, the best treatment is to take a dose of medication before starting the activity that produces pain. The dose may or may not be the same as your breakthrough pain dose. Work with your doctor and use your own experience to determine what dose best prevents pain before specific activities.

You can treat end-of-dose failure in one of two ways, depending on your medicine and your medication schedule. You can increase the dose of medicine, or you can decrease the amount of time between doses. Also, if you are using pills that are not long-acting, you might switch to long-acting versions that "smooth out" the transition time between doses. Talk with your doctor about the best choice for you.

The amount of medicine that you take will be very different depending on the route used. If you switch from morphine tablets to injections, for example, the new dosage usually needs to be cut to about one-third of the oral dose.

It is usually better to take one kind of opioid at a time, although you will need to take two if one is a transdermal patch. Taking only one opioid limits the side effects and makes it easier to calculate dose changes.

"My doctor stopped my Oxycodone and started morphine because my pain was worse. Does that mean that I'm dying?"

Although many people think that taking morphine means that death is approaching, that is not the case. There may be times when you need to change opioids in order to get better pain relief. Although opioids are part of the same class or group of medications, there are differences between them. For example, different opioids may work by acting on different nerve receptors in the body. Some, like morphine, attach to *mu* receptors; others to *kappa* or *lambda* receptors. If your pain is not responding to the medication as well as it once did, your physician may change or "rotate" these opioids to take advantage of these differences and increase your pain relief.

When this happens, your doctor may prescribe a slightly lower dose than the **"equivalent dose"** to your previous opioid. This is because equivalent doses are not exact and because your body may need less of an opioid that it is not used to having. Use your breakthrough medication for pain while you and your doctor adjust your new medicine.

"I'm afraid that giving morphine or another opioid will cause my dad to die faster. After all, my aunt had terminal cancer and died three days after she started taking morphine."

Opioids are really very safe drugs. If you use them as we have described, they are very unlikely to speed up dying, even if you need very large doses.

Some people feel that opioids must kill people because they are so often in use at the end of life, but this is not the case. What happens more often is that people delay taking strong pain medication until they are within days of death and having terrible pain. If the pain is relieved and they are resting comfortably when they die, it may seem to some family members that the medication was to blame.

Sometimes a family member will feel guilty after giving the last dose of pain medication before a loved one dies. Again, the prescribed dose of medication did not cause death; instead, it helped maintain relief from pain. Opioids provide a great deal of comfort and are quite safe when used appropriately.

How often to take pain medicine

Usually, you must take opioids around the clock to relieve and prevent pain. Some people try not to take opioids too often for fear that they will become addicted to the medicine. But waiting until you "need the medicine" or "can't stand the pain anymore" is NOT an effective way to take opioids. First, it means that you will have much more pain. Second, when your pain becomes extreme, it will take more medicine to relieve your pain. To get good pain relief with the least amount of medicine, take your medications, especially opioids, on schedule. Try to prevent pain rather than to have to treat it.

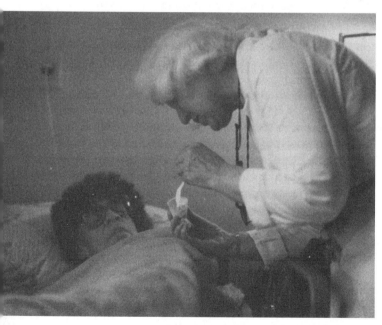

Fear of addiction

Many people are worried about addiction to pain medicine. Unfortunately, as our society has battled illegal drug use, people have become discouraged from taking legal medications when they really need them. You should not "just say no" to good pain relief. And you will not become an addict by taking your medicine as prescribed.

Addiction is a psychological disorder of drug craving and compulsive drug use even when taking drugs is harmful to the user. Addiction is really very rare in people who take opioids for illness. It is NOT the same as taking medicine because you have pain. It is not the same as tolerance or physical dependence, either.

Tolerance means that increasing doses of an opioid are needed to maintain the effects of the medicine. In treating pain with opioids, tolerance is a useful feature. Although people rarely develop tolerance to the pain relief that opioids provide, they do develop tolerance that causes most side effects to wear off a few days after a dose is increased.

Physical dependence means that the body becomes used to having an opioid present. Physical dependence happens to everyone who uses opioids for more than a few days, but all it means is that opioids should never be stopped suddenly. They should be weaned over a few days if they are going to be stopped. If they are stopped suddenly, you may experience **withdrawal**—a very uncomfortable flu-like syndrome that includes muscle aches, nausea, diarrhea, and sometimes vomiting or even muscle spasms. If a person suddenly cannot take opioids by mouth, the weaning needs to be done by some other route (by infusion or rectal suppository, for example).

> DYING WELL
>
> It was pain, raw and unyielding that drove him to ask for help.
> "Oh my God, I can't take this. I can't do this. I don't want to die
> like this. It's so dark, so horrible, it hurts so bad."
> The nurse drew up the morphine. "It's a beast, clawing at you, but
> we're going to take care of that beast right now."
> The needle pierced his skin, and in ninety seconds he relaxed and
> said "You mean it, don't you?"
> "Mean what?"
> "You'll be here."
>
> PAUL WILKES from
> *New York Times Magazine*, July 6, 1997

Controlling Pain

Side effects of pain medications

Opioids do have side effects; the most troublesome is **constipation**. Almost everyone needs stool softeners and laxatives to prevent constipation. You may also need an occasional enema (see the information on constipation in Chapter 8). Keep in mind that you will **NOT** develop tolerance to the constipating effects of opioids. As you increase the amount of your dose of pain medication, you should increase your stool softeners and laxatives.

Opioids can cause **drowsiness**. Usually, however, your doctor can prescribe a dose of medication that will relieve your pain without causing confusion or excess sleepiness. Do not be alarmed by increased drowsiness for a day or two after increasing your dose of medicine. Some of your drowsiness may be from not sleeping well because of your pain. You may be exhausted and need to "catch up" on your sleep. You may need a few days to develop tolerance to the drowsiness, which will then lessen. Very sick people can have somewhat diminished response times even when they are not feeling drowsy. However, if you generally feel well and you are taking a stable dose of medications, you probably can drive safely. Talk with your doctor before you drive a car or do anything else that might be dangerous if you are not able to respond quickly to an emergency situation.

If your drowsiness does not go away in two or three days, ask your doctor if another medication might be responsible or if you might benefit from taking a stimulant to counteract the sedating effects of the opioid. **Remember that patients should not have to accept sedation or coma in order to be comfortable unless they are very weak and near death, when the trade-off is often welcome.** If you are much stronger and active, there is probably something more that could be done for your pain.

Some people experience **confusion** or **delirium** when they take certain opioids. This usually limits the use of the specific opioid to a few doses because no one wants to take a chance that the confusion will continue or get worse. This is not the same thing as an **allergy**, although people are often told to say they are allergic to the medication to avoid its being given to them again. Allergies to opioids are actually very rare. However, the fact that someone becomes confused taking one opioid does not mean that all opioids will cause the same effect. Usually there is a dose of some opioid that avoids this problem.

If taking an opioid causes **nausea**, then you should consider trying another opioid or taking an **anti-emetic**, which is a medication that stops nausea. Often the nausea disappears as tolerance develops. Do not let an easily controlled side effect such as nausea keep you from taking your pain medicine.

A few people taking high doses of opioids develop **muscle twitching** (myoclonus). This occurs mostly when a person is in and out of consciousness prior to death. When that is the case, the tremors and twitching are more likely to bother family, friends, and staff than they are to bother the person having them. If, however, you are having myoclonus that interferes with your activities, then a muscle relaxant or change in medication may be helpful.

If you have lung disease or congestive heart failure, you may experience both pain and shortness of breath. Conveniently, opioids are used to relieve the feeling of breathlessness that people with heart and lung disease often experience. Nevertheless, extra care should be used when treating your pain with opioids. When you are very close to death, the opioids that provide comfort by relieving severe pain could cause you to breathe a little less effectively. Some people worry that this effect could potentially hasten your death, although medical evidence does not confirm that. If this is a worry for your caregivers, you should make it clear to them that being comfortable at that point is more important to you than a small possibility of living a short while longer.

> ...he was moribund and screaming...I had no morphine ...I finally instinctively sat down on the bed and took him in my arms, and the screaming stopped... He died peacefully in my arms a few hours later. It was not the pleurisy that caused the screaming, but loneliness.
>
> ARCHIE COCHRANE
> from "One Man's Medicine"

More medications that relieve pain

Pain that starts in the nerves themselves, called neuropathic pain, is best treated with **antidepressants** and **anticonvulsants** (antiseizure medications),

Although pain medications are effective, you may also want to try other methods that have proven helpful for people who have persistent pain. Many people find these alternative, or complementary, methods helpful. Your physician or hospice team can suggest which approaches would be best in your particular situation.

- *Heat and cold:* It used to be said that cold should be used on a new injury, such as a sprain, and heat used only after twenty-four hours. However, if either can reach a pain and provide relief, then use either or both. Be careful when applying heat to the skin of an elderly or sleepy person. Fragile skin may be burned at lower temperatures without the person realizing that a burn is happening.
- *Massage, reiki, healing touch:* These may help to reduce feelings of isolation, improve blood and lymphatic circulation, strengthen and tone muscles, and stimulate or calm functions of the nervous system.
- *Electrical stimulation (TENS unit):* This blocks pain by directing an electrical current into accessible nerves.
- *Yoga and other exercises:* Yoga focuses on the physical and mental practice of blending body, mind, and spirit and can be done very gently to ease muscle tension and improve strength and balance. Simple exercises—such as a ten-minute walk around the neighborhood—can also help to relieve stress and anxiety, as well as reduce pain.
- *Relaxation methods:* Many approaches are available, such as breathing exercises, meditation, guided imagery, visualization, affirmations, centering, and muscle relaxation exercises.
- *Biofeedback:* This technique provides guidance on direct feedback to control bodily processes and can be useful for relaxation.
- *Art therapy:* This encourages supportive, creative expression of emotions.
- *Music therapy:* This therapy can be a passive or an active experience of music that helps to achieve relaxation and a sense of well-being.
- *Acupuncture/acupressure:* Acupuncture is the therapeutic insertion of needles in patterns at acupuncture points to encourage the flow of energy; acupressure is a similar method that applies pressure to several points that carry energy through the body.
- *Hypnosis:* This is a way to achieve an altered state of consciousness through focused attention.

often in combination with opioids. These may be used in doses lower than the doses used to treat depression or seizures. However, if someone has neuropathic pain and also has depression or seizures, these medications may be prescribed in traditional doses to treat both conditions at the same time.

Steroids (prednisone, dexamethasone, and others) also help relieve pain, often in combination with opioids. The steroids reduce inflammation that can exert pressure on an already painful area. They also reduce **cerebral edema** (fluid in the brain tissues) associated with tumors or metastases in the brain, thus improving pain and some neurological symptoms. Steroids can also improve appetite and overall sense of well-being. Side effects of steroids usually depend on the dose and how long someone takes them. Most of the short-term side effects, such as elevated blood sugar, swelling of the legs and arms from fluid, difficulty sleeping, and confusion, can be managed. Because steroids can cause stomach irritation, your doctor might prescribe an anti-ulcer medication whenever steroids are taken.

Finally, when pain is coming from a specific place but is difficult to manage with the usual medicines, **nerve blocks** may be performed, usually by an anesthesiologist. A nerve block is performed by injecting the area of the nerve with an anesthetic to keep the nerve from transmitting painful impulses. This is just like anesthesia for dental procedures, but it can be longer lasting. Other nerve blocks can be performed by placing a catheter in one of the spaces around the spinal cord and instilling small amounts of opioids and anesthetics. If such a catheter is

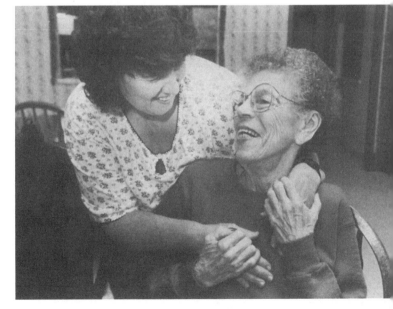

placed, a pump may be used to deliver small quantities of medicine continuously to maintain pain relief.

In summary, pain can almost always be managed well enough so that you can be comfortable and life can be meaningful. If pain gets to be overwhelming, usually it is because available treatments are not being used well.

8

Managing Other Symptoms

Although the world is full of suffering; it is also full of the overcoming of it.
HELEN KELLER

Various symptoms cause trouble at the end of life. Many can be alleviated most, if not all, of the time.

"I feel very short of breath, as if I just can't breathe"

Depending on why you are short of breath, various approaches may ease your breathing. Some helpful strategies are simple and straightforward:

- Do your best to stay calm.
- Keep your breaths as slow and even as you can.
- Change positions. If one lung is healthier than the other, lie on the side that keeps the "good lung" higher.

- Sit up straighter by supporting your back and arms with pillows or sitting in straighter chairs.
- Turn on the fan.
- Open a window.
- Keep the room warm, but not hot enough for it to feel heavy or stifling.
- Remove clutter so you don't feel closed in.
- Keep the curtains or door open to feel that there is a greater sense of space.
- Keep a journal about your shortness of breath. Keeping track of when it happens might help you to prevent it or reduce situations when it occurs.

In some cases, more medical approaches may be needed. Your doctor may need to prescribe additional medications to help relieve you of the sense of being short of breath. It may help to have fluid drained from around your lungs or in your abdomen. You may get relief from shrinking a tumor with radiation or steroids.

> They changed my oxygen mask and within minutes my breathing began to clear — a strange sensation, like removing thick cobwebs one by one.
>
> TIM BROOKES
> from Catching My Breath: An Asthmatic Explores His Illness

You might feel better using oxygen, either as needed or all of the time. Ask your doctor or care team if oxygen can be provided to you. Your insurance plan may need some information before they agree to pay for oxygen. Most hospices will provide oxygen as part of their service.

Remember that oxygen makes any flame quite intense, so special safety measures need to be taken. Do not allow smoking in a room with oxygen. Keep the oxygen equipment, tubing, and tanks at least ten feet away from all flame sources, including gas stoves and open flame fireplaces.

If you have persistent shortness of breath that isn't made comfortable with these approaches, you may breathe easier with a regular, low dose of opioids. Opioids include morphine, oxycodone, hydromorphone, and similar medications. Although they are frequently prescribed for pain relief, they also ease the feeling of being short of breath. Taking opioids at bedtime can help you sleep comfortably and keep you from waking up fighting to breathe. Some patients get the same sort of relief from medications commonly used to treat anxiety.

Some doctors resist using opioids for shortness of breath. If your doctor is concerned, you might share this book and encourage a look at texts on symptom management. You might also try just a low dose for a few days (or a few bedtimes). You may be able to try the medications in a situation in which someone can monitor any side effects four and eight hours after trying the medication. You could do this when you are in a hospital or when a family member or a hospice or home care nurse can check on you. A trial with this kind of checking might be reassuring enough to you and your doctor.

Shortness of breath is a common symptom among people who are dying. Some, however, have illnesses that make it even more likely that they will have much more severe or sudden shortness of breath. People with chronic heart or lung disease require more aggressive treatment to relieve the distress. Some illnesses, such as emphysema, are more likely than others to make you feel as if you just can't catch your breath. You may be afraid that you will feel as if you are suffocating—but you should *not* feel this way. No matter what disease or condition you have, you can make plans to cope with shortness of breath. Talk with your doctor or care team about what will help you if shortness of breath affects you or could affect you in the future.

Hospice and palliative care physicians agree that patients suffering with shortness of breath are helped by opioid medications, usually morphine, even if the patient becomes unconscious. If you have an illness likely to cause shortness of breath, you should talk frankly with your doctor about what treatment he or she is willing to make available. Having specific

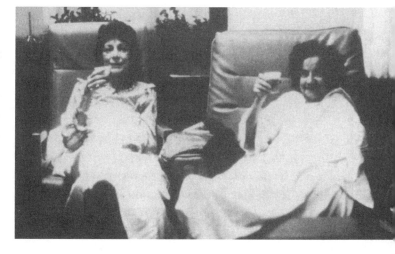

plans in place can help ease your worries and make it more likely that your symptoms will be treated. Making arrangements while you are short of breath just doesn't work well! If you are likely to experience severe shortness of breath at the end of your life, make sure that your doctors and nurses will treat your problem aggressively, even if it may lead to unconsciousness. Keep the medication in your home and have a way to have it administered relatively quickly. If your doctor and nurses are not comfortable with such a plan, you should try to get a palliative care or hospice consultation or even consider looking for another care team.

Frank James, a sixty-seven-year-old retired bricklayer with severe emphysema, called his doctor's office to see when Dr. Miller would stop by. Ever since Mr. James got so short of breath that a doctor's office visit was exhausting, Dr. Miller had been stopping by every month or so to check on him at home. They had a clear understanding that Mr. James would never again be put on a ventilator. Mr. James's sister, Clara, lived with him and had agreed to page Dr. Miller if there was a sudden change or a bad episode. So Mr. James was startled to hear the receptionist say, "Mr. James, Dr. Miller has had a health problem of his own. He's arranged for a new doctor, Dr. Winchester, to take over his practice until his own health gets straightened out." As his anxiety mounted, Mr. James felt his breathing getting hard and motioned to Clara to take the phone. She arranged for Dr. Winchester to come by a few days later.

After examining him and talking generally, Dr. Winchester said, "I see from Dr. Miller's notes that you have firmly decided not to go back to the hospital for shortness of breath."

Mr. James: "That's right. My time is close. This life is okay, but it's not great. When the angels come by next time, I'm going along."

Dr. Winchester: "What will you do?"

Mr. James: "I was supposed to page Doc Miller. What am I to do without him?"

Dr. Winchester: "When you get really short of breath again, and your regular medicines aren't enough, do you want to have a medicine that could make you sleepy but more comfortable? Even if there is a small chance that you could die more quickly?"

Mr. James: "Yeah. That's what I want. And that's what Doc Miller promised."

Dr. Winchester: *"Let's see what I can do. I don't live nearby like Dr. Miller. I can't be as sure that you can reach me quickly, and I have two other doctors covering for me after hours."*

After some investigation, it turned out that the local hospice could respond quickly. Clara was comfortable with working with the hospice team to get Mr. James the medication he would need. By the time Dr. Winchester talked with them the next day, Mr. James and his sister were reassured that they had a good plan, a caring doctor, and the opportunity to live fully in the time remaining. Clara called her son and her prayer group to tell them the good news.

When Your Loved One is Short of Breath

- Encourage him or her to stay calm—and you stay calm, too.
- Give oxygen if prescribed.
- Raise head and shoulders to at least a forty-five-degree angle by using extra pillows, or move to a sitting position with good back support. If you have an adjustable hospital bed, raise its head. Support arms on pillows higher than waist level to help the chest and lungs expand.
- Have the person sit up on the side of the bed with feet resting on a chair or stool and arms resting on an over-the-bed table or small table with pillows on it. Tilt head slightly forward.
- Turn on a fan or open the window to improve air circulation.
- Encourage slow, even breaths—in through the nose and out slowly through pursed lips.
- Limit the number of people in the room.
- Keep a clear line of sight to the outdoors if possible.
- Reduce the room temperature and remove heavy clothing or bedding without producing a chill.
- If prescribed, give the person medication for shortness of breath.
- If none of these strategies works, call the physician.

ADAPTED FROM A HANDBOOK FOR HOSPICE FAMILIES: WHEN COMFORT IS THE FOCUS FROM THE HOSPICE OF LANCASTER COUNTY

Managing Other Symptoms

"I just can't eat."

Digestive system problems are common in very sick persons. Some of these problems are related to symptoms of specific diseases. Some may be related to generally not feeling well. Others are related to medications. It is best to prevent them or treat them early, rather than letting them get to the point of making you uncomfortable.

Nausea/Vomiting

You may have nausea or vomiting as a result of certain medications, constipation, or bowel obstruction. Your medication may be the cause; ask your doctor about changing your medicines or adding an anti-emetic (anti-nausea) drug. Constipation can cause nausea and vomiting, so treat it promptly (see following subsection). Sometimes an imbalance in blood chemistry is the problem, so your doctor may need to check some blood tests.

Many people find that they have no appetite and that forcing oneself to eat is not pleasant. Usually you are best advised to follow your body's instructions. Try small amounts of a particularly appealing food. Also, recognize that food is often important for its symbolism (of home, friends, and

---

Mouth Dryness

Mouth dryness can be very uncomfortable. Here are some ways to relieve it:

- Use commercial products or liquid vitamin E to ease chapped lips.
- Use mouth swabs moistened with water or suck on hard, sugar-free candy to relieve your dry mouth. Some new chewing gums designed especially to deal with dry mouth might help. Ask your pharmacist for a pack. Do not give hard candy to someone who is confused or has trouble swallowing.
- Brush your teeth or use mouth sponges to clean your teeth, mouth, and tongue.
- Use only alcohol-free or low-alcohol-formula mouthwashes. Alcohol and petroleum-based products can be very drying and should be used with care, if at all.

---

traditions) and its bringing people together socially, often more so than for its nutrition. Unless particular foods make you sick, when you are close to the end of life, eat what you want, not what someone thinks you should.

Constipation

Constipation is commonplace and very uncomfortable. With limited intake, little activity, and the effects of medications, it is no wonder that your bowels may be sluggish. You may also experience abdominal cramping from constipation. Preventing constipation is very important. Do not wait for it to become a problem before telling your doctor or care team. They can come up with a regular program to prevent constipation or treat it very early.

If possible, and if your condition can tolerate it, make sure to drink several glasses of fluid every day. Also, get as much fiber as you can in foods such as fresh vegetables, fresh fruits, and whole grains. Dried fruits such as raisins, prunes, and apricots can help as well. Do NOT take fiber supplements without asking your doctor or care team if you should.

Talk to your doctor or nurses about using stool softeners, laxatives, and enemas to relieve constipation, especially if you are taking opioids. Always try to prevent constipation. Relief of constipation can improve your comfort, often even during late stages of dying.

Bowel Obstruction

Your bowels can get blocked sometimes, especially in abdominal cancer. If you might have many months to live, doctors will advise surgery. However, if you are close to the end of life, you can stay quite comfortable without surgery by using medications to slow bowel contractions and other means to prevent stomach overfilling, as needed. A little pathway may open up, perhaps with some help from steroids, so that fluids can be absorbed normally. Although bowel obstruction may be a final complication before death, dying this way can be made quite comfortable (see Chapter 11 on forgoing nutrition and hydration).

Mr. Horace Black came to an inpatient hospice with widespread cancer and a stomach obstruction. He had a plastic tube, suctioning his stomach, hooked to a vacuum pump. He was quiet and resigned. He had almost no family left, only a sister living in a nursing home nearby. *The hospice nurse asked him if he'd like to try going without the suction tube. He couldn't believe that this might be possible and talked with the doctor, who said it might actually be preferable to get rid of the tube. The worst that might happen would be some vomiting, and the tube could be replaced if he wanted it back. In fact, if he wanted, he could take a little food and drink.*

A few hours later, after some additional medications and with the tube gone, Mr. Black sipped a little fresh orange juice. Then this very reserved man called his sister and was overheard to say, tears running down his cheeks, "Rose, I'm alive again! Either that or I'm already in heaven! I'm free of that awful sound, and I'm actually tasting juice. Life is so sweet!" Things went well for him. He had little appetite but enjoyed small tastes of favorite foods. He died peacefully ten days later.

"What are bed sores and how can I prevent them?"

When you are very sick, you are prone to have skin breakdown wherever the weight of your body presses into the bed. You are at greatest risk if you move very little or if you are in bed or in a chair for a long time, especially if you also have been losing weight. Ordinary pressure on the skin as you sit or move across sheets may be enough to tear or break down your skin. It is worth a great deal of effort to keep skin well protected; skin breakdown is uncomfortable, a major indignity, and a major expense.

"I want to stay awake; there's so much yet to do"

Fatigue accompanies most fatal illnesses. Sometimes this tired, weak feeling comes from the disease. Other times, medicine can make you sleepy or slow down your thinking. It is certainly reasonable to try to save energy for the things that really matter to you. It is often not essential to make a trip to the physician's office or to continue a medication or exercise that is no longer helping, especially if doing so saps energy you need for something else.

Protecting Your Skin

- Change position at least every two hours. If you are in bed and comfortable in most positions, it is good to lie on one side, then your back, then the other side. If you need help, a skilled nurse can show your family members how to help you shift positions comfortably.
- Use pillows to protect the common pressure points—under the ankles to suspend the heels and between the legs to separate the knees.
- Apply gentle massage with moisturizing lotion or cream to the back, arms, ears, hands, legs, and feet—but not to any area with redness or sores unless your doctor or nurse agrees.
- If you are at great risk for skin breakdown, you may want to get a special "flotation" bed, which can be rented for home use.
- If you or your family notices newly reddened or broken skin on pressure points, a foul odor, or skin close to an ulcer that is warm and swollen, call your doctor or nurse. You may need special medications, dressings, or bed accessories (such as soft pads or heel protectors) to provide added skin protection.

Sometimes it is worthwhile to try a stimulant—caffeine or a stimulant pill. Talk with your doctor about trying out something like that if your fatigue seems to be the major block to your enjoying your family or some other activity.

Tips For Reducing Fatigue And Conserving Energy

- Plan activities and be sure to use your energy for what is most important to you.
- Meditation, prayer, yoga, and other mindfulness activities may help to decrease fatigue.
- Eat as well as you can. It may be easier to eat several small meals each day.
- Limit your alcohol consumption.
- Keep a fatigue journal to track your experiences.
- Plan for frequent periods of rest rather than one long nap during the day.

- Ask family and friends to call before they visit. Schedule time to rest both before and after their visits.
- Ask for a bedside commode to reduce or eliminate tiring trips to the bathroom.
- Ask family to rearrange furniture so that you can exert yourself a little less. For instance, set up a tray near your favorite chair where you can sit and eat some of your meals.
- Instead of giving up favorite activities, try shorter or easier versions.
- Tell your doctor about your fatigue. It might be time to change some of your medications.

"Sometimes I just don't feel like doing anything."

If you have no interest in what is going on, see only the bleak side of life, take no pleasure in things that you usually enjoy, or seem to feel no emotions at all, then you may be suffering from a treatable, clinical depression. This is different from feeling sad about your illness or the end of your life. Depression is a medical condition. It especially affects older people and people coping w ith serious illnesses. It can also be a result of having pain for a long period of time.

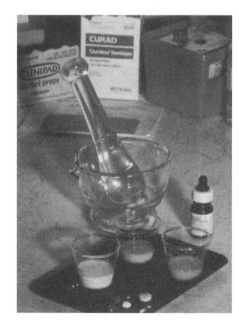

There are some things that depression is NOT. It is not a sign of weakness. It is not a sign of failure. It is not a sign that you have nothing left to share with those you love.

It is important for you or your family to talk to your doctor so that depression can be diagnosed and treated. Treatment is often effective, even in the last weeks of life. Not only will you feel better, but your family will feel better knowing you enjoyed the time you spent with them.

"I'm just so anxious about things. Sometimes I even feel panicked."

Anxiety is more than normal worrying. Anxiety is feeling so worried or fearful that it interferes with your functioning, coping, and enjoyment of life. If you typically feel anxious during periods of stress, you may be more likely to feel anxiety now. The coping skills that have helped you in the past may help you now. These may include getting reassurance, learning more about what is troubling you, or staying busy with activities you enjoy.

Some people have greater anxiety because they feel uninformed or overwhelmed. If you are feeling this way, it is very important that you tell your doctor and family that you might do better if you had more information or more help. Good communication is probably the most important remedy for anxiety of this nature.

If your anxiety is not managed, or if you have attacks of panic, then medication is likely to be helpful. Daily medications may help control general anxiety. Other medications are available for occasional episodes or when something out of the ordinary is likely to make anxiety or panic strike.

"Should I be worried about getting confused or just being 'out of it'?"

When you are very ill, it is easy to become confused. Confusion may be caused by a new medicine, a minor infection, or even a change in living arrangements. If this happens to you, your family should offer you soothing reassurance, perhaps reminding you where you are and what is going on around you. Your doctor should be called in case it is helpful to adjust medications or prescribe antibiotics. Sometimes the visions and experiences that the dying person has are comforting and meaningful: seeing family members who have died before, for example. You and your family may be grateful for these experiences.

If you are quite frightened or upset, however, you may feel better if your doctor orders a mild tranquilizer or if someone can stay with you at all times. Medications are often quite effective, even at low doses. Roughly half of

dying persons are unconscious for most of their last few days. This common "drifting off" while asleep is a peaceful way to die, especially if you and your family are at peace and all plans are made. Some people contend that a dying person is often still able to hear. Although this is unproven, your family can talk to you and say their good-byes, assuming that, in some way, you can hear them.

"Remind me—can anything good happen?"

A list like this can make you feel a little overwhelmed, even though each symptom can be treated. As you have read elsewhere in this book, it is not enough to have good symptom management. Good dying is not just avoiding bad experiences. Living well with a fatal illness involves having experiences that matter—having the chance to grow spiritually, getting to say some farewells and to feel the love of those who care about you, even just getting to see the flowers bloom one last time. You will have more chance at this if you are comfortable and confident of your doctors and nurses, of course. When you know that time may be short, every hour counts.

9
Living with Specific Illnesses

"I told my son, 'Spencer, I hope every mosquito that bites me this summer dies from the chemotherapy.' He quickly replied, 'Either that, Mom, or there are going to be a lot of bald-headed mosquitoes at Hide-A-Way Lake this summer.'"
DODY SHALL, *Seven-year breast cancer survivor*

Regardless of your illness, you are likely to share many concerns with others who face life-threatening disease, including the fears, worries, and needs for information and support that accompany this critical time in your life. Your particular illness will shape some of what you can expect to happen. It will affect how much can really be predicted. It helps to know that doctors often can give only very general guidance on how long you will live and what problems are likely to arise. Even more than birth, death is not always predictable or logical. Nevertheless, you should press your doctor and your care team to tell you the best and worst that your illness is likely to cause.

Organizations devoted to a particular illness can provide you with helpful information and resources, often connecting you to support groups based in your own community. Only a few, though, are prepared to deal with the problems that illnesses cause close to the end of life. We have included some of the addresses, phone numbers, and websites in Chapter 17. The Internet offers an overwhelming amount of information. Be cautious in relying on the information posted in newsgroups or on bulletin boards. Some of it will be no more reliable than advice you might get from a random person sitting with you on a bus. Check it out with your doctor or care team before you trust it. One reliable source of information is the U.S. government's site, healthfinder (http://www.healthfinder.gov/), which screens sites before adding links to them.

How long do I have?

Regardless of your disease, you will want to understand your prognosis—that is, the probable course of the disease. This conversation is likely to have occurred after the initial diagnostic testing or surgery or hospitalization. However, discussion of prognosis should remain an ongoing conversation during any treatment planning, especially when there is evidence of advanced disease. You and your doctor will often find it hard to talk about these issues. It is always easier to "put it off until the next visit."

> She got better. "Better" does not mean great; she walks with some difficulty now; she is fragile in ways she once was strong. . .
>
> —BOB GREENE, Mother's Day posting on CNN.com

This conversation might be easier if you include it in nearly every encounter. Try out something like this: "I understand that we are always pretty uncertain when looking at the future, but what I understand now about how this disease is likely to go is that I am likely to live with it for some months before it starts really limiting what I can do, and that then I will probably have just a few months left. Is there anything else you can tell me now? Is it reasonable to think that I will still be able to travel to be with my children this Christmas?"

Some days, you really just won't want to deal with the future. Even then, you can help the conversation next time by saying something like this: "With all the worries of the last few weeks, I can't really bear to think of things getting worse. Still, next time I see you, I would appreciate an update on how I'm doing and what problems are likely to arise, given how my disease is progressing and how I feel." By doing this, you create an opening that will make it easier for either of you to bring up the subject next time.

What follows in this chapter are summaries of important issues likely to arise in each of a series of common illnesses causing death. These thumbnail sketches are not meant to be complete but to give you enough information to guide you in knowing what issues to pursue for yourself.

How to Stay in Touch with Your Prognosis

- Don't ask, "How long do I have?" Ask: "Given my condition, what is the shortest and longest that I can reasonably expect?"
- At virtually every encounter, reconfirm likely symptoms and needs in general terms: "From what I know now, I'm making plans around a need for _____ (occasional severe illness, a few months of substantial disability, a risk of seizures, whatever….). Is that about right? Anything else?"
- When something new arises, ask: "Does this change what I can expect?"
- Expect that many doctors won't really know the answers. Ask your doctor, "How many patients like me have you followed through to death?" Don't accept: "There's no one quite like you!" If your doctor doesn't really have any experience, find someone (another doctor, a home health nurse, a nursing home nurse, a hospice professional, or a support group leader) who has "been there" before.

Heart disease

More Americans will die from diseases of the heart and the circulatory system than from any other cause. For most, the death will seem sudden, even if the person has been ill for some time. Most people with serious heart and blood vessel disease have episodes of serious illness—heart attacks or heart failure, for example—and then long periods in which nothing changes.

> I stepped from Plank to Plank
> So slow and cautiously;
> The Stars about my Head I felt,
> About my Feet the Sea.
>
> I knew not but the next
> Would be my final inch,—
> This gave me that precarious Gait
> Some call Experience.
>
> EMILY DICKINSON

By the time you realize that heart disease might well be the cause of your death, you will already have heard about improving diet and exercise, stopping smoking, and controlling blood pressure and fats in the blood. However, you are not particularly likely to have heard from a doctor about how your disease is likely to affect you over time. Many doctors haven't really thought about it; they work on the problem you have right now and get you "back on your feet." They may not think much about how your life is going until you are sick again.

This leads to all kinds of misfortunes for many people with bad heart disease. No one warns them that they might live a long time—or might be gone rather suddenly. You will think that you will get a decent warning of when your time is at hand, just like your Aunt Bertha with breast cancer or Cousin Harry with kidney failure. Not so. You may become too short of breath to walk stairs, or you may stay relatively well. Either way, you are likely to end up dying within a few days of being quite stable in your "ordinary" health.

Society has not really taken the opportunity to think about what it would be to live well with the high risk of sudden death. Certainly, you are not likely to want to stop all treatment—ongoing treatment and treatments of bad episodes keep you pretty comfortable and functional. On the other hand, you probably would like to avoid dying on a ventilator in intensive care. You want that decent opportunity to say your farewells and make peace with your life.

Serious heart disease is a signal that you really should make plans for the kinds of sudden events that can be emergencies. Your family needs to know whether you want the emergency rescue team called, whether you want resuscitation tried, and whether you want intensive care stopped if it seems that you have lost the ability to live outside of a hospital or nursing home. You should write down instructions for your family and put them in obvious places in your home (e.g., on the refrigerator or telephone). Also, be sure your instructions are filed in your doctor's medical records and your records at the local hospital.

Dying with heart disease requires that you say "farewell" in a "can't be sure" mode. Rather than the final farewells that movies portray as people die of violence or cancer, you need to draw people together and to finish your life work in a way that acknowledges that you might still live a long time, or you might not. Perhaps you can make a video for the grandchildren; that is an enduring gift. Or you could write some letters and put them with your will. Most people

respond pretty well to an open acknowledgment of the uncertainty of the situation. Perhaps you can call a loved one you have not seen in some time and say:

"My doctor says that I just won't know when my time is up. I would really like to see you and have some time to talk. It doesn't have to be 'good-bye.' Maybe I'll still be around for a decade. But, just in case I'm not so lucky...can you find some time to come visit for a few days in the next few months? Hearing that I have a

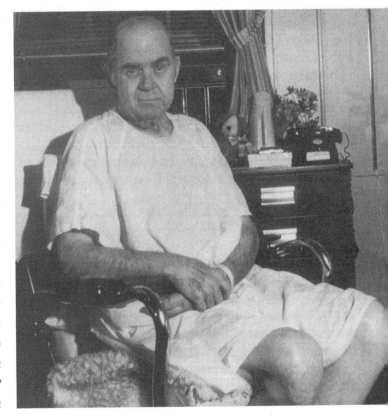

bad heart really makes me see things differently. I would like to spend some time with you."

People with heart disease may not have serious problems with chest pain. But you may well be troubled with fatigue, shortness of breath, or more generalized pain. You may have little tolerance for exercise. If you do have chest pain, that can usually be eased with medications. At the end, you might have serious shortness of breath.

One major decision that you should make in advance, if possible, will be whether to use a machine that will take over breathing (a ventilator or respirator). Sometimes, the odds of that working are so low that the doctor will advise against it. Sometimes the ventilator might well work in relieving the shortness of breath, but you may be too weak to live without the ventilator. You deserve the chance to talk this over with your doctor and to make plans. You will find more discussion about ventilator use and decision making in Chapter 11.

Because these decisions are difficult, you really need a doctor you can trust to have the skills to rescue you from episodes of shortness of breath and to help you when death will be the outcome. Ask the doctor directly whether he or she will use opioids or other medications to ensure that you will not feel a sense of suffocation, especially if you choose to avoid or stop using a ventilator. If the doctor is not willing or has never faced such a situation, you might do well to find another doctor, or at least a good hospice program with a care team that will stand by you. You also need to be sure that your family is aware of your decisions and will support them.

You need to move as much treatment as you can into your home (including into a nursing home, if that is where you live). To do this you need:

- A scale to take your weight every day (and the plans and medications to treat weight changes quickly).
- Important medications nearby for pain, shortness of breath, and weight gain. Your doctor can have you take them right after a telephone conversation or your care team can help you take them according to a preset plan.
- The decision made (among you and those who are around you) about whether you will go to the hospital in an emergency.
- The decision made and written down about whether to have resuscitation attempted.

Severe heart disease once killed people quickly. Now, most of us will live a long time after onset. A few will even get a chance to try a transplant. If you might be one, you will need to do even more thorough planning—both for survival through transplant and the more likely event of dying before transplant is attempted or shortly after.

Unless you have an implanted defibrillator, your dying will probably be rather sudden when it finally happens. If you have an implanted defibrillator (ICD), your heart will automatically get a shock if it starts beating in an uncoordinated way or stops. Mostly, this works to get a heartbeat going again and extends your life, but it also can get in the way of a peaceful death. At the time when you no longer want to keep shocking your heart to stay alive, simply have your care team turn off the defibrillator. This can be done from outside of your body with magnets or radio commands to the device. You can direct that the defibrillator be turned off in an advance directive (see Chapter 10) which specifies what circumstances should lead to it being stopped. Sometimes a patient chooses to have a defibrillator turned off after getting another serious diagnosis, thus choosing to risk a more sudden death rather than endure a slower dying. As always, be sure your care team knows your wishes and is ready to carry them out.

To have dying unfold in the way you want, you really must plan ahead. You need to make key decisions in advance and you need to ensure that you have a capable and experienced doctor and care team.

Cancer

Early in the course of dealing with cancer, treatments aim mostly at a cure or at least a longer life. With these goals, it is certainly worth going through a lot of discomfort. However, when cancer recurs or spreads despite treatment, it is likely to cause death eventually.

The benefits of trying more treatments aimed at controlling the cancer must always be weighed against the burdens those treatments will cause. Usually, a time comes when treatments to change the course of the cancer will not be helpful, even to make you more comfortable or improve your functioning. Even when there is "nothing more to do" to control the cancer, there is a lot to do to maintain comfort and give you the chance to do the things that are meaningful to you and your family.

My Father Breathes

When he taught us to swim
Breathing was the hardest part:
How to turn your head
Just so into a pillow of suffocating
Water and suck air from clouds
While keeping the complicated
Body afloat.
I think of those lessons
These days when cancer steals his breath
Frightens him into spasms of gasping
At air so ordinary and vital
We simply assume it's ours.
I offer instructions
For this most basic activity:
Breathe
In deeply through the nose
Gently out through pursed lips
Tongue rolled on the roof of the mouth.
I stand beside him whispering
"Breathe" like a prayer
While he clutches something in
And then
At least for now
Surfaces again.

JANICE LYNCH SCHUSTER

Doctors use all kinds of terms for cancer: malignancy, carcinoma, lymphoma, tumor, and so on. Most people just see cancer as a word for a bad disease that can act like a parasite and destroy the body. About one-quarter of Americans will die from cancer. Compared with some other life-threatening diseases, cancer can often be "managed" for a period of time. Most people are still able to take care of themselves and stay mentally alert until close to the end. For most people, with most cancers, pain is a real concern—but it can be controlled.

The term *cancer* refers to many diseases, each with its own distinctive characteristics. What is common to all is that cells change and grow in an abnormal fashion, multiplying uncontrollably. The continuing growth of these deviant cells leads to the development of a mass or growth called a tumor. Two unique characteristics of cancer cells create its life-threatening nature. First, cancer cells may spread to adjacent areas and invade normal tissues and organs, depriving them of nutrition and competing for space. Second, these cells may travel to a distant part of the body where they begin the development of another tumor, called a metastasis. The most common sites of metastatic spread are the bones, lungs, liver, and brain.

The most common signs and symptoms of advanced cancer are fatigue, weakness, loss of appetite, loss of weight, pain, nausea, constipation, sleepiness or confusion, and shortness of breath. Pain and shortness of breath are important symptoms to be prepared to treat. Make sure that your doctor and your other caregivers are good at preventing and treating them.

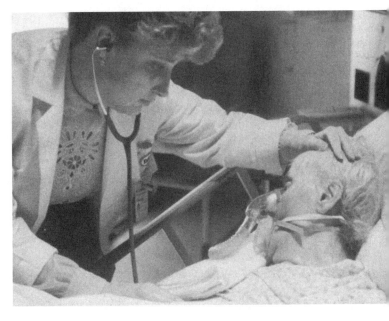

A symptom that is very disabling for many people with cancer is fatigue. This fatigue is more than being a little tired, and taking a nap or going to bed a little earlier is not enough to make it better. It is useful to rest as you need to while exercising gently when you are able. Save your energy as much as possible for important activities and events. But if fatigue continues to be a problem, talk with your doctor about medications that can help.

Some types of cancer—certain lymphomas, leukemias, and breast and prostate cancers—can become chronic illnesses. Long-term management using a combination of surgeries, medications, and radiation can often slow the progression of these diseases while alleviating symptoms. People often live for many years with some of these illnesses.

When treatments won't really change the time course of the cancer, you still need comfort care, or what doctors call *pallia-tion*, the relief of symptoms that interfere with your quality of life. In fact, you should aim to live well throughout the course of your illness, pursuing those personal goals that you can achieve while staying comfortable.

> The tongues of dying men
> Enforce attention like deep harmony.
>
> WILLIAM SHAKESPEARE
> from *King Richard II*

Treatment planning, how you and your doctor plan to manage and treat your disease, must be updated throughout the entire course of your care. Cancer is often unpredictable. Furthermore, someone with advanced cancer who is receiving supportive and comfort care may also need quite intrusive and technologically advanced treatment for specific emergencies, such as a broken bone, seizures, or tumors that compress the spinal cord. Occasionally, individuals who have not yet become debilitated can benefit from a short course of chemotherapy or radiation to reduce the size of a troublesome tumor. At all times, the benefits of any treatment must be weighed against its burdens. You don't want to refuse a treatment with minimal side effects that will help you a great deal. You don't want to be subjected to treatments that are worse than the disease!

Cancer has a special place in our culture as a particularly evil menace. You may feel that way, or you may tell yourself, "I had to die sometime, and this is not the worst thing that could have happened." Sometimes having brochures from the American Cancer Society, the National Cancer Information Center, or other resources helps. You should know whether there are any implications of your having this cancer for your family—some cancers tend to run in families and some do not (and some are still unclear). You might or might not care to know whether anything you did contributed to the illness. You might want to consider how you will respond to insensitive people who blame you for your situation, something that often happens to smokers who develop lung cancer. Many people with cancer find it helpful to meet with others with their disease, perhaps in a support group, in order to hear how others deal with the challenges they confront.

Lung disease: emphysema and chronic bronchitis

The most common serious lung disease is known as chronic obstructive pulmonary disease (COPD), emphysema, or chronic bronchitis. These are a group of related progressive and irreversible diseases that affect the ability to breathe in oxygen and breathe out carbon dioxide. Common symptoms of lung disease are: cough with phlegm, shortness of breath with any exercise, and wheezing.

Often, someone with lung disease will experience these symptoms for ten years or more before they become so bad that activities of daily living become difficult. Most people with lung disease find their difficulty breathing to be the most troublesome symptom. As the disease becomes severe, walking even short distances may be impossible, and breathing may become difficult

Lynn, Harrold, Lynch Schuster

even when resting or lying flat. Although there is no cure for the underlying disease, there are various methods available to treat shortness of breath.

Often, you will have oxygen at home, which can be used most of the time and as needed to help alleviate the difficulty breathing. The amount of time you spend using oxygen can be increased as the disease progresses. Various drugs open the air passages and make breathing easier. People with lung disease often find that these drugs give temporary relief to their shortness of breath, loosening mucus and aiding in the production of sputum, which relieves blockage of the air passages. These drugs do have side effects and may not be right for everyone with lung disease. Also, family caregivers can be taught a technique known as chest physiotherapy, in which they tap on the back of the person and turn them in specific positions to help bring up phlegm and clear the lungs to help prevent bronchitis and pneumonia.

> It might not be the worst way for any of us to live, even those of us who are much younger than she is; it might not be a bad idea for us to live as if someone has told us, "It may be two days. It may be two weeks." Imagining those words is a pretty good reminder that we should savor every hour we are given.
>
> —BOB GREENE, Mother's Day posting on CNN.com

As the lung disease becomes more advanced, you might not have enough oxygen circulating in your bloodstream, a condition that doctors call *hypoxia*. Also, you might not blow out enough carbon dioxide as you breathe, which doctors call *hypercapnia*. Together, these two effects lead to the feeling of shortness of breath and sometimes to decreased alertness. These problems with breathing can lead to confusion, unusual behaviors, tremors in the hands, and seizures. Physicians can provide oxygen therapy, medications to reduce shortness of breath, antiseizure medications, and medications to decrease the tremor.

Persons with lung disease can also become very anxious because of their difficulty breathing. This anxiety actually makes breathing more difficult. Medication can be given to reduce anxiety until the breathing improves, and meditation or guided imagery often helps you regain control.

Persons with lung disease may also experience pain. Often, pain is located in the chest as a result of coughing and excessive use of the chest muscles for breathing. At times, persons with lung disease cough so violently that they can fracture a rib. Medication or injections can usually ease these pains.

There are times when it will be important to call your doctor right away. Alert your doctor if you:

- Develop a fever.
- Cough more frequently than usual.
- Produce more sputum or see a change in sputum color to a green or rusty brown color.
- Experience increased chest pain on breathing.

These worsening or changing symptoms may be signs of a sudden worsening of lung disease. Especially during winter months, you will be more susceptible to infections, including bronchitis and pneumonia, which are the most common cause of setbacks. Persons whose lung disease has become worse because of infection can be treated with antibiotics and steroids. Depending on your symptoms, you may benefit from hospitalization and aggressive treatments, such as ventilator assistance.

One alternative to intubation and ventilation that is available for patients with lung disease who are very short of breath is called "BiPAP," or bilevel positive airway pressure. With this treatment, patients are fitted with a tight mask on the nose or the nose and mouth. The BiPAP machine then sends oxygen at a high enough pressure to keep the airways open. When you inhale,

the pressure helps the oxygen get into the lungs better. The pressure then decreases when you exhale. Another, similar alternative is "CPAP," or continuous positive airway pressure. As the name implies, oxygen is given at a continuous pressure to keep the airways open without a change for inhaling and exhaling. For some people, using BiPAP or CPAP can be enough to get over a period of difficult breathing. Others use it every night and even during the day at home. Ask your doctor if one of these might help ease your breathing.

Because of the nature of the disease, physicians often cannot tell how close people with lung disease are to death. Lung disease can usually involve several emergency episodes in which a person will be acutely ill, requiring "rescue" care to try to keep him or her alive. The underlying ability of the lungs to function will slowly decline, and the disease will eventually lead to death. Only a few people will get successful lung transplants.

People with lung disease and their family members need time to think about the illness, the prognosis, and options for treatments. If no discussion occurs until you are admitted to the hospital for an acute episode, you will be too ill, and decision making will fall to your family or doctor. Not only does this place a large burden on your family, but it also can lead to decisions that you would not have wanted. You should talk with your doctor and your family about your preferences for hospitalization and ventilators regularly, because you may well find that your priorities and preferences change. You will find it helpful to read the discussion in Chapter 11 about how to make decisions concerning various medical treatments.

You may also choose not to use cardiopulmonary resuscitation (CPR; attempting to restart the person's heart if it stops beating). As the lungs become more and more damaged, the benefits of CPR and ventilator decrease until they are no longer beneficial at all.

Health care providers can help with home care or hospice, with visiting nurses, oxygen and other breathing treatments at home, antibiotic therapy, and medication to relieve anxiety, pain, and difficulty breathing.

Both you and your family may find it better to be in the comfort of familiar surroundings with adequate treatment for relief of symptoms, knowing that the disease is not curable and that hospitalization will not alter the course much. Alternatively, you may decide to try the hospital for treatment but to stop if you are not doing well. Either way, plans need to be made with your family and physician to handle symptoms and events that may occur near death. For example, doctors can prescribe various treatments for shortness of breath, medication can be kept on hand for pain and to relieve anxiety and help with sleep, and drying agents can be prescribed if you have a lot of secretions.

Toward the very end of life, you may become less and less alert and may stop eating and drinking. You may become confused, may not recognize loved ones, or may become agitated and restless. Usually any such symptoms last only a short time, and they can be managed with medications. But you really need to have a doctor or hospice that knows how to handle shortness of breath as part of dying. They have to be willing to give opioids to relieve shortness of breath if that is what you need. (See also the discussion about heart disease earlier in this chapter.)

Kidney failure

Loss of kidney function leads to serious illness, affecting many aspects of physical well-being. The kidneys filter by-products of body chemistry and adjust the amount of liquid in the bloodstream. Many people have progressively diminished kidney (sometimes called "renal") function as they grow old, but usually this slow decline can be managed with diet and drugs. When the kidneys fail completely, you cannot live for long unless you have dialysis or a kidney transplant. A transplant that works relieves the person of kidney failure. However, transplants are not always available, appropriate, or successful.

> "The first time I saw the kidney machine I thought it looked like a big washing machine."
>
> S . HAYWOOD

Dialysis is the name for the process of artificially replacing the main functions of the kidneys. Hemodialysis refers to filtering the blood through a machine. Peritoneal dialysis refers to using fluid exchanges through the abdomen. Either procedure can be used to sustain life for years, but they do burden you and your caregiver, and each procedure has complications.

Sometimes a person whose kidneys no longer work decides not to continue or even not to start dialysis and to let death come from kidney (renal) failure. If you are considering this option, you need to know what is likely to happen. Usually, dying from kidney failure is fairly gentle, and most symptoms can be suppressed. The characteristics of your renal failure and your other medical problems help to predict which symptoms may arise.

As the by-products of the body's chemistry accumulate in renal failure, these substances cause an array of symptoms. You almost always lose energy and become sleepy and lethargic, but you may find it hard to sleep at night. Over time, the typical patient just slips into deeper and deeper sleep and gradually loses consciousness completely. However, early on, mild confusion and disorientation are common and usually require only reassurance as treatment. Sometimes, though, upsetting hallucinations or agitation arise. These can be treated very quickly with tranquilizers and antianxiety drugs. Certain minerals in the bloodstream can also accumulate and cause twitching of muscles, tremors and shakes, and even seizures. The tremors are usually of no importance to your comfort, but their onset can signal a need to prevent seizures. Medications to prevent or treat seizures are usually quite effective. Some patients develop mild or more severe itching before they become too sleepy to notice. This can be treated with creams, massage, and antihistamines. Sometimes a fine white powder can be seen on the skin, but it is not the cause of itching and is of no importance. Appetite decreases very early, again to no one's surprise. The accumulation of acids in the bloodstream causes rapid, shallow breathing; this is not an uncomfortable feeling, and the rapid breathing is not changed by oxygen.

Many people with kidney failure pass very little or no urine. If you pass little urine and are not on dialysis, you have to be careful to avoid problems with salt and water overload. Restricting your fluid intake to less than one quart of liquid each day will keep you from having much trouble. Fluid overload results in swelling of the body (edema), particularly of the legs and the abdomen. The excess fluid can also cause congestion of the lungs and the heart, leading to rapid breathing and shortness of breath. Sitting upright helps relieve the breathing difficulties, at least for a while, as it shifts the fluid away from the chest and toward the legs. It is often impossible for persons in this condition to lie flat. Oxygen and morphine may also ease any feelings of struggling to breathe.

It is important to know that persons with some urine output have lived surprisingly long times after stopping dialysis—sometimes for months. People with no urine output are likely to die within a week or two. If this is your choice, or the choice of someone you love, try to be sure that you have

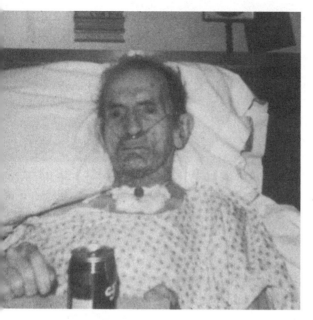

a doctor and nurse who are familiar with the problems that might arise and that medications to treat those problems are readily at hand, especially if you are in a nursing home or at home. In such situations, it is helpful to have a knowledgeable and experienced hospice team involved, as they will have procedures to get you any urgently needed medications. You probably will have a kidney specialist by this point, and that doctor may be a real help, both in making decisions and in keeping you comfortable. So, on the whole, when you have to die, allowing kidney failure to take its course is not generally a hard way to go. In years past, before dialysis became available, kidney failure had a reputation of being a gentle death.

Liver failure

Liver failure results in impairment of many functions we take for granted. Liver failure mostly arises slowly, over many years, but its progression is usually unnoticed. It can happen as a result of infections, cancer, alcohol or other toxic substances, and genetic causes. Often, when symptoms first appear, very little liver function is left. Much of the treatment of liver failure is focused on salvaging whatever liver function remains and avoiding overtaxing the liver. A few people with liver failure will qualify for, and successfully get, liver transplantation. Some people with careful attention to avoiding further stress on the liver may live for years, but most will die from the progression of the liver disease.

The liver has a multitude of functions: it helps digest food, filters and eliminates certain toxic chemicals in the blood, makes essential proteins, and maintains the level of energy-making compounds in the bloodstream. People with advanced liver failure are jaundiced because *bilirubin* accumulates in the skin, turning it yellow. The whites of the eyes become bright yellow-orange. Jaundice itself is not painful, but the abnormalities can cause quite troubling itching of the skin. Because certain compounds are not being put into the gut by the liver, bowel movements change from brown to chalky yellow-white. These brown com-

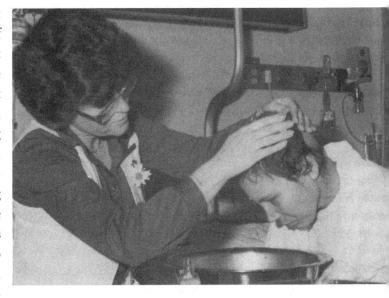

pounds showing up in the urine make it appear quite dark.

With liver failure you may:

- Feel weak, slow, and lethargic
- Experience muscle tremors and twitches and, in some cases, seizures
- Feel quite itchy
- Become confused, sleepy, or lapse into a coma
- Have trouble with bleeding
- Develop swelling in the belly and legs

Often, you can delay the onset of confusion by keeping the bowel movements very frequent—for example, with a laxative called lactulose. Sometimes the itching of the skin responds to drugs that bind up some of the toxic chemicals. Nausea and vomiting, when they occur, usually can be suppressed with antiemetic drugs.

Many people with liver failure develop severe swelling in the abdomen because fluids that usually pass through the liver cannot do so. Fluid in the belly (called *ascites*) can stretch the skin tight enough to be uncomfortable or can press against the lungs, making it necessary to remove part of the fluid with a needle. Because the liver is not making the proteins needed in the blood, fluid often seeps out of the bloodstream into the tissues, causing generalized edema. This swelling affects the belly, legs, and arms, and sometimes the face. Elevation of the legs, diuretic medications, and fluid and salt restriction may help these symptoms.

Bleeding is fairly common, because the failed liver is no longer able to make essential clotting substances. For example, there may be oozing from the gums when teeth are brushed, and large bruises may appear on the skin. In some cases, bleeding becomes the life-threatening event, usually with bleeding into the stomach. Treatments for this kind of severe bleeding may include interventions to block the blood vessels and transfusions of clotting proteins and of blood.

Unlike some illnesses for which there is a particular treatment to consider stopping, such as a ventilator or dialysis, most liver failure patients will not have a single clear issue for decision. Nevertheless, you can decide to forgo any further transfusions if bleeding occurs and to stop any other aggressive treatment that might sustain your life when complications arise. You should decide about resuscitation and hospitalization. Mostly, living with liver failure is the challenge. Dying from liver failure usually includes the fairly rapid onset of confusion and coma and thus is a merciful end. Having plans in place in advance for medical treatment decisions and for saying good-bye to friends and family is important to do.

HIV/AIDS

At one time, AIDS was a quick death sentence. Then there was a time when it was a rapidly progressive chronic disease with various difficult pathways through the end of life. In the last decade, the course of AIDS has changed again. With new drug regimens, many people are living for much longer, and how the usual person will die is again unclear. It still seems likely that persons with AIDS will probably die of complications of the disease, but often this will happen only after many years of living with the HIV infection. The very last phase is likely to include infections, tumors, or mental confusion. If you want to, you can take a strong hand in shaping what treatments will and will not be used when AIDS becomes advanced.

AIDS has become a "high-tech" disease. The medication regimens and machinery involved are difficult even for experienced health care professionals to manage. You will be well served to seek out doctors and teams who have lots of experience with AIDS patients, because they will be up to date on the best information as it becomes available. They also will be familiar with your needs and the challenges you face. Even if you are in a rural area or otherwise can't have an experienced team as your primary source of care, you might well find an experienced team in a nearby city to consult occasionally.

Because some people still believe (incorrectly) that HIV infection is contagious to people nearby and because family members are often unable to leave work, you may have to rely somewhat on paid caregivers and non-family volunteers. "Buddy" programs in the community can really help. Most people with AIDS will live a long time, but you will probably be sick from time to time and will have long periods when you have limited energy. You will do better if you keep connections to friends and family.

> "There are many who believe that this disease is God's vengeance, but I believe it was sent to teach people how to love and understand and have compassion for each other. I have learned more about love, selflessness and human understanding from the people I have met in this great adventure in the world of AIDS than I ever did in the cutthroat, competitive world in which I spent my life."
>
> ANTHONY PERKINS Actor

AIDS has affected mostly people who are relatively young. Thus you are not as likely as retired persons to have substantial financial resources and permanent housing. Yet you may have young children, and treating AIDS is very expensive. Almost everyone with AIDS needs to consult knowledgeable and experienced social workers who can help to secure support services for you and your family. Likewise, plans must be made for the care of any dependent children, some of whom may have been infected as well. Social workers are helpful here, too.

The situation may seem quite overwhelming. Caregivers often doubt their ability to meet the physical and psychological needs of AIDS patients.

Living with Specific Illnessess

Yet astonishing networks commonly are created, and caregivers ordinarily feel useful and positive about their work. Caregivers may worry about becoming infected. This is really exceedingly unlikely if everyone learns a system called *universal precautions* and uses it consistently, even when it seems a little silly or a little troublesome.

Bereavement seems harder for AIDS patients and their families. Many victims (and their caregivers) are young and frequently must deal with the losses of friends and family members who have also died of AIDS. Caregivers who are HIV-positive are being asked to confront their own futures every time they care for a loved one with advanced AIDS. For them, anticipatory grieving may be much more intense.

Not many years ago, it was very awkward to deal with death certificates with "AIDS" as the cause of death, and it was often even difficult to arrange funeral services. Now, you and your family are much less likely to run into these problems, but you still would do well to inquire and plan ahead. Preplanning funerals and handling of the body and arranging things having to do with the care of dependent children are especially important for many people with AIDS. Many of these things are much easier to do when the person dying can still sign legal papers and make decisions. It is often a great burden to family and friends to have to handle everything through the courts and official channels.

Remember, you often can't avoid feeling angry, and you will need to grieve. The situation is tragic. The intensity of your feelings is a reflection of the intensity of the situation. Just be sure to reach out for support and to try to express your appreciation when support is offered.

Patients with AIDS frequently take many medications which are troublesome because of their demanding timing and their side effects. Because of the unpredictable nature of the disease, it is sometimes hard to know which medications provide comfort or suppress the illness and which ones are ineffective or causing problems. Active, aggressive treatment often continues right up until death. When you can't keep track of why you are taking certain medicines, you may need to review them all with your doctor or nurse and see if some can be stopped or their timing can be simplified.

Depression or depressive symptoms are very common among people with AIDS. You should know the warning signs of these disorders and seek help if they occur. The desire to commit suicide can itself be a symptom of depression. So any decisions about assisted suicide or stopping treatment should be delayed until a physician can make an evaluation and treat underlying mental health disorders.

HIV/AIDS sometimes causes dementia or confusion. Again, it is important to use health care providers who are familiar with the management of AIDS and with these psychiatric disorders.

Physicians try to evaluate symptoms and treatments by keeping in mind "the big picture." You should do the same. Will the medication or test significantly enhance your quality of life or enable you to do something important? Is the treatment or test being used to prevent a symptom or to extend life? How does the medication make you feel? Remember, how you die is less important than how you live, right up to the end.

Special concerns for survivors of war and trauma

Millions of men and women have served as members of the military, in law enforcement, and in emergency services. Others have been similarly traumatized as civilians enduring war or torture. When they face a serious illness, their experiences may affect and influence how they deal with end-of-life issues. Perhaps the most important thing a family member or friend can do for such a survivor is to listen to whatever stories he or she decides to tell. Even if repetitious or a bit indecipherable, hearing the story has to count as a privilege and should not meet such objections as "Let it go," or "Forget about it." Even though it was "all a long time ago," the feelings of guilt, remorse, and loss may still be quite fresh.

Deborah Grassman, a nurse practitioner with more than thirty years' experience caring for veterans, offers observations that might be helpful to veterans' families and friends:

- Military service (and other strong experiences in a group) can provide a lifelong sense of identity, pride, and belonging. When clinicians and others thank a person for his or her service or suffering, they honor the patient's life.
- Military service may always be present in the veteran's experience. He or she may have served sixty years ago, but the memories of that

experience may be as fresh and as relevant as if it had happened yesterday. In particular, combat veterans may have memories and emotions that are closer to the surface as they near the end of life. Telling the stories to an empathetic listener helps.

- In battle and other dire circumstances, there is not time to grieve. Consequently, veterans and other survivors may find themselves grieving again—or for the first time—for the long-ago deaths of comrades. The power of these emotions may surprise even the patient.

- Soldiers are expected to be stoic, not to allow emotions to show or to get in the way. But that stoicism can keep a veteran from acknowledging pain or asking for pain management. People around the patient must make it natural and expected to use medications and other methods to be comfortable.

- Many veterans and other survivors find themselves having to come to terms with the "moral injury" of having killed or having had to make decisions or take actions that were morally reprehensible. Telling the story and hearing forgiveness by family or religious counselors obviously helps. When the survivor cannot tell the story, an empathetic forgiveness or a more ritual-based ceremony may help.

- Many veterans and other survivors have suffered from problems with alcohol or other drugs, or with mental health problems such as post-traumatic stress disorder (PTSD) or depression. Families have suffered the effects of the veteran's mental illness, too. Family members can often recognize and acknowledge this suffering and directly forgive the patient for it.

Dementia

More than one-fourth of those who live into old age will have some dementia, most often because of Alzheimer's disease or strokes. Dementia poses the most difficult treatment and planning questions for most people, future patients and caregivers alike. Persons with dementia die from an array of different complications, which may be treatable in earlier stages. Yet the treatments can be frightening, especially if they require that the person leave familiar surroundings.

The life saved, at least at the end, seems so limited that it is often not clear exactly which treatments should be included in "good care."

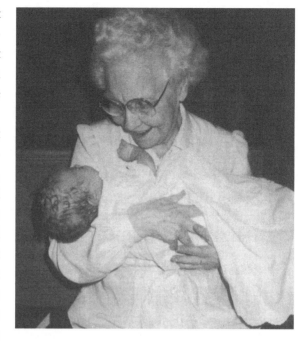

Everyone agrees that good care requires keeping the person clean, providing food and warmth, trying to keep him or her safe, and attending to things that cause pain. However, at some point, persons with dementia often stop eating enough to get by. Should they be fed with tubes? Some feel that such feeding is essential, even if it requires placing a tube in the stomach surgically to avoid having to restrain the person's hands. Patients often pull out a tube placed through the nose, but a surgically placed tube can be hidden under a dressing. Others feel it is really an affront to drag out the end of the person's life when he or she can have so little awareness or enjoyment. The courts have ruled, over and over, that using artificial nutrition or hydration is a treatment decision, just like chemotherapy or surgery, and that families and doctors can choose whether or not to use this kind of treatment.

How do people with dementia die when they are not fed artificially? What evidence we have indicates that they do not die more quickly and that they do not feel thirsty or hungry. Their dying without tube feeding tends to feature less struggling with restraints (which are often used to keep feeding tubes in place) and less trouble with an excess of fluids in the lungs, which causes shortness of breath. Without tube feeding, they probably lose a little more weight and might be at more risk of infections or skin problems, but these effects are also unproven. Mostly, people treated with or without feeding tubes end up sleeping away most of the last few weeks, and nothing very dramatic happens. If you find it quite perplexing to sort out whether a family member should have artificial nutrition, consider these things:

- Is he uncomfortable now?
- Could I tell if he were uncomfortable now or later?
- Would the situation be clearer if we tried tube feeding for a week or two?
- What do I think he would advise if he could have foreseen this?
- If the tube feeding were not readily available, would family members have wanted to seek it out?

If you are clear about what you want or if you feel that you might want to have all options available, be sure that your doctor, home care help, and nursing home (if appropriate) all agree. It can be very difficult to get a patient out of a nursing home or into the care of a new doctor if family and professional caregivers disagree about whether the patient can go without artificial feeding.

> While some changes have to be accepted through such adjustments in our own images and ideals, others can be resisted, met more actively, influenced for better or worse. A major challenge in taking care of demented people is telling the difference between the two kinds of change.
>
> JAMES AND HILDE LINDEMAN NELSON
> from *Alzheimer's: Answers to Hard Questions for Families*

The same kinds of questions come up about the use of antibiotics and surgeries, and even about hospitalizations. These treatments somehow are usually a little easier to turn down once the patient is quite demented. Still, family members need to have given the issues some thought and need to have forged a relationship with providers willing to follow the family's choice. You might also find it helpful to read the general discussion about deciding to forgo treatment in Chapter 11.

Dementia poses special problems for finding meaning. Usually the patient is living just in the moment, and issues of meaning and spirituality are beyond his or her capabilities. The family members, if they are providing care, are often quite stressed, often worn out. Enduring in the face of these challenges can be victory enough, but support groups, spiritual counseling, and recourse to one's faith often enable a sense of accomplishment in getting through a very difficult time.

Dying in very old age

When you are very old and dying, you may have different concerns than would a younger person. You may find that your wishes about care near the end of life are in conflict with those of your family members or friends. You may find that you have come to feel comfortable with the thought of death, especially if your spouse and close friends have passed away. Younger relatives and friends may wish to seek out new medical treatments for your disease, whereas you may be more content to put off dealing with medical things and put comfort first. Your son or daughter, for instance, may wish to try every treatment to keep you alive, in part because that seems to be what it takes to be a good child. Even older adult children must grapple with what it will mean to be motherless or fatherless.

Conversely, you may find yourself alone. You may no longer have family and friends alive and may count on acquaintances or paid help for caregiving support. As you become weaker with your illnesses and age, you may find that you feel isolated from your community. Your routine may change. Instead of going to the supermarket on Mondays, a club event on Wednesdays, and church or synagogue over the weekend, you can only muster the energy to make all the arrangements for a trip to the doctor's office every month. Make sure you communicate your needs to members of your community.

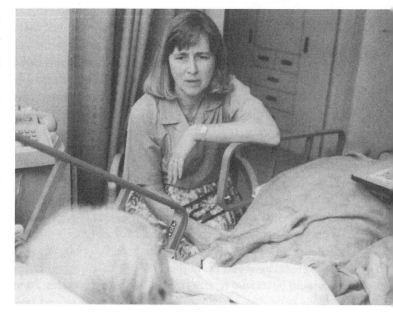

People from church or other organizations to which you belong may feel awkward dropping in uninvited but would be pleased to help you with a chore if asked.

You may wish to maintain your independence for as long as possible and avoid asking others to help. However, making connections now can prove valuable should your strength diminish.

Also, having many supports decreases your chance of becoming isolated. Ask neighbors to call you before they head to the grocery store so that they can pick up small items for you. You may even ask for a nonessential item, such as candy, so that you can look forward to a visit (and give some of the candy to the child who does the delivery). More advice is given in Chapter 5.

Advance planning is fairly obvious but often ignored. You really need to have plans in place for what to do if you are suddenly very sick and likely to die. Will your doctor come to your home? Is there a point when the various illnesses or your overall condition is enough to make hospice available to you? Can you have a skilled nurse who will come? Will you go to a nursing home at some point? There are a lot of uncertainties, and many of the possibilities may seem fairly troubling. However, remember that few will actually happen and that it is better that they work out in the way you want, rather than having some unknown emergency room doctor deciding your fate. If you are having trouble answering these questions, you can find more guidance in Chapter 10.

Your physical appearance is probably still important to you. Ask a neighbor to take you for haircuts or manicures. Having someone talking with you and making you look better will uplift your spirits.

Although you may enjoy getting dressed for outings, take care not to over- or under-dress. Pay attention to the weather, and use layers accordingly. You may feel inappropriate if you do not wear a suit to events to which you usually do so, but it would be unwise to wear one in 95-degree weather. As you age, your natural thermostat does not work as well as it used to, and you could overheat. Also, numerous medications could make your blood pressure drop and make you feel quite dizzy if you stand up quickly. Similarly, you should prepare for cold weather by always having a sweater or jacket available. You may or may not have been in the habit of routine exercise. Although you may no longer be able to take long walks, you need to do some exercises of the upper or lower body in order to maintain muscle strength. This routine is important to prevent dependence on others. You may be more motivated to exercise if you do it with music. Playing the same song every time you exercise will help to establish a routine.

As you age, your senses of taste and smell diminish, so that you will find it more difficult than a younger person to enjoy food. Much to your surprise, you may find that you enjoy adding strong flavors—vinegar, hot spices, aromatic spices, and pepper. Also, you may have dentures and find it difficult to chew certain foods, such as meats. Supplemental protein drinks, cheeses, eggs, or peanut butter can be good substitutes. Multigrain crackers eaten with the peanut butter or cheese may decrease the likelihood of constipation. Do not concern yourself with eating a low-cholesterol diet. You should eat what tastes good, even if it is ice cream.

> "But our machines have now been running 70 or 80 years, and we must expect that, worn as they are, here a pivot, there a wheel, now a pinion, next a spring, will be giving way; and however we may tinker them up for a while, all will at length surcease motion."
>
> THOMAS JEFFERSON, from a letter to John Adams, July 5, 1814

Vegetable juice or vegetable soup may be easier to digest than cooked vegetables. If possible, take a multivitamin with minerals each day. If, however, these pills are too large to swallow, have a family member cut them in half, or get the liquid or chewable forms made for children (and have your doctor or nurse help figure out how much to take).

You may find salty foods, such as crackers or nuts, more tasty than others. Do not restrict these if they taste good unless you have certain illnesses, such as congestive heart failure or hypertension, and your health care provider has recommended decreasing the salt in your diet. Be sure to ask the health care provider about whether dietary restrictions still apply. Your doctor may have told you years ago to be careful about salt intake or cholesterol in your diet, but the situation may be different as you age. For instance, your mild high blood pressure and subsequent need for salt restriction may disappear because you have lost weight.

When your appetite is poor, the thought of a large meal may worsen it. If a neighbor or friend brings over a large meal, or if you receive it from a community service agency such as Meals on Wheels, you can dish part of

---

Simple Exercise Program

- Ten arm circles forward (in the evening, do these backward)
- Ten leg lifts (sit in a chair, lift leg up, straightening knee)
- Ten shoulder stretches (use fingers to crawl up wall above your head)

Living with Specific Illnessess

the meal onto a dinner plate and eat only that amount. Save the rest for another time. Unlike a child who is eating to grow, you are eating just to enjoy yourself and to give yourself energy to manage the things you want to do each day.

Like other elders, you may be living with more than one illness or condition. You may suffer from osteoporosis and osteoarthritis, as well as a new-found cancer. You may have coped fairly well with one set of chronic diseases but find yourself overwhelmed by the prospect of dealing with another illness. Also, you may be concerned that treatments and medications may interact. This is a valid concern. Be sure to inform your doctors and nurses about how you cope with your other illnesses.

Many older people have some urinary incontinence. This, unfortunately, can worsen with many medications and some medical treatments. For instance, radiation or surgery done to treat prostate cancer usually worsens urinary incontinence. Do not give up your life because of this condition. Some persons with urinary incontinence dislike going out of the house for fear of having an accident. This further isolates them from their communities. Try out the new pads and underwear that can really keep you secure. Also, discuss this condition with your health care provider and ask whether certain medications are still needed. For instance, diuretics, which are often used to treat hypertension, can worsen incontinence. Ask whether they are still necessary or whether you can skip a dose occasionally. There are medical and surgical treatments for incontinence, but often patients are reluctant to discuss the condition.

If you are elderly, you may be the last remaining member of your generation, or at least the last person living in your house. As you get your affairs in order, it is, of course, important to make a will, but it is also necessary to give certain loved items to friends or members of your family. Don't assume that your only great-grandchild will find the antique doll in your closet and keep it for her own. If you have a strong opinion about who gets what, write it down. You don't want family members squabbling. You may enjoy giving the gift while you are still alive!

As an older person, you may have strong religious convictions. You may regret not getting out to your place of worship as often as you used to. You may miss both the spiritual and the fellowship aspects of the services. Communicate with religious leaders and ask whether the services can be brought to you. Ask them to tape the services so that you may listen.

Tell them that you would like a few members of the choir to come over and sing. Ask the pastor for a reprint of his or her sermon. Try to stay connected with the congregation.

Getting to live to old age is probably the supreme accomplishment of our society. Once, very few had the chance, but now most will. However, we do not yet have the social arrangements that ensure that you can live comfortably and meaningfully in your eighties and nineties and beyond. You and your family will have to create some novel social arrangements directly and find what will work best for you, your illnesses, your family situation, and your finances. It seems to help to keep the spiritual issues in mind, rather than letting medical problems and practical arrangements take over all of your attention. Push yourself and your family, at least a little, to enjoy some time doing things for one another, telling stories, voicing love and forgiveness, and sharing pleasant times. Those will be the shared experiences that get you through hard times, and those will be the times that your family and friends will remember with fondness.

10

Planning Ahead

I slept in a bed
in a room with paintings
on the walls, and
planned another day
just like this day.
But one day, I know,
it will be otherwise.
JANE KENYON, from *"Otherwise"*

Most of us do not plan for serious illness and death, and many of us feel that
if we don't talk about bad things, they won't happen to us. However, talking,
planning, and being better prepared for the last phase of life can let you live
fully and more comfortably. Have you thought about the services you want
during a severe illness, especially at the point at which you are not likely to
live much longer? Have you talked with your family about plans to ensure
that you will get the care and treatment that you want? When you are very
sick, you are likely to have some times when you cannot say what you want.
When you have not planned ahead, and your wishes are unknown, it may be

impossible to have things go as you would have hoped. Worse, it may not be possible to avoid circumstances that you most wanted to avoid. By making important decisions about your care ahead of time, you have a greater say in that care. You can help your family to avoid conflict and confusion about what to do.

Why do I need someone to speak for me?

One of the most important things to do is to name someone to speak and act for you in situations in which you are not able to do so. If you should become unable to speak for yourself or make decisions for yourself, this person will be your legal surrogate, or proxy. Choosing a legal surrogate is one of the most basic and important tasks in making advance plans. Your proxy will need to be able to act in ways that reflect your wishes and desires—not his or her preferences or values. You may want to have several of your family members discuss decisions about your care, in addition to appointing one of them. In any case, your doctors should always know who to turn to for decisions when you cannot decide for yourself. If you have no close family—or if your family doesn't work together very well—it is important to figure out who should be your "voice" and to involve that person in treatment decisions all along, throughout your illness. Although people tend to rely on family members, you may feel that someone else is in a better position to act as your spokesperson—she may

be nearer than your own family members, for instance, and be able to get to your side during an emergency. In any case, you should not feel obligated to choose one person or another. Choose the person who is most able.

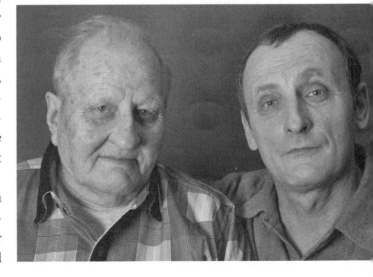

At times when you cannot make or communicate your wishes or decisions, you will need

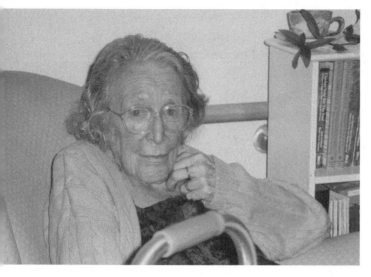

someone else to do so for you—and your doctor should always know who this person is. You can select this person (and talk to him or her about your decision) before writing your decision into a durable power of attorney or health care power of attorney. This document gives another person authority to make decisions if you become unable to do so. Most people appoint a family member or close friend. If you don't have anyone, a minister or lawyer may be willing to serve. Make sure the person you choose will support you in the way that you want, understands your treatment choices, and knows what you value.

Giving someone else this authority can be even more important than writing down your preferences. After all, none of us know for certain what changes in our situations may occur or what decisions will have to be made. Your spokesperson should be someone who can make your values and choices clear in a variety of situations. Otherwise, you risk having decisions made contrary to your wishes or by people you would not have chosen.

Remember that your proxy has authority when you cannot make your own decisions and not before. Many people fear that naming a proxy will allow someone else to override the patient's own spoken wishes if they still make their own decisions, but this is not the case.

You can give your surrogate clear authority by signing a durable power of attorney for health care or health care proxy. These documents do not have to give explicit guidance to your proxy about what decisions to make. Many states have developed forms that combine the intent of the durable power of attorney (to have a decision maker) and the intent of the living will (to state your choices for treatment at the end of life). These combination forms will probably be more effective than either of the two when used separately.

Your proxy should meet several criteria, including the following:

- Be legally able to make decisions for you.
- Be willing to act assertively on your behalf.
- Be able to separate his or her feelings from yours on points on which you do not agree and still speak for your preferences and choices.
- Be available: live close by or be willing to come when necessary.
- Know you well.
- Understand what is important to you.
- Be willing to pursue what you value.
- Be willing to talk *now* about your wishes.
- Be able to work with your professional caregivers and family members to carry out your wishes.
- Be able to handle responsibility and conflict.

ADAPTED WITH PERMISSION FROM *COMMUNITY CONVERSATIONS ON COMPASSIONATE CARE: AN ADVANCE CARE PLANNING PROGRAM*, DEVELOPED BY THE COMMUNITY-WIDE END-OF-LIFE/PALLIATIVE CARE INITIATIVE AND EXCELLUS BLUE CROSS BLUE SHIELD.

"What should I keep in mind when choosing a proxy?"

By talking deeply and openly with your proxy, you will lay the groundwork for someone who can truly speak on your behalf, based on conversations with you about very specific issues related to your illness and prognosis.

To be an effective proxy, the person you choose must know what is important to you. Knowing this can not only guide her in making decisions but can also comfort her when those decisions involve issues such as ending life support or forgoing medical treatment.

As a starting point, you might want to invite your family to sit down with you and have a heart-to-heart conversation about your values. Talk about what is important to you and why. Write down your answers, if you can, and file them where others can easily find them. If possible, make copies of your values statement and share it with people who are most important to you. Ask your family if they'd be willing to complete the values history questionnaire,

A values history questionnaire

1. What do you value most about your life? (For example: living a long life, living an active life, enjoying the company of family and friends, etc.)
2. How do you feel about death and dying? (Do you fear death and dying? Have you experienced the loss of a loved one? Did that person's illness or medical treatment influence your thinking about death and dying?)
3. Do you believe life should always be preserved as long as possible?
4. If not, what kinds of mental or physical conditions would make you think that life-prolonging treatment should no longer be used?

    - Being unaware of my life and surroundings.
    - Being unable to appreciate and continue the important relationships in my life.
    - Being unable to think well enough to make everyday decisions.
    - Being in severe pain or discomfort.

5. Could you imagine reasons for temporarily accepting medical treatment for the conditions you described?
6. How much pain and risk would you be willing to accept if your chances of recovery from an illness or an injury were good (50-50 or better)?
7. What if your chances of recovery were poor (less than 1 in 10)?
8. Would your approach to accepting or rejecting care depend on how old you were at the time of treatment? Why?
9. Do you hold any religious or moral views about medicine or particular medical treatments?
10. Should financial considerations influence decisions about your medical care?
11. What other beliefs or values do you hold that should be considered by those making medical care decisions for you if you become unable to speak for yourself?
12. Most people have heard of difficult end-of-life situations involving family members or neighbors or people in the news. Have you had any reactions to those situations?

ADAPTED FROM THE VERMONT ETHICS NETWORK

Advance care planning basics

When you are healthy:

- Identify and document someone to make decisions for you (your surrogate).
- Talk with your surrogate about your preferences for how you want things to go, both good and bad.
- Let your doctor know if you have religious beliefs or traditions that influence your decision making.
- Write down your preferences.

When you are diagnosed with a serious, chronic illness:

- Do all of the above.
- Think about what is important to you now—your values, beliefs, and needs.
- Talk to your doctor and family about possible treatments and their burdens and benefits.
- Ask your doctor about time-limited trials for certain treatments.
- Ask your doctor about your prognosis.
- Introduce your surrogate to your doctor/nurse.
- Talk to your doctor about how your illness is likely to progress and turn out.
- Discuss next steps and follow-up measures.

When you are diagnosed with an eventually fatal illness:

- All of the above, with a focus on the following steps:
- Discuss potential treatments and their likely effects or results.
- Ask your doctor to review the possibilities for time-limited trials of certain
- treatments or interventions.
- Talk to your doctor and family about what you would like to do or accomplish in the time you have left, and how they can help you fulfill those hopes or plans.

too, so that you can engage in a real conversation about what is meaningful to each of you and why.

How can you get started? First, think in very general terms. Have you talked with your family about how you want to live, given the circumstances? Do they know what kind of medical services you want to have or want

ADVANCE CARE PLANNING: Determining and documenting your goals and wishes for specific treatments based on your medical condition and personal preferences. With an advance care plan, clinical care is shaped by your choices, even if you become unable to make decisions for yourself. By anticipating emergencies, decisions will rarely have to be made in a crisis, with inadequate information or reflection.

ADVANCE DIRECTIVE: A legal, written document made by a competent individual about preferences for future treatment if that person is unable to make decisions at the time. "Advance directives" include the two forms which most states recognize as legally important: the living will and the health care proxy (or durable power of attorney).

DURABLE POWER OF ATTORNEY FOR HEALTH CARE, HEALTH CARE POWER OF ATTORNEY, OR HEALTH CARE PROXY: *A document* that gives another person legal power to make medical decisions when you no longer can make your own. The written form used to appoint the proxy is often called a "durable power of attorney" for health care decision making. Some states have a list of the order of family members to serve as a proxy when one has not been named.

PROXY OR SURROGATE: The person you name as your spokesperson may be referred to as your 'proxy' or 'surrogate'.

LIVING WILL: A written document that gives instructions for treatments to be used or avoided at end of life when that individual becomes unable to express his wishes for health care treatment. Often people use a preprinted form, but it is most useful when the dying person adds specific instructions related to his situation.

FORGOING LIFE-SUSTAINING TREATMENT: Choosing not to have specific treatments that might have been used to try to extend your life. This can be done by withholding treatments, which is a choice not to start the treatment. It can also be done by withdrawing, or stopping, a treatment after it is started.

LAST WILL AND TESTAMENT: A legal document to determine what will be done with your money, property, and other possessions after you die. If you do not write a will, the laws of the state will determine how your wealth is passed along to family members. The will, however, is not read until after you die and cannot be used to direct services while you are still alive.

PHYSICIAN-ASSISTED SUICIDE: An end of life brought about when a physician hastens a patient's death by providing the necessary materials (drugs) or information that allows someone to take his or her own life. This is illegal in most states. (See Chapter 12.)

Overcoming Barriers to Completing Advance Care Plans

Barrier	Keep in mind
I don't know enough about what I face or how to plan.	The Handbook helps you get started. Talk to your care team, too, about your situation and what your community has to offer.
It's just not that important to me right now.	Whether or not you have a life-threatening illness now, making plans is important. Acute illness and injury may strike at any time, leaving you unable to make or voice your own decisions. You are likely to make better decisions as you think more about the possibilities.
I just don't have time.	Planning for serious illness is as important as budgeting for your future, writing a will, or any of the other things you do to secure your future. Try to make it a priority.
I don't know how to raise the issues with my family.	Let them know you have been reading this book, that you have been thinking about your future in terms of your health, and that you really need to talk to each other about what's next.
I don't want to think or talk about it.	Avoiding the issue will not make it go away. The issues will still come up, and no one will be prepared—unless you take action ahead of time.
It's just too hard.	You are not alone in these feelings. But the benefits are so important—you'll have peace of mind, your family will be relieved of the burden of not knowing what to do, and you can help avoid confusion and conflict. Most important, you'll get the support you need for what you most want to do.

ADAPTED WITH PERMISSION FROM *THE COMMUNITY CONVERSATIONS ON COMPASSIONATE CARE: AN ADVANCE CARE PLANNING PROGRAM*, DEVELOPED BY THE COMMUNITY-WIDE END-OF-LIFE/PALLIATIVE CARE INITIATIVE AND EXCELLUS BLUE CROSS BLUE SHIELD.

to avoid? Have you discussed advance care planning with your physician? Does he know what you prefer to be done or not done? What kind of life do you want to lead—and what would prevent you from doing so? Which circumstances are you willing to tolerate, and which would be unbearable? Do you want every possible treatment tried, even when it involves mechanical support for body functions or even when it is not likely

Planning Ahead

to work? Do you want to die at home, even if doing so might mean going without some treatments or supports? Many of us don't take the time to figure out our wishes and hopes for the last part of our lives. Others write living wills but don't tell anyone what they really want that document to accomplish. Considering the possibilities and talking them over with family and clinicians makes it much more likely that you can live well through to the end of life, despite serious illness.

What if...?

Discussions about what kinds of treatment you want are more likely to be well developed and helpful when they occur long before decisions about your care and treatment actually have to be made. You might call this *"what if?"* planning. *What if* I should become too sick to eat except through a tube? *What if* my doctors say I will have only a short time to live? *What if* I can't talk or write or signal my thoughts? *What if* I can't be kept comfortable at home? *Then,* who do I trust to make important treatment decisions for me? This *"what if?"* planning may feel uncomfortable or scary. But it will help you have the life you want and to feel more in control. It also can be a very special gift to family and loved ones, who can be spared the burden of making choices without knowing what is most important to you.

Many of the choices you will make about the last phase of life will involve medical treatments. But these decisions are not likely to be the most important ones. Your ideas and hopes about the end of your life—being with your family, or making peace with God, for example—are the more meaningful ones. Your values and beliefs should guide medical choices whenever possible—not the other way around.

One way to approach these kinds of choices is to consider the questions on a ***values history questionnaire*** like the one on page 154. These are not questions that you are likely to find in most living wills. Your answers will not be simple yeses or nos. Although this questionnaire may look complicated, it can help guide you in a conversation with your spokesperson or anyone else who may have to make decisions for you when you cannot. Completing a questionnaire like this—even part of it—will help you think about how you hope things will be. Your answers will also be a useful way to get started talking with your family. One starting point is to ask the most basic of questions: What is most important to you? What matters most to you, even in the midst of illness or poor health? What do you hope for and what do you fear? What makes your life good? And what can help to make your dying "good"?

If you have signed a standard living will, you may think that you do not need the values history questionnaire. Advance directives, such as living wills, are legal documents, and the values history questionnaire is not. However, despite the precise legal language, living wills are often difficult to interpret. Conventional living wills include words such as *terminal, extraordinary,* and *heroic* that mean different things to different people at different stages of disease. Thus your answers to the values history questionnaire can be useful to your proxy, who needs to understand what you mean in your advance directive, taking into account your stage of disease and overall condition. You are often best advised to complete a values history *and* a legal advance directive.

I have strong views, but they aren't about medical treatments!

Most of the work on advance care planning has focused on decisions about medical treatments and naming a surrogate. Sometimes thoughtful people object that they have strong views about how to live that are not readily translated into treatment decisions. For some, their commitment to a religion and its precepts is supremely important, but applying these precepts to their situation is going to require knowing the details at the time. For others, the commitment to values of family or society would often trump self-interest, but again, sorting out how to translate those to medical treatment

decisions will require knowing the family situation or the effects upon the community in a way that will necessitate making judgments at the time.

Obviously, if you have these concerns, you can name a legal surrogate (or surrogates) you trust. You can require that the person consult with certain other people whose knowledge and commitment would help sort out the issues. You can also give the decision maker guidance about the principles you want used. For example, you can say that you want all decisions to be in accord with the rules of your religion or that decisions be made to preserve assets enough to support your spouse and disabled son. You can even say something like, "I have lived my life in the service of the poor. To the extent possible, I would prefer that my assets not be used to sustain my earthly life beyond the minimum needed for a decent and dignified dying so that whatever wealth remains can be turned to good use by (the organization to which I'm leaving my assets)." This sort of construction places the burden of judgment on your proxy but also gives that person (or persons) authority to act in a way that might otherwise seem unjustifiably generous at your expense.

How can I be sure my choices will be followed?

First and foremost, tell your family and doctor what is important to you and write it down. From a legal perspective, it is better to write down what you want than to trust that everyone will remember what you said. A written statement gives your choices clarity, visibility, and validity. Be as precise as you can, both about what treatments you want and about what you hold dear, so that everyone will remember what you said. Be sure to update the forms as necessary to reflect changes in your circumstances or desires. Most statutes that authorize these forms require that they be dated and witnessed by one or more people.

Remember, too, that you can always change your mind. Your choices may change with your experiences. For example, people often choose aggressive care at the start of an illness, but then change their minds when the disease is not responding to treatment. It makes sense that your choices about your care might change as your condition changes. Preparing advance directives and talking about how you and your family plan to cope with serious illness and death can help to make the end of life a time of comfort and dignity—not a time of hurried choices. (See Chapter 5 on how to get the help you need.)

What else matters with advance directives?

Written advance directives are often unavailable or can't be found when important decisions need to be made. What happens to patients who are at home when emergency treatment becomes necessary but their advance directive is only in their hospital medical records?

In most areas, emergency medical teams will try CPR on all people found to be in cardiac arrest (the term meaning the heart is no longer beating and the person is either dead or will be within minutes). However, this may not be in accord with the wishes of persons who have been seriously ill. Because of this, many states now have ways to advise emergency responders such as police officers, firefighters, and emergency medical technicians (EMTs) about your directives.

Some states offer bracelets that you can wear to indicate your wish not to be resuscitated if you are found unconscious or otherwise unable to communicate. In other states, emergency responders look for Do Not Resuscitate (DNR) forms in designated areas in the home, such as on the refrigerator or next to a person's bed. Similar to living wills, DNR forms allow individuals to document preferences for care. Ask your doctor or call your local emergency medical services organization to find out about local policies.

Are there forms my doctor needs to complete?

In some states, physicians can complete orders that direct treatment you should or should not receive in an emergency situation out of the hospital. First created for the state of Oregon, Physician Orders for Life-Sustaining Treatment (POLST) are now used in several other states. (You can find out which ones by checking at www.ohsu.edu/polst .) The POLST form is printed on brightly color paper that is included with or attached to your medical record and goes with you when you are transferred from one health care setting to another.

Unlike your advance care plan, the POLST is a doctor's order, which has medical authority wherever and whenever you are being treated. The POLST covers significant issues about care that you do—or do not—want to receive if you become very sick. It addresses your wishes surrounding CPR; other medical interventions, whether to transfer you to the hospital or to the intensive care unit (ICU); the use of feeding tubes and artificial hydration; and the use of antibiotics. Some states have adapted the form to comply with their own regulations.

I had a living will in Ohio and now I'm in Florida. Do I need a new one?

Just thinking through the issues and writing down your instructions is a major step in guiding the services you will have. Probably, doing that will be enough to guide your family and doctors. However, you should still rewrite your advance directive if you move to another state. Some states have said exactly which types of advance directives the law will recognize as binding. State laws differ. Some states will recognize the laws of the state in which the directive was executed. So if you move or cross state lines for health care, find out about this issue by contacting the local Area Agency on Aging, a state chapter of the AARP, a patient advocate at a nearby hospital, or the National Hospice and Palliative Care Organization (www.caringinfo.org).

What about planning for where to live when I am more disabled?

Most life-threatening illnesses can cause worsening disability. You are wise to make plans for how you will cope with disability. Those plans might require fixing up a first-floor room as a bedroom or putting grab bars in the shower. They might require thinking through whether a family member might move in or whether to convert a room to accommodate someone who could stay overnight. If you see the possibility of an assisted living facility or nursing home in your future, visit several while you are still "in the driver's seat." You will learn a great deal about which one will suit you best and how to live well there. As you see more disability coming your way, it is a good idea to talk with an experienced social worker or home care nurse—someone who has "been there" with lots of other people. Their suggestions will be very helpful in making sure that you can live where you most want to be for as long as possible.

What about planning my finances?

If you have only modest wealth and income, you and your family need to know what care is covered by Medicaid. Your best source of information is likely to be an experienced social worker. If, however, you have some

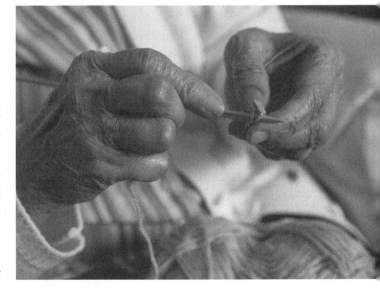

property and savings, you really need to do some planning. This usually requires the help of a lawyer, though it may not cost much if things are pretty uncomplicated. The lawyer, who might specialize in estate planning or elder care issues, will help you think through your goals, both the goals you have while you are still living and those for after you have died. The kinds of arrangements that you can make are quite varied and sometimes complicated, but they are also often effective in securing good care while you need it, financial security for your spouse, and a legacy for others. Good financial planning takes some time, so try not to put this off until death is very close. The lawyer can help you to designate someone to manage your financial affairs should you become unable to do so.

My mother had a living will but the doctor ignored it. Is this common?

Some people assume that advance directives have been ignored because care was complicated or included some things that someone did not want at end of life. This is not true; in fact, doctors usually follow clearly stated directives. Directives aren't "followed" when they are too vague to indicate exactly what should be done, when the medical circumstances were not covered in the document, or when the document was not available in an emergency situation.

For example, many standard forms use the word *terminal* to describe the time near the end of life when a person would or would not want certain treatments. But *terminal* is not easily defined. Even if a state law defines it as having only a certain number of months of life expectancy, it is still difficult to know what the patient wanted to avoid when filling out the form. Such imprecise and vague language doesn't really give much direction unless other conversations have made the meaning clear.

Advance planning helps doctors know what you want instead of having to guess. You might say that you do not want to be given antibiotics if you develop pneumonia and have advanced dementia. You might want a brief period in which you receive artificial hydration and nutrition but not have a permanent feeding tube placed in your abdomen. Advance directives can be very specific in their language, and this can help to avoid ambiguity or uncertainty in your care.

Is it legal to refuse life-sustaining treatment?

Legally, you have the right to choose not to have any particular medical treatment. American courts have defined a broad array of interventions as being "medical treatment." For example, when people become unable to breathe on their own or unable to eat solid foods or drink liquids, they are sometimes put on a respirator to assist breathing or are given nutrients through tubes. This has been defined as a medical treatment. Courts have ruled that patients and families may refuse use of them.

Some people may consider it invasive or unnatural to have tubes inserted or to be hooked up to machinery. Others believe that if something can be done to extend their lives, they want it to be done. These are personal decisions that each person may make for him- or herself.

What else should I plan for?

Doctors and others on the health care team will typically focus on medical treatment decisions. You, however, should have a very different agenda much of the time. Often, you will find it rewarding to make plans about who you want to see, what you want to do now, what should happen near the time of death, and what should happen after death.

These plans are all too easy to put off if you spend too much time and energy on thinking about medical treatment. If you find you have a great deal of anxiety over a specific medical treatment issue (resuscitation,

---

What might you plan?

- To enjoy nature and be in touch with the spiritual side of your life.
- To leave a record for future generations.
- To heal old wounds.
- To share time with those you love.
- To have the funeral or memorial you would like.
- To have your last days at home (and therefore have what you need there).

---

for example), stop and ask your doctor whether this is really likely to matter much. Often, the honest answer is that the treatment won't make much difference (and the struggle is really over a symbol). Remember, enjoying *this* day is always important. Making plans for the people you cherish may be much more rewarding and important than anguishing over medical treatment decisions.

All of this is sort of depressing, isn't it?

Most of us would agree that we don't enjoy making decisions about dying. Yet not making decisions will not prevent them from having to be made. By making these decisions in advance, you may feel more confident that you will have some control over how you live, even when very sick. Your loved ones will also feel more secure because they know what you want. Think through your choices for treatment at the end of life and then give this gift to your family. Don't force others to guess about your wishes when they are facing an emergency.

11

Deciding about Medical Interventions

If I'm lucky, I'll be wired every which way
in a hospital bed. Tubes running into
my nose. But try not to be scared of me, friends!
I'm telling you right now that this is okay.
It's little enough to ask for at the end.
Someone, I hope, will have phoned everyone
to say, "Come quick, he's failing!"
And they will come. And there will be time for me
to bid goodbye to each of my loved ones....
RAYMOND CARVER from *"My Death"*

Not everyone would agree with this poet's sentiments, and especially if the person dying were to be "wired every which way" for months and months. How, though, do you decide what is "just the right amount" of treatment?

Many interventions are started because there is still some real chance that the patient will improve. Even if the patient is dying, some interventions may be used in hopes of improving comfort or buying a little more time. So artificial life support—which can look like being "wired every which way"—may become an issue, even if you have plans not to use such interventions when you are "terminal" or the situation is "hopeless."

Artificial nutrition ("tube feeding"), IV hydration, antibiotics, and breathing machines (ventilators) are usually put in place because there is the expectation—or the hope—that a patient is going to recover from a temporary setback. Deciding to use these interventions in the course of a serious, chronic illness demands careful consideration. Once these interventions have been started, it can be hard to decide if or when to stop.

You need to know, though, that you can stop medical interventions whenever you decide to do so. This chapter provides information you can use to help you make these decisions and to think through the issues.

Thinking about the issues

As with all medical treatments, the likely benefits and burdens should be weighed when deciding whether or not to continue tube feedings, IVs, or ventilator breathing. The burdens these interventions cause should not be ignored just because they might be keeping someone alive.

Artificial treatments are often very effective. Many people are alive because, in their time of sickness, a machine—to provide nutrition, water, or air—got them through. Indeed, when there is any doubt about whether a treatment will improve comfort or quality of life, a time-limited trial is often very useful. Trying an intervention for a reasonable period of time allows you to see whether there is a benefit to using it. The key is to define the time limit before starting the treatment, so that everyone is expecting a reassessment then. You might decide with your doctor, for example, that you will try a ventilator for a week or ten days and then, if your situation does not improve, the ventilator will be removed.

Some people worry that once they start an intervention, they will not be able to stop it. Legally and ethically, not starting and stopping are seen as

> "On one hand, you're the doctor, and you want to provide hope," he said. "On the other hand, you can inflict a great amount of harm. There's a great potential to cause even more pain with pointless treatments."
>
> DR. DAVID MINTZER
> from *Final Choices: Seeking the Good Death*
> by Michael Vitez

Lynn, Harrold, Lynch Schuster

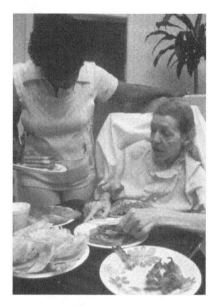

the same. If a treatment is not improving comfort or quality of life, then there is no reason to continue it. Sometimes people feel that if they stop an intervention such as a feeding tube or a breathing machine, then they will have "killed" their loved one. Again, the law does not see stopping these procedures as homicide or suicide. You are under no legal obligation as an adult to take any medical care (unless your disease is a risk to others).

The natural progression of the disease is what prevents you from eating, drinking, or breathing normally. Stopping treatments that replace these natural functions gets technology out of the way and allows the disease to follow its natural course. Even if these interventions have been in place for months or years, it is ethical and legal to stop them and allow natural death to occur.

Time-limited trials

If death is not expected in hours to days, you and your family may consider a time-limited trial of artificial nutrition (food) and hydration (liquid) to see whether it improves your comfort, alertness, or energy. To give tube feedings for a short period of time, a tube is usually threaded through the nose into the stomach. For longer periods of tube feedings, tubes may be placed through the abdomen directly into the stomach. This is a surgical procedure performed by a gastroenterologist or a surgeon, depending on the patient's other medical problems. IV catheters are usually placed in the veins of the arm or hand to give artificial hydration. If IVs are going to be used for nutrition, as well as hydration, they usually must be placed in the large veins of the arms, neck, or chest.

You and your family should agree in advance with your doctor about what you hope to accomplish from trying tube feedings or IV fluid. You should

Deciding about Medical Interventions

also determine, in advance, how long to wait to see if you are feeling any better before removing the tubes.

Tube feedings, IVs, and breathing machines are obviously not the same thing as eating, drinking, and breathing naturally. Not only are they mechanical and not responsive to our feelings of hunger, thirst, and breathlessness, but they can also be troubling, uncomfortable, and efficient—just what human contact is not.

The way we talk about these interventions makes it easy to forget that they are, in fact, medical procedures. We talk about "feeding" patients—but the patients are not chewing, swallowing, or tasting as nutrition passes through feeding tubes. We also discuss how patients are "breathing" on ventilators, making it easy to forget that the machine is moving the air for them. The words can be misleading because they can make these machines seem almost natural.

There is no question that feeding tubes, for example, help thousands of people recover from or live with what otherwise might be a fatal condition. Sometimes people who suffer a stroke cannot swallow at first, and a tube is inserted to provide hydration and nutrition. Often these patients can learn to eat again, and the tube is eventually removed. Sometimes a patient with throat cancer might not be able to swallow after successful treatment of the disease. He or she may have a feeding tube and still carry on otherwise normal activities. Few would question whether feeding tubes are appropriate in cases such as these, but there are many cases in which feeding tubes and IVs are more of a burden to the patient than a benefit.

When food seems like love

In all cultures and throughout all history, offering food has been a sign of caring and hospitality. Our mothers made sure we were well-fed as children. Most people enjoy eating with family and friends, especially on special occasions. In most religions, food is part of sacred rituals. It is no wonder, then, when someone we love is unable to eat and drink naturally, that we feel compelled to "feed" them in some way. It seems to be basic caring.

As death approaches, though, you will not keep up your strength by forcing yourself to eat when it makes you uncomfortable. If eating is a social event for you, or if providing food is one of the common ways of expressing

Some potential benefits of not using tube feedings and IVs near death	
Effect on the Body	Benefit
Less fluid in the lungs	Easier breathing
Less fluid in the throat	Less need for suctioning
Less pressure on tumors	Less pain
Less frequent urination	Less risk of skin breakdown and bed sores
Increase in the body's natural pain-relieving hormones	Increased comfort and less pain

caring in your family, your loss of appetite may be distressing to you and your loved ones. You might enjoy small amounts of home-cooked food—dishes that mean something special to you. However, you should also know that a decrease in appetite is natural, and eating less may increase, rather than decrease, comfort.

Because most dying persons are more comfortable without eating or drinking at the end of life, forcing food or liquids is usually not beneficial, especially if restraints, intravenous lines, or hospitalization would be required. Not forcing someone to eat or drink is *not* letting him or her "starve to death." The person is not feeling hungry, and his or her tissues cannot use the nutrition.

The benefits of dehydration at the end of life

The truth is, for those who are dying, the time comes when it might be more compassionate, caring, even natural, to allow dehydration to occur. Forcing tube feedings and IVs on dying patients can make the last days of their lives more uncomfortable.

The evidence from medical research and experiences of clinicians suggests that dying people are often more comfortable without artificial hydration, whether provided by a feeding tube or IV. Until this generation, everyone who died a natural death died without artificially supplied fluids. The stopping of eating and drinking has always been part of the last phase of a terminal condition. Only recently have people been afraid that not providing food and fluid through a tube would cause someone to "starve to death." There is no medical or clinical evidence that not using a feeding tube or IV leads to a more painful death. In fact, the research says just the opposite can happen.

The main burden associated with dehydration at the end of life is a dry mouth. Very few dying people feel any thirst. Good mouth care, ice chips, or moistened sponge swabs relieve any discomfort from a dry mouth.

Mr. Gordon was a ninety-nine-year-old concentration camp survivor with stomach cancer, admitted to an inpatient hospice for end-of-life care. Mrs. Gordon, ninety-four years old, stayed with him day and night and often wondered aloud how she would live without him. As the days passed, Mr. Gordon ate less and less, despite his wife cajoling him to "eat to keep up your strength." Although Mr. Gordon had never written an advance directive, he and his wife agreed that he did not want a feeding tube, as that would not do anything to cure or treat his cancer.

When Mr. Gordon became comatose, his daughter and grandson were called from their home hundreds of miles away. Mr. Gordon's grandson stayed with him for a while, then left the room and tearfully insisted that the doctor put in a feeding tube to "give him a few more days."

The doctor explained that tube feeding might or might not give Mr. Gordon "a few more days," but it would be more likely to cause pain from having the tube in place, diarrhea from liquid feedings that Mr. Gordon's stomach and intestines could no longer tolerate, and shortness of breath from fluid buildup.

Mr. Gordon's grandson admitted that he was not ready for his grandfather to die. He found it hard to believe that artificial feedings would not strengthen Mr. Gordon. Mr. Gordon's daughter reminded her son of how peaceful Mr. Gordon looked. She compared that to having pain, diarrhea, and shortness of breath. Although Mr. Gordon's grandson did not want his grandfather to die, he did not want him to have pain or other discomfort. In accord with Mr. Gordon's decisions, no feeding tube was placed. Mr. Gordon died the next day, peacefully, surrounded by his family.

Tube feeding and the dementia patient

Increased difficulty with eating and swallowing is one of the signs that an Alzheimer's patient has moved into the final stages of the disease. She may tend to choke on food and drink and, therefore, run the risk of a respiratory infection. She may lose interest in food or forget how to swallow. These signs mark the end of a very long and sad disease process. By this point, the patient is totally dependent on others for care, incontinent, unable to recognize family or to speak intelligibly, and generally "doing poorly."

Some caregivers may want to address the decrease in food and fluid intake with a feeding tube. Family, doctors, or nurses may even say that they do not want the patient to "starve" to death. Providing tube feeding is certainly an acceptable way to provide care. However, this dying is part of a very tragic disease, and the inability to eat is a natural and expected part of its last stages. Inserting a tube will not stop the progression of the dementia. Indeed, it won't reduce the risk of aspiration of saliva into the lungs, causing pneumonia. Because dying without additional hydration is often quite comfortable, many choose to allow the patient to experience a natural and peaceful death, which is what happens without artificial feeding. The patient takes whatever she can tolerate when spoon feedings and sips are offered by a caregiver. Sips of water and ice chips are often enough to relieve a dry mouth.

Artificial feeding and the permanently unconscious patient

Many people can be supported with artificial feeding even though they are not conscious. Some stroke patients may never again respond to any stimuli. Some people have suffered hypoxia (lack of oxygen) or head trauma and become permanently unconscious. Three well-known court cases involved Ms. Karen Ann Quinlan, Mrs. Nancy Cruzan, and Mrs. Terri Schiavo, who lived for years supported by feeding tubes though they were never aware of their surroundings. These patients are said to be in a persistent vegetative state or to have had permanent loss of consciousness. Are we obligated to keep such patients alive even though there is no hope of their recovery to a conscious state? If we do choose to withdraw the tube feeding, would these patients experience a painful death? Would we be "killing the patient?" The answer about the patient's experience is clear: the patient does not have any awareness, including pain.

The courts and consensus statements by clinicians have ruled it acceptable to withhold or withdraw tube feeding from such patients. This is not taking an action to kill the patient; rather, it is allowing a natural death to occur. The real struggle for the families of these patients is an emotional and spiritual one. If the patient could choose, would he or she withdraw treatment and allow a natural, peaceful death? Are we continuing the artificial feeding for others or for the patient?

> My own belief is that the use of heroic and experimental medical technology is often a moral outrage, showing callous disrespect for the sacredness of human life and pathetic inability to face the reality of human death.
>
> PEGGY STINSON
> from *The Long Dying of Baby Andrew*

Choosing to stop eating and drinking

Occasionally patients do make a deliberate choice to stop taking in food and fluids, and they may actually say they are doing this to speed up the dying process. These are people in the last stages of a fatal disease. They do not suffer from a mental illness or other condition that has affected their reasoning. They are not "suicidal" in the usual sense of the word. They have concluded that the burden of living as they are has become so great that they would prefer to die rather than to live a little longer in this way.

This choice is usually disturbing to family members and to medical personnel. In such instances, the family and caregivers need to be sure that the patient is not suffering from depression or pain. Perhaps these conditions could be adequately managed; once under control, the patient may no longer want to hasten death.

It is also important to consider carefully whether the other burdens that the patient may be feeling can be relieved. These burdens may be emotional issues, such as discord in the family, or spiritual issues, such as a need to feel forgiven. A chaplain or other counselor may be helpful in sorting out these kinds of issues.

After the emotional, spiritual, and symptom management issues have been adequately addressed, the patient may still refuse to eat. If this happens, it usually is in the very last days of the course of the disease. Just as a patient can refuse surgery or chemotherapy, a patient also can refuse to eat.

The patient was forty-two years old and had been suffering from a slowly disabling neurological disease for ten years. He had concluded that the burden of living had become so great that he was ready to die. He had a loving wife and a large, caring family, and he even continued to

> Of all the wonders that I yet have heard,
> It seems to me most strange that men should fear;
> Seeing that death, a necessary end,
> Will come when it will come.
>
> WILLIAM SHAKESPEARE
> from *Julius Caesar*

work as a consultant out of his home. He was confined to his wheelchair or to bed. He was totally dependent on others for all of his care. He took large doses of drugs just to be able to be moved out of bed in the morning and keep his vital systems going. He experienced repeated infections and occasional hospitalizations. He was a man of deep faith and regularly worshiped with his congregation. He knew his disease was fatal and that his condition would only get worse.

He rejected the idea of suicide for moral reasons, as well as the burden it would place on his family. He chose to stop all his medications and let the disease run its natural course as quickly as possible. Over the weeks following this treatment plan, he became weaker and more frail. His heart and other vital systems were failing. Six days before his death he stopped eating and drank only sips of water. He was fully conscious during his last days. He had pushed his body to its physical limits and knew that to refuse to eat and drink would allow his death to come more quickly. He died peacefully in the night, his wife sleeping at his side.

Decisions about ventilators

Ventilators push air and oxygen into the lungs and often save lives. Even so, people with very serious diseases may prefer not to start using a ventilator or to have one removed. Reasons not to use a ventilator include:

- Ventilators may interfere with your ability to speak and swallow.
- Ventilators do not reverse the disease process itself.

- Ventilators are uncomfortable.
- If you are very sick, it can be hard to recover enough to come off the ventilator.
- You may have to have sedation to tolerate the breathing tube.

These are all things to consider when deciding whether or not to try a ventilator.

Reasons to try a ventilator may be your degree of disability or the level of discomfort you have. At the same time, you may be very anxious about going on a ventilator.

As with feeding tubes, you can tell your doctor you want a time-limited trial on a ventilator. For one or two weeks, a ventilator can be hooked up through your nose or mouth. For a longer period, you would need a tracheostomy (a hole in your throat) to insert the tube.

Ask your doctor how comfortable he or she would be with complying with your request to remove the ventilator. Can your doctor keep you comfortable as the ventilator is removed? Does your doctor have experience with using medications for sedation, so you won't ever feel short of breath? If not, is there a palliative care or hospice team that can help you? Can you go home or stay at home? Be sure your doctor will do what you want.

As with other decisions you will make at the end of life, this one is complex because of the emotional issues raised by stopping a ventilator. Nevertheless, you can choose to forgo a ventilator or to have a time-limited trial with a planned withdrawal.

Decisions about resuscitation

When a person's circulation stops, death occurs. If someone's heart stops, he or she will die unless circulation is restarted within minutes. Because a person's sudden collapse must be addressed so quickly, many people are trained to make the efforts needed to restart circulation right away. Usually, treatment is what people in the community would want.

However, when you are seriously ill, you may find this procedure—called cardiopulmonary resuscitation, or CPR—to be worthless or even deeply disturbing. Although you may be grateful for the time you have, or at least willing to endure whatever time you have, you might not want someone to disrupt your time of death with a flurry of activity that is doomed to little success.

Once you have decided against trying resuscitation, how can you prevent people from trying anyway? You need to have a clear discussion with your doctor and those near you to be sure that everyone understands that you really don't want resuscitation tried. It is rarely successful in those who are very sick, and life after resuscitation is often short and uncomfortable. Therefore, deciding against resuscitation is quite reasonable. However, because resuscitation has to be started right away, there is a presumption in favor of using it whenever the situation is unclear. It is up to you and your doctor to see to it that your plans are clear!

At home, you will have less risk that resuscitation might be tried unless someone panics and calls the emergency medical system. As mentioned in Chapter 10, there are usually ways to ensure that the emergency crew will follow your wishes, but you have to know the procedures in your area and follow them.

In a hospital, you should ask for a "do not resuscitate" (DNR) order. If possible, ask your doctor to phone this order ahead of your admission. When you arrive at the emergency room or the admissions desk, you or your proxy or family member should check to be sure that an order is in place as soon as possible. When you get to a hospital room, ask your nurse and any doctors who see you to be sure that your order is in place. Most hospitals have some way to identify patients who have requested DNR orders—a bracelet, perhaps. Ask about the process and be sure it is followed.

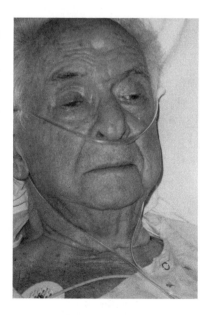

In a nursing home, the situation may be parallel to a hospital, or more may be entrusted to your main nurse. Ask how you can be sure that no one will misunderstand what you want. In a nursing home, you need to be clear about whether you should be sent to a hospital if you become quite ill. If you decide that you would want to go to a hospital only to relieve symptoms or not at all, be sure to make that clear, as well as your decisions about resuscitation.

The many meanings of "DNR"

Deciding whether or not you want a DNR order sounds so simple. Yet this decision causes much anxiety for families and health care providers. Why? Because these decisions are often put off until the patient is too sick to make them, and making the decision often means acknowledging that you are likely to die soon.

To hospital staff, the DNR decision is usually a sign that things are pretty bad. Yet it is important that this decision be made. Without a written order, doctors and nurses will attempt resuscitation. Nurses and doctors who are likely to have to try the resuscitation are reasonably upset over the prospects of having to do such brutal procedures without any real chance of success.

So, if you are the patient or a proxy or family member, you have some real control in this situation. First, figure out whether you really want resuscitation tried, on the basis of its chances of success and how you envision the end of your life. Then, if you want no resuscitation but you don't want to be counted as one who has given up, insist that the doctor write an order that makes that clear.

State clearly what you do and do not want done. Then the doctor can make clear in the record that you want no resuscitation but you do want diagnosis and treatment for anything else that comes up.

Other decisions to forgo interventions

This advice holds true for almost any intervention. You need to know what it will accomplish and what burdens it will cause. You often will want to try it out before deciding that it is not "worth it" for you. This holds true for simple treatments such as antibiotics or insulin, for routine interventions such as tube feeding, and for dramatic rescue efforts such as ventilators or chemotherapy. The principles are the same, and the need for a compassionate and knowledgeable doctor is also constant.

12

Hastening Death

If, following the quality-of-life, take-me-out-and-shoot-me principle, we end up using assisted suicide to preempt the infirmities of old age and terminal illness, how well equipped will we be to encounter infirmity elsewhere? How to become fluent in help if we have banished helplessness from our vocabulary?
RAND RICHARDS COOPER, from *"The Dignity of Helplessness"*

Many people feel that if they were faced with a life-limiting illness, they would want to end their lives quickly rather than wait for the disease to take its course. Some people fear dying in pain, whereas others dread becoming dependent on their family and friends. People are afraid of dying alone or being attached to life support in a hospital. Some fear running up huge medical bills that will bankrupt their families, and many fear the loss of dignity that comes with being very ill and dying.

When the future feels so bleak, it is no wonder we sometimes want to change course quickly. It is also understandable that people want to take control over the end of life by controlling the exact day and hour of their death. As a society, we praise independence and freedom; if we have been in control for most of our lives, losing control at the end seems almost unbearable. Intentionally hastening one's death is legal in three states—Oregon, Washington, and Montana—and in the Netherlands and Switzerland. These states and countries have strict requirements that patients must meet before they can request and receive a prescription for a lethal combination of drugs. Having a physician administer a lethal medication to a patient is not legal anywhere in the United States, and a physician is probably not legally allowed to administer a lethal medication to a noncompetent patient anywhere.

If you live in one of these jurisdictions, you should talk with your family, physician, and care team about your thoughts and questions concerning *physician-assisted suicide*. No matter where you live, however, it seems more important and helpful to first ask whether suicide is really the only way out of pain and suffering. As there are almost always alternatives, is it the best way?

In the abstract, physician-assisted suicide may be a good subject for debate, but when you are dying, or watching someone you love die, the issue hits home. You may feel overwhelmed, helpless, and afraid. Hastening your death may feel like a relief. People facing fatal illness often consider it, even if they have no desire to follow through with action.

Perhaps it would be helpful to think about how you feel about this before it becomes an urgent question in your own life. You may then have time to better understand your options and to discuss your hopes and fears for the future with your family and your care team.

People sometimes think that if they are being cared for by hospice, they will be able to ask for a lethal injection or an overdose of pills. However, hospice does not offer such assistance. Instead, hospice is an alternative to the technologically driven death in a hospital that so many dread.

Many people are afraid that they must be willing to hasten their deaths if they want to have good symptom relief. Good symptom management, however, very rarely shortens life, and even then only by a few hours (see Chapter 7).

Considering suicide: when you just cannot face another day

Living with a chronic illness and the knowledge that you are dying is hard to do. You may feel cheated, betrayed by your own body and the world. You

> ### Suicide, Physician-Assisted Suicide, and Euthanasia: what's the Difference?
>
> SUICIDE is taking your own life by your own hand and in your own way. You do not ask or expect others to help you.
>
> PHYSICIAN-ASSISTED SUICIDE is carried out by asking a doctor to write a prescription for a lethal combination of drugs, which you administer to yourself. The doctor has to help by ordering the drugs and providing instructions.
>
> EUTHANASIA is the act of killing someone who otherwise would suffer terribly from an incurable disease. This is sometimes called "mercy killing" and an example would be an injection meant to cause death.

sometimes feel that your doctor is just not doing enough, or that a cure should still be possible. Being treated for serious illness can be expensive, uncomfortable, and disheartening. Being sick requires many sacrifices and changes. Often, you have to ask others to do things you once did for yourself. Some days, you may feel so full of despair that the idea of just dying now seems like a reasonable alternative. In fact, attempts at suicide are often tied to clinical depression, a disease that makes people feel sad, unworthy, guilty, and overwhelmed. Depression and sadness are not the same. Depression is a complete lack of positive or hopeful feelings, often accompanied by the lack of energy to care.

Many dying people who focus on suicide are depressed. Some have alcohol and drug abuse problems. Among older people who commit suicide, many not only are depressed but also suffer from long-term physical disabilities. Still others are depressed because of medication they take to treat diseases (such as hypertension). Most of the depression that leads patients to consider suicide can be treated effectively with medication and therapy. Most dying people are not depressed, and most who are depressed can be helped (often within days or a few weeks).

Being depressed is like wearing blinders or trying to read in the dark. Your perspective is just not what it should be. You may not even be able to remember times when you were happy and felt that life was worth living. You may feel that you have been depressed for years. It is certainly a time when the future seems irrelevant and bleak.

Hastening Death

Many health care professionals can diagnose and treat depression, though you should know that depression is often overlooked. It can help for you to ask: "Is this depression that makes me feel so low?" Your doctor should talk to you about your symptoms and find a treatment. Some antidepressants require several weeks to take effect, but most people begin to have some relief within a week or ten days of starting medication. Your doctor can also prescribe stimulants that may help you feel better more quickly. Even if you are near the end of your life, you can be treated for depression. No matter when it strikes you, depression can be a treatable illness.

You can also get help by calling a local or national suicide prevention hotline or finding a community mental health center. These hotlines offer confidential help from trained and friendly volunteers who will listen to your troubles and lead you to resources. By asking for help, you open the door to support and hope. Getting help for depression can give you time to think about your life more clearly. Often you will come up with adequate options for the fear and loss of control you feel.

Your doctor might recommend that you join a support group in your community. Talking to others who share your experience and concerns can take a weight off your mind. Sharing your feelings—and just being with other human beings—is a powerful way to heal.

If you are not depressed, you may still feel that dying is taking too long or may want to have more control over how and when the end will come. If so, you should consider not only the other issues discussed in the rest of this chapter but also the possibilities of allowing death to come more quickly by stopping treatments. Ordinarily, people who are very sick can stop a medication, can decline artificial nutrition and hydration, or can accept sedating levels of drugs. These are not so definitive or confrontative as suicide or euthanasia, though they are usually fairly effective in avoiding prolonged dying (see Chapter 11).

I Want to Spare My Family

If you are terribly sick and suffering, it is understandable that you might want to "get it over with." You might feel that dying quickly will spare your loved ones the burden and pain of your suffering. Such feelings are common, given the emotional and financial toll of living with a life-threatening disease. Although the burdens of care can be overwhelming to family, it is also true that caring for another human being often enriches us, making us more compassionate and kind, or showing us strengths that we did not know we had.

No matter how you die, your family will suffer. In the depths of your despair, you may not envision the effect a decision for suicide would have on them. Suicide can devastate the survivors. Spouses and children often feel responsible for not relieving your emotional pain. They are often angry at being cheated out of a chance to talk to you and help you. The guilty feelings last for years, marking their future relationships. Religious beliefs might lead others to judge you very harshly, and your family may bear the brunt of such judgment.

If you ask your family if they feel burdened or overwhelmed, they might say they are. They are also likely to say they'll do anything for you and that you should put aside your worries. In fairness to the people you love, talk to them. Tell them that you think suicide may be the best option. Very often, they won't agree, and their perspective may help you see both other ways to continue to live and less destructive or dangerous ways to hasten death (see Chapter 11 on forgoing treatment).

I Want to Be Sure to Die Comfortably. Wouldn't Suicide Be a Guarantee?

Some of us want everything possible done to keep us alive. Others want to die when nature decides it is time, and we do not seek or want aggressive or curative care. No matter how you envision your death, no matter what you do to prolong your life, you should be able to rely on your care team to give you the pain relief and emotional support you need to die comfortably. Each of us will define an "acceptable dying" in our own way, but you should feel that you will have the basics: that you will not have severe physical symptoms, that your family will have help in providing care, and that you will have the support needed to be at peace with yourself. The information provided throughout this book will help you to shape a good death for yourself, without having to undertake suicide on your own or with a doctor's help (where that is legal).

> But be glad for me if I can die in the presence
> of friends and family. If this happens, believe me I came out ahead. I didn't lose this one.
>
> RAYMOND CARVER
> from "My Death"

Nevertheless, you might not be able to find a health care arrangement that inspires trust, or maybe you just don't want to take any chances. Then you should know that suicide attempts—even physician-assisted suicide—can fail. Sometimes the dose of pills is not enough, or you vomit some of the medication. Sometimes you sleep for a long period and awaken. Then you risk brain damage without having succeeded at causing death. This prospect may lead you to seek a doctor's help in giving a lethal injection. However, because this is illegal throughout the United States, you are exceedingly unlikely to find a doctor who will comply. Although patients might be able to accumulate pills on their own, the doctor's involvement in giving a lethal injection is illegal, and it carries such severe penalties that few will even talk about it.

Thus trying to control the hour of your death can be an uncertain proposition. Most people find it better to get good, reliable care.

Don't the Laws Now Allow Physician-Assisted Suicide?

As of 2010, physician-assisted suicide is legal in the United States only in Oregon, Washington, and Montana. In 1997, the U.S. Supreme Court issued rulings on physician-assisted suicide and sent the issue back to the states to decide. The Supreme Court decided that it could not identify a constitutional right to request a physician's help in dying. Therefore, the states are responsible for determining whether to bar or allow physician-assisted suicide.

At the same time, the Court reaffirmed that Americans do have the right to refuse or end life-sustaining treatment, such as ventilators and feeding tubes. The Court pointed out that there is a difference between letting someone die naturally and helping someone to die sooner than if the disease ran its usual course. Refusing treatment lets your disease run its natural course. Having someone's help in suicide, the Court ruled, is different.

The Court also emphasized the importance of pain control for dying people. The Court's ruling may well have created a right to pain and symptom management—or at least it keeps the states from erect-

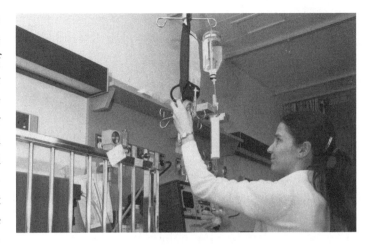

ing barriers to pain management. Many doctors are already hesitant to prescribe opioids (also called narcotics) because they fear the state will revoke their licenses or their prescribing privileges. The Court's ruling was intended to reassure people that good pain management is not physician-assisted suicide in any legal or ethical sense.

In reality, should you try to hoard pills to overdose, you are not likely to be prosecuted, and certainly talking about suicide is not against the law. In most of the United States and the world, however, any action taken by a doctor to directly cause your death—deliberately prescribing pills, giving a lethal injection, or even being present at your suicide—is illegal. In states and countries in which particular actions are allowed, the conditions are quite constrained.

What about states in which aid in dying is legal?

In 1997, Oregon voters were the first in the US to assert their desire to make physician-assisted suicide legal. Oregon's law has several requirements. The patient must be "capable" of making the choice. The patient must make this choice voluntarily, without pressure from family or health care providers. The patient must be a long-term resident of the state. One result of the Oregon law is that the state and its doctors and hospitals worked hard to improve end-of-life care for all residents.

The Oregon law also includes a two-week waiting period to ensure that a patient has really considered suicide and definitely wants to die. This safeguard actually limits the usefulness of physician-assisted suicide, because people who might seek physician-assisted suicide (PAS) are often very near death and either die within two weeks or become unable to express their wishes or to ingest a lethal dose of medicine.

Since 1998, 950 Oregonians have pursued PAS. These patients were overwhelmingly older white adults, highly educated, and suffering from cancer. The most frequent reasons for opting for PAS were the loss of autonomy; the loss of ability to participate in pleasurable activities; and the loss of control over bodily functions.

One study of survivors of patients who had legal PAS found that many appreciated the time they had to say good-bye to their loved one and to plan and prepare for the death. They felt their grief was lessened slightly by knowing that their loved one had chosen to end his or her life, that the choice was legal, and that the patient avoided prolonged suffering.

However, people who disagreed with their loved one's decision regarding PAS did not have less grief. If you are considering PAS in a place in which it is legal and your family is not in agreement, it could be very important for you to talk with them about your thoughts and hear more about what your choices mean to them.

The physician-assisted suicide statutes are available only to long-term residents of states and countries in which it is legal. You cannot move to one of these places at the end of your life in order to use PAS.

What Are Some of the Arguments against Legalizing Physician-Assisted Suicide?

Legalizing physician-assisted suicide is a part of the debate about improving end-of-life care. It can't be seen as a quick and easy way to protect patients from inadequate care arrangements. Too many people still suffer needlessly, often because doctors and families just do not know how to serve people who are dying. Many suffer because doctors fail to provide adequate medication for pain. To legalize physician-assisted suicide, some believe, would make real reform, such as better pain control, less likely. Without those reforms, patients end up with no prospects of living well while dying. In this scenario, making physician-assisted suicide an option is offering a rather coercive choice.

Many people fear that physician-assisted suicide will create a climate in which some people are even more deliberately pressured into committing suicide. The very old, the very poor, minorities, and other vulnerable populations might be encouraged to hasten death, rather than to "burden" their families or the health care system.

Again, this would not be a genuine choice, but it highlights a social concern about how our society cares for those who are elderly, poor, or vulnerable. Making suicide legal does not solve the underlying social problems. Even for those who have adequate financial and social resources, having physician-assisted suicide available could create a troubling new situation. Seriously ill and disabled persons could feel that they had to justify a choice to stay alive. They could feel that PAS is, in some sense, "expected" by family or friends. As a society, we have never asked people to justify their being alive, and it seems likely that asking them to do so would run risks of being quite difficult or demeaning.

Finally, the safeguards built into the proposed statutes would be very difficult to implement. "Terminal illness," "competent" patients, and "voluntary action" are each quite ambiguous categories. Waiting times and restrictions on the help available risk could create tragic situations that push public opinion toward loosening restrictions.

A 1997 study conducted by the American Medical Association found that more than half of Americans believe physician-assisted suicide should be legal. However, when people are told about alternatives to the technological treatments so many of us fear and about the availability of pain control and hospice care, their support for physician-assisted suicide goes down to under one-fifth. This study showed that, when people understand all of their end-of-life choices, they were less likely to opt for suicide.

What Arguments Support Physician-Assisted Suicide?

Supporters of PAS believe that this is fundamentally an individual choice—that having control of the timing and manner of activities in your life includes having control of your death. They believe that individuals have the right to make life-and-death decisions for themselves without government

> In our system, it is easier to get open heart surgery than Meals on Wheels, easier to get antibiotics than eyeglasses, and certainly easier to get emergency care aimed at rescue than to get sustaining, supportive care. It would be so easy to encourage dying persons to be dead rather than to find them services. If it were easy to get good care, the question of whether one should be able to choose to be killed would be troubling and important. But it is not easy to get good care.... Accepting a responsibility to work to change the shortcomings of the present system argues against reducing the pressures for change by removing the sufferers through death.
>
> JOANNE LYNN
> from "Travels in the Valley of the Shadow"

interference. Supporters of legalization may also be responding to the fear of being in terrible pain and agony, of being hooked up to life-support equipment, and of becoming a financial or emotional drain on their families. They see PAS as an alternative to becoming dependent on others or to having a very poor quality of life.

Sadly, our current health care system and its practices leave people suffering unreasonably and unnecessarily at the end of life. Too often, people suffer from avoidable pain and other symptoms in their final days, and such suffering can occur even with good care. People advocate for PAS as a more reliable way to guard against these possibilities.

Sometimes just having an option for suicide limits anxiety and allows the patient to enjoy life more fully. Making physician assistance legal might make it easier to monitor and regulate.

Of course, dying people and their families have every reason to consider the policy questions of legalizing physician-assisted suicide. However, most are constrained to live within the law, as it is in their jurisdiction now.

I Don't Trust Doctors

If you are fortunate, you will have doctors, nurses, and others who are easy to trust. Maybe you've known them for years, or maybe you have needed them urgently and they have always come through. Instead, though, you may feel uncertain. You may have no regular doctor or nurse, or you may have needed help badly at some time and they let you down, or you may have heard stories of bad care. What can you do?

First, trust and confidence don't usually arise immediately. Talking about your fears and being well informed are helpful. With serious illness, there are some special fears worth noting. First, morphine and other opioid medicines are very useful and very safe. When your doctor starts using them, death may still be far off, and using these medications usually prolongs life. Higher doses of morphine or other opioids may well be needed near death, but there is no evidence that using enough to stop suffering also causes death (see Chapter 7).

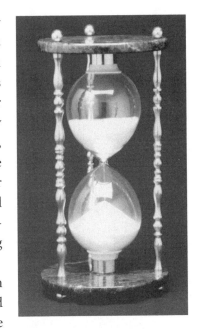

Second, despite the current changes in health care, doctors are still well protected from the costs of your care. Some people have come to fear that new health payment arrangements make doctors prone to resenting patients whose needs lead to big bills. If you are worried about this in your situation, try to talk with your doctor or with a social worker or chaplain. Perhaps they can show you that the care your doctor is recommending is the same as what doctors generally recommend for people with better insurance. Perhaps they can help by talking frankly about the limits that your financial situation creates.

Finally, though, it is reassuring to know that the conflicts over expensive care have mostly been about particularly high-cost procedures, which are very rarely an issue for people who face serious and eventually fatal illness. For most care, doctors and nurses generally provide about the same care to rich and poor, and to persons of different social and ethnic groups. Remember, your doctors and nurses are people who chose a career in serving people coping with illnesses like yours.

Obviously, your main concern when you confront the end of life will be to get excellent care. If you also want to consider the issues in suicide, physician-assisted suicide, or euthanasia, you owe it to yourself to read more and to find some people—doctor, chaplain, counselor, family—who will be willing to talk with you.

13

Coping with Events Near Death

The last Night that She lived,
It was a Common Night,
Except the Dying; this to Us
Made Nature different.

We noticed smallest things, —
Things overlooked before,
By this great light upon our Minds
Italicized, as 't were.

EMILY DICKINSON

Earlier generations may have had so much experience with dying that most people knew how to recognize approaching death. When people died at home, families also knew more about how to deal with the practical aspects of the time near death. Now, however, this knowledge is just not commonplace. Many of us have watched people die only on television or in the movies, neither of which gives a very realistic view of the process. This chapter gives some practical facts and advice to family and friends of people who are near death.

How will I know when death is getting close?

Just as doctors usually cannot pinpoint the day when a baby will be born, they cannot predict the exact day or hour when you or your loved one will die. You might need reassurance that it is simply not always possible to know when death is near. Some illnesses make prediction difficult. However, in many illnesses, there are a few hours or a few days when it is evident that death is close. The person dying usually is no longer eating or drinking, except for perhaps a few sips of liquid now and again. The person may be sleepy or confused for much of the time and is usually in bed. If the person is dying from cancer or progressive failure of an organ, he or she will usually have lost a substantial amount of weight. If life support is being stopped, the physician should be able to tell you what to watch for in order to estimate about how long it will be before death.

> I am too tired
> To move on, or to mind the paths traveled.
> Where I find moonlight and gentle breezes,
> I shall unload, lay down, and rest in peace.
>
> HELEN CHEN
> from "Reflections in the Dusk"

Many people near death will have cool hands and feet and a persistent purplish discoloration in the parts of the body resting on the bed. Many also will have uneven breathing, sometimes stopping for many seconds and at other times breathing rapidly. This kind of breathing and discoloration can persist for a few days, but these signs usually also mean that the person will die within a day or two.

Some people have some jerking motions or even seizures from metabolic abnormalities near death. As disturbing as it may be for others to watch this happen, the dying person is probably not aware of it. The involuntary motions usually do not need treatment unless they seem to cause problems for the patient.

If the dying person has been taking opioid medicines, these will usually be continued, because ending opioids abruptly can lead to uncomfortable symptoms. The dose may be decreased, especially if the kidneys are not working well. It may be increased if the patient appears to be in pain. If the dying person is no longer able to swallow, opioids can be given by suppository, injection, skin patch, or intravenous infusion.

Probably half of patients develop very noisy breathing near death, which is sometimes called a "death rattle." This is the result of relaxation of the muscles of the throat where saliva and other secretions naturally collect. This does not cause the person to feel as though she is struggling to breathe. In fact, most dying patients are not aware of this noisy breathing. However, if family or caregivers find it unnerving, the doctor or nurse can help reduce the noisy sound, either by giving medication or repositioning the dying person in bed.

What should family and friends do when death is close?

You, and your family and friends, will need to answer this question for yourselves. Many patients are frightened of being alone, or just want a loved one nearby to help ease their passage. Some want to be touched gently. A few simply want to be alone. Some family and friends find comfort in reading, reminiscing, saying prayers, or singing. Some just want to be there, sharing the precious time. What any one patient or family member wants may change over time or as other visitors come and go.

Unless it is absolutely unavoidable, family and friends should not spend much time on medical treatment decisions at this point. It is best to have had any such discussions earlier in the course of a disease, or just to limit the time spent on them now.

> You have grown wings of pain
> and flap around the bed like a wounded gull
> calling for water, calling for tea, for grapes
> whose skins you cannot penetrate.
> Remember when you taught me
> how to swim? Let go, you said,
> the lake will hold you up.
> I long to say, Father let go
> and death will hold you up.
> Outside the fall goes on without us.
> How easily the leaves give in,
> I hear them on the last breath of wind,
> passing this disappearing place.
>
> LINDA PASTAN
> from "Go Gentle"

Sometimes families or patients have to remind the professional staff in a hospital that this is precious time and should not be taken up with such issues as drug doses or formal advance directives. Remember, too, that this can be a good time to call on religious support, including the hospital chaplain.

Music is very helpful for some patients and families. One elderly lady was comforted by a Gregorian chant tape, another by special harp music. Some prefer gospels or modern music. Most families and patients seem to benefit from listening to music.

This is a very good time to say farewells and to ask forgiveness, if these things have not already been done. People who visit can say to the dying person that she lived well and is loved. Often it seems that dying people can still hear, even when they no longer seem to be awake. So saying things to a person who seems to be asleep is reasonable, and it can be important for those left behind.

Some patients and families have a sequence of people who, one by one, come through to say good-bye. Others have more unplanned visits. Some have religious rituals to follow; others make up their own style as they go.

Is it important to be there at the moment of death?

Many people feel that they should be present at the very moment that a dying loved one draws his or her last breath. However, whether this is important depends on the preferences of the family and friends and the dying person. Trying to be there can be quite wearing, as the exact time of death is so hard to predict. People sometimes keep up a death watch for days and finally have to get some coffee or some sleep. Often, that is when the person finally dies. Perhaps she was "waiting" and needed to be "on her own" a little in order to let go. Perhaps the timing was just chance.

Important things are rarely said just at the time of death, so it is not likely that survivors will miss hearing something important if they are not there. On the other hand, a few patients really do say remarkable things in the few days ahead of death—seeing persons long dead, giving comfort to family, or making peace about a long-hidden failing. It is important to the patient and the family for these things to be shared.

Families often use this time also to share feelings and perspectives that do not usually have the opportunity to be heard. They can begin to sort out new relationships and do some practical planning, too. Families and patients should give instructions to caregivers in hospitals and nursing homes about who should be called, if possible, when death is close, and who should be called when the person has died.

How does a family member know that the person has died?

> We sometimes congratulate ourselves at the moment of waking from a troubled dream; it may be so the moment after death.
>
> NATHANIEL HAWTHORNE
> from *The American Notebooks*

Often the patient takes a breath, sighs or shudders, and is dead. Many people have another effort or two at breathing but really are not moving air. A few have movement of limbs or trunk for up to ten minutes after death.

Still, how can a family member know that the person has died? If there is no air moving, the person is dead. There is no urgency to making the determination, so an observer can just sit and watch for a few minutes. Family and friends may want to spend a few minutes crying, praying, or meditating.

Most of us are too unfamiliar with death to be comfortable deciding that it has happened. In a hospital or nursing home, someone who can check with a stethoscope can be summoned. In hospice or regular home care, usually a nurse can come to the home within an hour or so.

If the death takes place at home, the family really needs to plan ahead so that no one feels any need to call 911 or involve the emergency rescue system. Emergency technicians will often find it difficult to size up the situation quickly, so just when the family needs comfort and time, they instead have to explain themselves to an outsider.

Families may find more comfort if they call the doctor's office or the hospice. Often it helps to have spoken to the doctor in advance about this need.

Many people really need to hear someone else say that the person is dead. "Pronouncing" a person dead is important. Even if it is perfectly obvious, family should still be able to ask, "Is he dead?" and hear from someone else that he really is. Again, talk with the doctor about how this will be done.

What happens then?

After a death, there are more decisions and activities than most families really expect. Take some time to remember the person who just died, to be in touch with loved ones, to pray, or to do whatever is significant and helpful to the survivors. Within a few hours, usually, the body will be moved to a location that handles dead bodies—a hospital morgue, a funeral home, or a medical examiner's morgue. If a person expects to die at home, make plans ahead of time with a funeral director.

> The winter after you left us was the longest, coldest, snowiest one that anyone had ever seen in these parts. It seemed fitting, somehow. It makes you feel small. It reminds you, So many things are out of your hands.
>
> SARAH L. DELANEY
> from *On My Own at 107: Reflections on Life without Bessie.*

The next of kin may need to be involved in decisions about an autopsy. If the doctor or nurse says there is no need to notify the medical examiner, or if the medical examiner declines to do an autopsy, the next of kin should still consider having an autopsy done. Autopsies help answer questions about what really happened. They also keep doctors and other caregivers "on their toes," as autopsies can turn up conditions or changes that would otherwise have been unknown. The body after an autopsy still looks normal and can be shown in an open casket if that is the family's wish.

If the person died in a hospital, an autopsy may be available at no cost to the family. If the person died in a nursing home or at home, the situation is more complex. If there was trauma involved, the medical examiner may require an autopsy and will perform it at no cost. If not, sometimes the doctor can arrange for a free autopsy. More often, however, there is a fee (of a few thousand dollars) which the family must pay. Sometimes one just cannot find a way to get an autopsy. Obviously, this situation is complicated enough to warrant having considered it in advance whenever possible, especially for deaths at home.

If the death is sudden or unexpected or, in some places, just at home, there is often a legal requirement to notify the medical examiner (sometimes called the coroner). The medical examiner will then make a determination about whether to examine the body and whether an autopsy is required. Family members have very little authority to stop public officials who want an autopsy, because they are concerned with public safety.

Families or patients must make the other decisions about how the body will be handled. More often now, people are choosing cremation, perhaps because it is much less expensive than traditional burials. Again, planning ahead will help make this transition a smoother one. The dying person and family may have made plans and may even have prepaid for services.

> He searched for his accustomed fear of death and could not find it.
>
> LEO TOLSTOY
> from *The Death of Ivan Ilyich*

Without pre-planning, the family will need to make decisions quickly about caskets, location of burial, services, announcements, and so on. Many people have pointed out that this is not a good time in the lives of families to be negotiating costly items. It is all too easy to spend more than is really warranted by family or patient preferences. There are now federal and state regulations that generally require that funeral home directors give customers notice about the costs of services, about which services are actually legally required, and about the full range of casket prices.

Finding a funeral home director who is both reasonable and kind is well worth some time, as that person can make the first week or two after death so much easier on the survivors.

Some people will have joined a memorial society, a private association that helps members with low-cost funerals and memorials. Also, remember that Social Security, veterans' benefits, and other benefits may be available to help with funeral costs.

So many families are overwhelmed with the number of issues that arise just after death. Their experience leads to a reminder to consider these issues in advance whenever possible. It may seem terribly uncomfortable to be arranging a funeral with the person still alive. However, this is becoming the usual way that families proceed. It certainly helps ensure that reasonably prudent choices are made and that the family has fewer serious disruptions in the emotionally difficult times just after the death. Here is a short checklist that might help:

WHO NEEDS TO BE NOTIFIED, AND HOW? Consider asking the professional caregivers to help with giving notice to a few family and friends. Think about setting up plans so that those notified then call others.

HOW WILL PEOPLE GET TO THE FUNERAL? Will some family members need travel tickets? Bear in mind that airlines and some other travel services often give discounts to people who are traveling for such emergencies, but the traveler will usually need a letter from a doctor or an official death notice.

WHO WILL PROVIDE FUNERAL SERVICES OR THE EQUIVALENT? Will this be a cremation or a burial? If cremation, families may seek out a service that provides transportation for the body and delivery of the ashes without many other services. If the body is cremated, the ashes can be scattered in a special place, buried in a graveyard, or kept in a special container or urn.

Consider also whether the body is going to have to be moved across state lines. If so, the family will often need to have a funeral director in the city where death occurred and a funeral director in the city where the burial will occur. International or long-distance transportation of a body is complicated and generally requires help of the U.S. embassy abroad and skilled funeral directors at each end of the trip.

WHAT KIND OF MEMORIAL SERVICE WILL THERE BE? If it is to be in a church or synagogue or other public building, speak to someone there to find out what will need to be arranged.

DID THE PERSON HAVE CLOTHING IN WHICH HE OR SHE WANTED TO BE BURIED? Making plans like this ahead of time is often quite meaningful.

DO YOU HAVE SOMETHING YOU FEEL IS APPROPRIATE TO WEAR TO A FUNERAL? People discover that their wardrobe has nothing that seems appropriate. One certainly need not wear black any more in most religious traditions, but it still often seems that one should be somber and conservative.

ARE THERE ANY RINGS, JEWELS, OR SPECIAL MEMENTOS TO BE PLACED WITH THE BODY? Some people like to leave a wedding ring, others choose to remove it. Some like to slip a letter or note in the casket or to place a favorite picture or blanket.

ARE THERE DEPENDENT PERSONS WHO NEED IMMEDIATE ATTENTION? Children and disabled or elderly dependents may be left adrift for daily care by the death. Caregivers and more distant family need to consider this possibility, especially with the elderly person left at home who may not be known to health care personnel or even to neighbors.

ARE THERE PROPERTY MATTERS NEEDING IMMEDIATE ATTENTION? Sometimes there is real urgency to get rent or taxes paid, house or car made secure, animals fed, and so on.

HOW MANY DEATH CERTIFICATES WILL BE NEEDED? Even for small and uncomplicated estates, people often find they need two dozen. Funeral directors can help, but families should get many more than they think they need because it is often more costly and troublesome to get them later.

WHO WILL ARRANGE A DEATH NOTICE OR OBITUARY IN THE RIGHT NEWSPAPER(S)? Often, funeral directors will help make these arrangements for or with the family. Consider the need to make notices in places where the person used to live. Get the phone numbers and even a written draft of what needs to be said. Families often find that they need a little time to get dates and sequences of life events just right. Although many newspapers used to print obituaries at no cost, more are now charging fees for anything more than a brief notice of death and the details of funerals or other services that will occur. Ask what the charge will be so that there are no surprises.

IS THERE A WILL? If not, should one be written before the person dies? A will is almost always helpful in settling the estate. It is astonishing how much estate even people of modest means will have (a car, a few stocks, a savings account, a debt owed to the person or a debt to be paid by the estate, and so on). If a will exists, does the person still affirm it? Where is it? How will it be read after the death?

SHOULD CHARITABLE DONATIONS IN LIEU OF FLOWERS BE ENCOURAGED? If donations, to what cause or charity?

WILL THERE BE AN OPEN OR CLOSED CASKET? If closed, will there be a private time for family to have it open? Is there a picture appropriate to have at the service? If the body is to be cremated, think about whether you and your family want to see the body one final time. Visitations and viewings are likely to require the time, effort, and cost for embalming. A quiet time for family members to say good-bye might be arranged at little to no cost.

WHERE WILL THE BURIAL BE? Who owns the plot? What permissions and notices are needed?

IS ORGAN DONATION APPROPRIATE AND DESIRED? Organ donation (heart, kidney, lung, liver, etc.) can be arranged in advance or at the time of death. Tissue donation (bone, cornea, etc.) can often be arranged even hours after death. Donations are essential to the well-being of others and can fulfill a dying person's wishes. Depending on the cause and circumstances of death, some organs may not be usable. However, corneas, skin, and bone are often usable when other organs are not.

WHAT WILL BE ENTERED AS THE CAUSE OF DEATH? Usually the doctor decides this, but if many factors contributed to causing death or if the main cause is somehow embarrassing, family members could talk with the doctor and negotiate a resolution.

Can family keep some information out of the obituary?

People often do not realize that there are two ways to announce a person's death. The first is a death notice, which is a paid listing in a newspaper. The second is an obituary, which is a news story, usually written by the newspaper staff. Families purchase death notices, in which they can say almost whatever they please, as long as it is appropriate in length and in

The dying need but little, dear, —
A glass of water's all,
A flower's unobtrusive face
To punctuate the wall,
A fan, perhaps, a friend's regret,
And certainly that one
No color in the rainbow
Perceives when you are gone.

EMILY DICKINSON

good taste. Although many newspapers used to publish death notices at no cost, more newspapers are charging a fee in exchange for allowing families to write more personal and lengthy information. Many newspapers will take information for death notices or obituaries only from funeral directors unless the family comes in person and brings a copy of a death certificate. This safeguard is meant to limit the unfortunate experience of false death notices.

Although it is common to hear the term *obituary* used to refer to a family-written "death notice," obituaries are technically news stories, and the family has little control over them. Usually, the newspaper decides for itself whether to write and publish the obituary, and it often has a formula for what is and is not included. Family will have little control over whether the obituary states the cause of death or the circumstances, or whether unfortunate aspects of the person's life are characterized.

How long can one wait before burial or cremation?

In some traditions, burial should be very prompt, within one day. In others, a few days are allowed for family and friends to gather. In modern America, refrigeration (and embalming, when it is chosen) helps to make it reasonable to wait for a few days. In some traditions, a prolonged time of praying with the body present is considered optimal, although these practices are causing some friction with public authorities. The usual funeral and burial occurs well within a week.

However, it is becoming more common for burial or cremation to proceed within a few days, with a more thoughtfully planned memorial held a few weeks or months later.

Can family know what was learned in an autopsy before burial or cremation?

People also do not realize that it often takes two months after the death to complete an autopsy. A preliminary set of findings is available shortly after the body leaves the morgue, but real understanding usually requires making laboratory tests and microscopic examination of various tissues, and that takes more than a month. Often, family members have to remind the doctor or pathologist that they want the autopsy results. Sometimes, the best way to get them is to set a meeting time specifically for this purpose. Even when done with great sensitivity, this will be a little cold and jarring, so it might be wise to bring along a trusted friend or counselor.

How does a family follow religious and other important traditions?

Families need to know their own traditions and to express their needs or to use facilities that are familiar with those traditions. Again, planning ahead will be of great comfort. There is rarely any health reason that prevents family from being in contact with a dead body, so those who are moved to participate in bathing the body or in preparing for burial are more limited by popular squeamishness than by real risks. Those who do help with bathing or dressing the body often find it to have been an important labor of love and a significant milestone in coming to terms with the death. If this is important to a particular family member or friend, be sure that the funeral home director knows the plans and agrees to make it possible. Sometimes, the best time to do these things is in the place where the person died, and that may

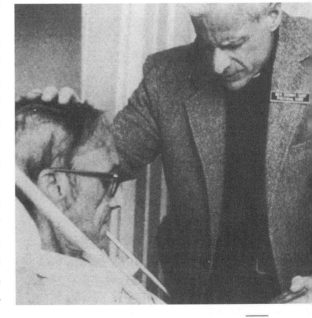

> The Bustle in a House
> The Morning after Death
> Is solemnest of industries
> Enacted upon Earth,–
> The Sweeping up the Heart,
> And putting Love away
> We shall not want to use again
> Until Eternity.
>
> EMILY DICKINSON

require agreement from other administrators as well. Many people in modern times are only vaguely familiar with the rituals of their own traditions. When someone in the family is dying, this is a very good time to re-examine the family's traditions and to explore possibilities with suitable religious leaders. There is much latitude now in how memorials and funerals are handled, so families can adhere to a particular tradition or can modify it as appropriate.

Music and art are often an important part of memorializing the dead. Families might well want favorite music played and religious or family pictures displayed.

What does one do at a "viewing" or "visitation"?

A viewing is a time when the body is present and friends and family can come and say last farewells. Visitations are usually a set time period when friends and family can gather to commiserate and share recollections of the dead person's life. The body may or may not be present at a visitation. This time might also be at home rather than in a funeral home or religious building. Once, bodies were kept at home and the life of the family continued as usual until the body was buried. Now, it is much more common for the body to be in a funeral home. Even with cremations, the visitations are often at a funeral home. Families can arrange these things in other ways, but they usually are willing to listen to whatever the funeral home director recommends.

Those who come to see family and say their farewells will usually be expected to sign a guest book, to approach the body if it is present, and to speak, as appropriate, to the closest friends and family. Some traditions are more rigid or more openly emotional, but one can usually see those variations fairly quickly. Usually visitors can count on being forgiven for some awkwardness and on being gratefully received in the community of the bereaved. It is hard to offend anyone if you are trying charitably to share in grief.

After funerals, families often invite others to join them at home or at a religious building or a restaurant for a shared meal, to talk, remember the dead, and share a sense of fellowship and community.

Are there things that must be done right after the burial or cremation?

The law requires only that someone attend to the settling of the financial estate, but religious and family traditions may well make a number of other demands. In some religious traditions, family members stay at home and receive visitors or say prayers for a substantial period of time. In some traditions, too, certain survivors are expected to wear special clothes or to abstain from certain activities for a prescribed period. Because these mandates are uncommon and vary substantially, family and friends might want to tell others in the death notice or in a handout given at other ceremonies.

As to the estate, family is well served when the deceased person leaves behind a will that at least names someone to have the authority to manage these affairs. If there is no will, generally close family will have to go to their county courthouse and get instruction in how to have someone named as "executor."

That person will have to report to the court what the person owned and how it

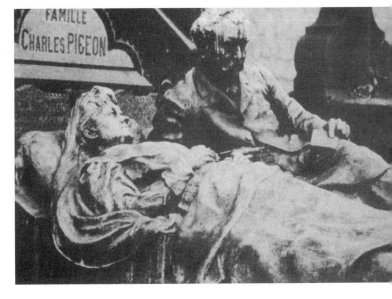

was handled. In the United States, if wealth is passing to a spouse, tax laws are fairly lenient. If wealth is passing to others, however, taxes are often substantial. If the estate is worth much, the family should have a lawyer's advice (in advance of death is much better, of course). Working through the issues in this chapter ahead of death is often quite calming and reassuring, and it is nearly always helpful to the family.

14
The Dying of Children

I'm afraid my baby is going to die. I'm afraid my baby is going to live.
PEGGY STINSON, from *The Long Dying of Baby Andrew*

Children aren't supposed to die—they are meant to outlive their parents. They are so innocent, and the world can be so cruel. Parents may wish they could take their child's place. Many wonder what they did wrong. Some question their belief in God. Most would do anything to keep their child alive. In this chapter, we address the challenges you face as a parent of a very sick child.

If there is a chance for cure, you and your child will want to pursue it. Your child should live, not just exist as long as possible. Your child's life should be comfortable, and it should be a life that both your child and your family value. Life at all costs is not usually the only goal. This can make it difficult and complicated to make decisions for and with severely ill children.

In the United States, eighty-five thousand children die each year. Some die of problems that are detected at birth, such as birth defects and prematurity.

Others die from injuries such as car accidents. Still others die from cancer and rare disorders that may not be detected at birth but that have a progressive course of deterioration. Each of these situations has its unique problems.

Infants

> A person's a person
> no matter how small.
>
> DR. SEUSS

Families have to share in making decisions for seriously ill children. However, an odd set of historical events and court cases in the 1980s led to a series of federal regulations restricting what families could decide for their infants if the decision might allow an earlier death. Called the "Baby Doe regulations," they have confused the medical and legal professions ever since. The latest version of these regulations states that life-sustaining treatment for an infant may be withheld only when one of these conditions is met:

- The infant is chronically and irreversibly comatose.
- Treatment would merely prolong dying.
- Treatment would not be effective in correcting all of the infant's life-threatening conditions.
- Treatment would be futile in terms of the survival of the infant.
- Treatment would be virtually futile in terms of the infant's survival, and the treatment itself would thus be inhumane.

Unfortunately, it's hard to know exactly what these regulations mean. You may want more than one opinion. Often neonatologists (doctors who care for newborn and very young babies) do not treat children after they are discharged from the intensive care unit. Therefore, some may be only vaguely aware of the long-term possibilities, of the burdens suffered by handicapped babies, and of the effect on the family. Thus it falls to the family of a tragically ill baby to gather all the information needed to make the best decisions for

Lynn, Harrold, Lynch Schuster

the baby and the family. Sometimes nature just takes away any choices and the baby dies despite treatment. But sometimes babies have an astonishing ability to linger if they are given medical support. Parents care deeply and want to do the best they can for their critically ill baby. Here are some ways to help your baby and your family.

> "Every blade in the field —
> Every leaf in the forest —
> Lays down its life
> in its season
> as beautifully
> as it was taken up."
>
> HENRY DAVID THOREAU, from a letter to Ralph Waldo Emerson, 1842

Ask if your baby is in pain. Babies can and do feel pain, and they have a stress response to it. Be sure he gets medication that prevents pain whenever he needs it. Even very tiny or very sick babies probably benefit from being sung to and being touched. Ask your nurse how to hold your baby. You may have to learn how to ignore tubes or wires.

Be wary of getting fragments of information about your baby. It helps to have one doctor or nurse who is expected to give you a good overview of your baby's situation at least once every day. Ask questions and don't hesitate to ask for more explanation when the information offered is too complex. Doctors and others should be able to answer all your questions in a way that makes sense to you.

If your baby will not survive, you still can have a family-centered death. You should be able to have as many of your family and friends with you as you want. Even small children (especially brothers and sisters of the baby) should be allowed to be present. The children ordinarily should be allowed to touch and hold the baby, kiss the baby, have pictures taken of themselves with the baby, preferably with a clock and a calendar nearby so you have a record of the date and time. Children do much better if they are involved. They are much stronger than most people think and do not need to be "protected" from death. In fact, they may suffer a greater loss if they have not been a part of their brother or sister's life and death. Ask for booklets that help you explain to your other children what is happening. Answer questions honestly and be patient if they ask them over and over, even years later. Be sure to include them in the religious ceremonies that are important to your family.

The Dying of Children

One three-year-old was asked if she was sad about her baby sister dying. She said, "Yes, but she ain't goin' nowhere; she's staying right here," as she pointed to her heart. Their eighteen-month-old sister played in the room, climbing on chairs. In the future, she will be able to look at pictures of the three girls together and know she was there, part of the baby's life, a sister forever.

If many people want to visit your baby, you may need to move to an area outside of the ICU. These needs probably can be accommodated. These are, after all, your family's last days with your baby.

Consider making hand- and footprints of your baby, affixing a lock of hair to a piece of paper with a poem or other decorations, or taking pictures of the family holding your baby. These acts will have special meaning, especially if you never got to take your baby home. Many people find that they have not only lost their babies but also their chance to feel like a "Mama" or "Daddy." This grief from not feeling like a parent can be overwhelming, even if you have other children. Pictures and other mementos are tangible evidence of your baby and your loving actions as a parent.

Sudden causes of childhood death

Yesterday your child was normal, healthy, facing a normal future. Suddenly, he is overwhelmingly ill as a result of a car accident, drowning, blood infection, or other problem. Children can pull through often enough that doctors and parents hold out hope for a long time. However, you may be faced with the realization that your child is not likely to recover. Now you have to make some decisions about how the very end will be lived. Use what you know about your child to guide you. What did he like to do? What made him happy? What can your family tolerate?

If the child will not be surviving, most people want to try to have a family-centered death. Your entire family should be able to visit at the same time, though perhaps that will require moving from ICU.

One child, a fourteen-year-old Pakistani boy, had drowned and was being kept alive until family could gather. His family and community came to honor him and provide a peaceful death, forming a circle around his bed and chanting. Then they drew closer to him (all thirty-five people in the room, of all ages), crying. When the breathing tube was removed, they poured holy water in his mouth and continued their chants. When he took his last breath twenty-seven minutes later, everyone looked out the same window and a peaceful hush fell.

Fatal chronic illnesses with intact intellect

There is a lot of living to be done after being diagnosed with a chronic and ultimately fatal illness. First and foremost, your child is a child. She needs to do kid things—play, draw, be with friends, be disciplined, have responsibilities, go to school. Sometimes these activities, though the most important to your child, get lost in the intense effort to treat medical problems. Wherever possible, squeeze these activities in.

Your child is likely to have good days and bad. You might both find it helpful to figure out what makes for a good day and to do what you can to have one. For some children, this might mean going to school. For others, it might mean seeing familiar faces in the hospital units where they have come to spend a lot of time. Still others will simply want to be at home with you. Each child will have a different idea of what a good day is, and each family will have a different way of shaping one. Knowing that you have done your best to make your child's life "good"—comfortable, content, safe—may offer you some reassurance. It allows you to respect and honor your child's wishes in a way that feels normal and good to her or him.

One sixteen-year-old wanted desperately to graduate from high school. A call to the school by the hospice team resulted in a cap-and-gown ceremony and graduation party. This same girl wanted to ride on a motorcycle but needed good pain control to do it. She again was able to accomplish this very personal goal because she was allowed

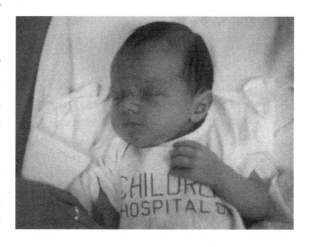

The Dying of Children

209

to express it, knew she had a limited life span, and had excellent, child-centered caregivers and parents who respected her and her wishes.

Your family has all kinds of needs. Ignoring these needs for the sake of a child who will be ill for a long time can actually harm him. For instance, not taking time to enjoy your marriage can damage the marriage, and the child may lose one of his parents, his pillars of strength. Well siblings need your attention, too. They need to feel loved and valued. Some regularly scheduled, dedicated time with each child fosters goodwill toward the ill child and prevents healthy children from worrying that they no longer matter. Instead of insulating the well children from the ill child, let them help care for their sick sibling. This experience fosters a sense of confidence and value that lasts into adulthood.

Communication

Everyone should try to talk about their feelings and fears about the illness. Open discussion also allows the sharing of anxieties and the accomplishment of important goals.

Penny, a sixteen-year-old girl with an unresponsive form of leukemia, was doing poorly on her therapy. Her friend, Lindy, a nineteen-year-old, was dying next door of ovarian cancer. Lindy was in a hospice program; her symptoms of severe vomiting and pain had been brought under control. She was making a video for her friends and family and asked Penny to come in for a hug good-bye. Lindy died an hour later, having left a loving legacy. Penny, though, was never allowed to express her views. Her family could not bear to contemplate her death. She died a few weeks later in the ICU after six hours of aggressive attempts to revive her.

Talking about death does not make it happen, though many people are afraid it may. Talking about death allows the child to complete important emotional tasks.

Children are sensitive to the needs of their parents, too. They often feel guilty about financial pressures, marital problems, or causing fear and pain in their families. They may feel that they are bad for having become ill or that the illness is a deserved punishment for bad things they have done. You should talk about your child's fears and soothe her. Children can be very resilient, and even the child who is ill often has a lot of strength to share.

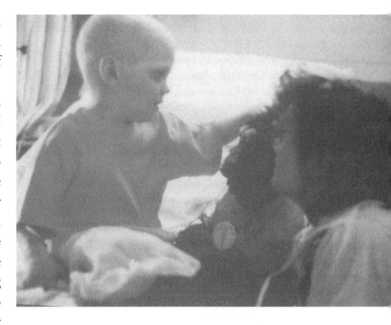

What if your child says, "Daddy, am I going to die?" You first reaction may be to answer, "Of course not!" But this answer may shake his faith in you. Your child can be very frightened if he feels you are hiding the truth. "Why do you ask?" is an answer that lets your child talk about his fears and perceptions. The child may have a new symptom, may have heard of a hospital friend dying, or may just be testing your willingness to talk. Children as young as three years old are often aware that they are dying without having been told.

Young children have spiritual lives and have important questions to ask. "Why is God doing this? Where am I going? Will I be happy and comfortable after I die?" These questions are best addressed by you, the parents. Answers consistent with your family's beliefs are the most reassuring to your child. Not knowing the answers is okay. Letting your child see your pain is okay. You can comfort each other in your uncertainties and in your love for each other. Chaplains can often be of help, though it is important for the parents to talk with them first.

With a few exceptions, the law does not recognize people under the age of eighteen as being able to make their own decisions. Although they may be immature compared with their peers in many ways, even very young, chronically ill children become especially mature regarding their own health. Parents often see this and feel it. Doctors may not understand the need to consult the child regarding her opinion on further treatment. Yet, ask a child-life specialist or a pediatric social worker, and you'll find that the best course includes asking the child. Your child knows what hurts

and what she feels is worth continuing to fight for. Deciding medical care for them without their input, even when they are very young, ignores their humanity and perspective. Your child can help you gain a better appreciation of her interpretation of what is happening and her suffering. Do not expect your child to make her own decisions about medical treatment, however, she may not understand the long-term positive effects of the treatment. Decisions are best made with mutual respect and collaboration between child, parent, and medical team.

When one nine-year-old boy correctly perceived he was dying, his medical needs were such that he could have gone home. His doctors, however, thought there might still be a slim chance. The child underwent all kinds of tests and treatments. His mother kept asking whether it wasn't time to let him be, but her questions somehow never got answered. The boy was never asked what was important to him. Did he want to go home to his bed or see his classmates one last time? Did he have a special movie he wanted to see? Was there a special friend or relative? He died five days later, in intensive care, monitors still beeping.

Many families want to know what their child's chances of survival are. When they ask their doctors, the answer may be, "Most children with cancer live. But I don't know for your child. It's either life or death—100% either way." Your response to this should be, "I understand what you are saying, but it is not enough information to allow my child and our family to make the best possible decisions. Can you give me a better idea?"

For children with cystic fibrosis or other serious, chronic illnesses, the answer may be, "You never know, you have pulled through so many times before." Yet, when your child is in the hospital more frequently and for longer periods of time, with repeated episodes on the ventilator or in intensive care, chances are getting slimmer. Begin to ask your child, when she feels well, what she wants to do next time she becomes ill. Check in intermittently to see whether the goals change as the child becomes more debilitated. Though it is difficult to hear, and difficult not to put your own needs first, you may hear great wisdom if you listen to your chronically ill child.

When treatments are experimental, they are just that. In other words, we don't know that they will help. You have to be careful to judge experiments as carefully as you judge your other choices.

At some point, a chronically ill, dying child and the family often benefit from hospice. Be sure to ask about hospice and investigate it long before you need it. If it is a welcoming, life-affirming, knowledgeable program, you may want to use it even before it is clear that death is at hand. Prepare for death even as you hope for life.

Rare disorders

The problem in many fatal childhood conditions is uncertainty. Some children have rare and even undiagnosable problems. There actually may be no statistics the doctor can cite for you. But the doctor, child (when feasible), and parents together, even in these cases, can review the child's course and see when the hospitalizations are becoming more frequent and longer and when the enjoyment of life for the child seems to be fading. At these times, the goals of care must be revisited. Perhaps going to the hospital is no longer the best choice. Perhaps some medications could be stopped. Perhaps blood tests hurt too much to continue them.

One three-year-old had a syndrome so rare that only a dozen people were known to have had it. He had been hospitalized only a few days each month. The boy then became more ill, never leaving the hospital for weeks. His mother stayed with him and his older siblings went to live with their grandparents. The family was torn apart by no longer spending any time together. The boy was receiving tests or medications every thirty minutes all night and day, and the mother was a sleepless wreck. Several teams of doctors were working on the child, none checking the schedule of medications and tests of the others. A palliative care nurse noted this and created a more humane schedule, reducing the number of tests and medications and grouping the others together.

The Dying of Children

213

The child was moved to a room where the whole family could stay day and night. For the first time in six weeks, the ill child, his brother, sister, and both parents were together. At the end of eight weeks, it was becoming obvious that he was not going to live, despite all the aggressive treatments. His family gathered advice from doctors and grandparents and others and decided to stop treatments and tests. Family and friends gathered for the little one's final day.

Disorders with impaired consciousness

Caring for children with neurodegenerative disorders is challenging, to say the least. Perhaps nothing is more painful than watching a previously "normal" child deteriorate before your eyes as you stand by helplessly. In these syndromes, a child who had learned to roll over and perhaps was sitting loses his skills. Older children, previously able to attend school, become unable to participate and then become progressively more dependent. Some children have their brain function robbed suddenly, in an accident, a fire, or a near drowning. These conditions share two problems: an increased likelihood of contracting and dying from pneumonia and the possibility of the child being so severely impaired that he is unable to feel hunger or

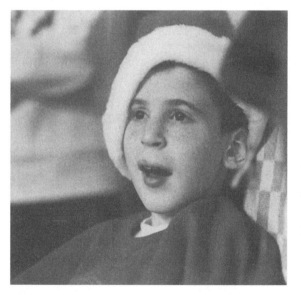

thirst or to respond to warmth or love.

Care is exhausting—financially, emotionally, and physically. Respite care may be available in your area. The social worker probably is the best source of information, but do not be afraid to pull out the phone book or check the Internet. Medicaid may offer financial help.

Asking friends and relatives to come stay for an afternoon or to allow you to get a full night's sleep is a good idea.

At some point, you will probably question whether recurrent hospitalization is helping or harming your child. It is important to find doctors, nurses, and social workers who can help you decide when you have done as much as you can and can help you through the dying. Allowing a child with severely impaired brain function to die naturally of pneumonia can be a loving gesture. It is the most likely cause of death, whether or not treatment is attempted. Symptoms can be controlled, using morphine if needed for breathing discomfort, with the addition of acetaminophen (Tylenol™) for fever and pain. Morphine does not hasten death, but it does help to ensure comfort. Finally, when a dying child has become so ill as to not feel hunger, there is no need to continue with tube or intravenous feedings. Stopping the feedings can enhance comfort by decreasing the amount of secretions your child is struggling with, decreasing the skin breakdown and hygiene needs, and preventing vomiting (see Chapter 11).

Parenting a dying child

No words can describe what it is like to know that your child is not going to live to be an adult. Your pain can be lessened by concentrating on living fully; being respectful of all involved, including the child, yourself, and the other children in your family; communicating with your child and family openly; re-evaluating goals of medical care at intervals; ensuring excellent symptom control; getting respite when needed; and insisting on informed decision making. At the time of death and

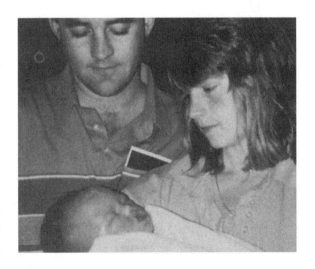

just afterward, do the important things that make lasting memories of your child for your family. Most of all, parents need support and help. Losing a child is extraordinarily difficult, and most parents appreciate some help in the journey. You can comfort your child during her lifetime and heal with your family in the future.

15
Dying Suddenly

Things can be going along, and then all of a sudden everything is changed.
MADELEINE L'ENGLE from *A Severed Wasp*

Many people believe that they want a death that comes suddenly and unexpectedly. But this can be difficult—certainly for families. Neither the dying person nor the family will ordinarily have been prepared. Instead, they assumed that there would be time to deal with dying someday—"when it is time." Those left behind may regret not having had the chance to say goodbye. Few people will have had any chance to say farewells or ask forgiveness or just to tenderly affirm a bond. Survivors may have many concerns: Did the person suffer? Did he have any last words? Could she have been spiritually prepared? Survivors may have many unanswered questions about those last minutes or hours. Survivors may have many regrets and questions and no obvious way to answer them. This chapter is addressed to survivors.

What can you do to cope with the sudden death of a loved one? First, be assured that time does help. You will need to endure for a while—the overwhelming sense of unreality, or numbness, or anger will lessen. So will the wild swings of emotion that you may be feeling. You will gradually begin to make good choices, to move forward in your own life. With sudden death, you may be more likely to keep questioning the events that led to death and to feel that your loved one's life was not "finished."

Some people have found it helpful to act out what would have been said or done if only they could have been there or if only they had had a few minutes to talk. Some survivors dream of the person or see him everywhere for a while. You might take that occurrence as an opportunity to write down what you would say, even to put it in an envelope and tuck it away.

Sudden death often leaves practical matters in real disarray. There may be children to take care of, financial matters left unsettled, or property to handle. With any luck, there will also be some trustworthy family or friends to help. Share your emotions and check your decisions with someone who cares about you but is not directly affected by what has happened. They can tell you if you are making good sense. If you are really on your own, then reach out to some professionals—chaplains, social workers, teachers, professional counselors. Everyone deserves someone to lean on after a sudden loss. You should also consider continuing with some professional support for a while. Many people find they need to push themselves into counseling or support groups at first, but later they say that this support turned out to be a lifeline and a great comfort.

Sudden death is not a common way to die now, but it is common enough that it affects almost every family. Sudden death happens in a variety of situations, some of which we discuss.

Violence

"The forces of hate and violence must not be allowed to gain their victory—not just in our society, but in our hearts. Nor must we respond to hate with more hate. This is a time of coming together."

REV. DR. BILLY GRAHAM
Prayer Service, Oklahoma City

When a loved one dies from violence, the survivors commonly experience a nearly overwhelming mix of shock, grief, fear, rage, frustration, and helplessness. Not only have you lost the person you love, but you have also lost some of your sense that the world can be safe. You may be fearful that the same thing could happen to you or to someone else you love. You may feel vulnerable and violated. You may experience frustrated rage at the person who did such a terrible thing, or at God for allowing such persons to exist. You may be angry at the authorities for having so little control. You may take on some of the guilt yourself, thinking that if you had only been there, come sooner, said something differently, this terrible death would not have happened.

After a violent death, survivors will often have to deal with investigators and the press. This can sometimes add an invasion of privacy to your other burdens. It may also be helpful to have evidence that people care and may give you an opportunity to talk about your loved one.

If an arrest is made, you hope that justice will be done. But the frustration can be great if the person responsible is unknown or not caught. A long period of time may pass before the person is brought to trial, and there may or may not be a conviction.

People often have savage, vengeful fantasies about the person who murdered or otherwise caused the death of a loved one. This is an understandable part of the grieving process, but you really must reach out to others to avoid acting on this impulse and to avoid taking it out on yourself.

Accidents

An accidental death can leave survivors feeling shock, grief, and a sense of supreme unfairness. The world may seem much more unpredictable and unsafe. If there was a clear reason for the accident, it feels like someone must bear the blame and guilt of having been careless or thoughtless. You might pursue

legal action to ensure that this kind of accident never happens again or to be certain that the person responsible is punished. There can be a comfort in knowing that others will not be hurt. It can also become a source of bitterness that a loved one's death is what it took to make a change.

Of course, sometimes the surviving loved one is also the person who feels most to blame for the accident. If you are the survivor in such a situation, you will need to hear many times that others do not hold you responsible and that you can forgive yourself. You will need to feel the special love of a family or community to begin to make sense of such an event. Take every opportunity to reach out to others, and find a professional counselor who you can trust and talk with in the months following the event.

Natural disasters

Any sudden death makes one feel uncertainty and fear. The world abruptly feels quite unsafe. A natural disaster forces you to feel how small and unprotected we are against the forces of nature. It may seem that fate picked your own little corner of the world to attack. Added to the loss of a loved one, you may have to endure the loss of cherished belongings—even the loss of a whole way of life. You might have to postpone grieving for the dead because of the immediate needs of finding shelter, locating other family members, or dealing with insurance companies.

Survivors of a natural disaster often find comfort in the fellowship of other survivors and in the companionship of community rebuilding. This sense of reconstruction can be the beginning of the healing and repair of families shattered by the loss of loved ones.

Suicide

Death from suicide often hurts terribly because the person who has died has so completely rejected his family and friends. If the suicide comes after serious physical or mental illness, though, you may feel both grief and a sense of relief that a long period of suffering has ended. On the other hand, you may feel really angry toward the person who has died, particularly if he or she either gave no warning at all or had actually engaged a lot of your time and energy trying to help. Guilt is common; you wonder if there was something more someone could have done.

If the suicide is unexpected, you may wonder whether you and others missed a signal or a silent plea for help. You may spend a great deal of time trying to understand what life must have been like, no longer wanting to live. Why didn't he love me enough to stay? Why wasn't my love enough for her to want to stay? You may feel ashamed, feeling that this reflects shortcomings in you and your family. Some people will hide the actual cause of death from others who may not understand or might judge harshly.

Families that have been affected by suicide should usually seek help from a mental health professional in the ensuing year. Family members benefit from a nonjudgmental but insightful outsider who can help sort out the conflicts and watch for signs that the survivors might be developing serious problems in coping.

Multiple deaths

When you have to endure the pain of the loss of more than one family member or friend, such as might happen in an accident or a natural disaster, grieving becomes more confusing and complicated. Many people find it so painful that life seems especially hollow. Sometimes a survivor wishes he could just die also. It may seem as if the dead persons are in a better place and that it is the survivors who feel left behind. Sometimes you don't know which person to grieve for first or most, or you feel guilty over missing one person more than another. The losses are so much that you cannot

believe that something this terrible could happen and leave you still living. You may have lost the family system that you had, and you may feel disoriented without having that familiar structure when you need it most.

You may desperately want to understand what happened—and why, even when there is no "why." You will need to lean on friends and family to hear your grief and maybe to give practical help. A professional counselor can also be very helpful. In these circumstances, you must be gentle with yourself and expect that merely enduring is enough for a while.

During chronic illness or recuperation

When you believe someone you love still has time to live, despite a severe illness, their sudden death will feel startling. When your loved one was stable just a few days ago, you can feel cheated and angry that you were robbed of the time you thought you would have together. Having already endured the anxiety of the illness and begun to face the eventuality of death, it often seems unfair not to get more warning.

It may sound odd, but families of most people who die after years of serious heart failure and of about a quarter of people who die of cancer say that the person died "suddenly." Even doctors do not always recognize that their patients might die in the midst of treatment, so it is likely that no one told you that your loved one might die suddenly. Nevertheless, the death is not a complete surprise. Once you think about it, you may realize that you knew that this would happen eventually, even if you hadn't expected it so soon.

You can take some comfort in knowing that the person was spared the worst that the disease could have caused. At times, you may be frankly relieved that death came suddenly, particularly when your loved one had been ill for some time and faced a long period of suffering. But this relief can cause guilt, too. Survivors are often afraid that the feeling of relief will seem like happiness that death occurred. It is valuable to realize that these feelings of relief are motivated by love and concern. Relief that suffering was avoided does not make the grief less real or wrenching.

Sudden infant death syndrome

The death of a child is a heartrending loss. People might expect their parents or grandparents to die, but no one expects children to die before their parents. When an infant appears healthy, as in the case of Sudden Infant Death Syndrome (SIDS), parents are especially stricken. You fear you did something wrong or didn't do something that should have been done.

About SIDS

An enormous amount of research has been done looking into the possible causes of SIDS. To date, only a little is known for sure; SIDS:

- Cannot be predicted or prevented.
- Is not hereditary.
- Has existed through the ages and in all countries.
- Is not caused by suffocation.
- Infants do not suffer.
- Is the most common cause of death among infants age one week to one year.
- Has been associated with low birth weight.
- Is more prevalent among some groups, including Native Americans and African Americans.
- Is more prevalent among the poor and less educated.
- Is slightly more common in the winter months.
- Is sometimes, but not always, preceded by a slight cold.

Sometimes the appearance of the baby who has died from SIDS can be confusing. Although some infants look as though they are just sleeping, if some time has passed before it is realized that the baby is dead, blood can pool in the baby's face. To inexperienced eyes, this can look like bruising. It is not surprising, although it is very hurtful, that emergency workers, the police, or even family may think that someone deliberately hurt the baby. Such confusion can lead to terrible misunderstandings or accusations. Sometimes parents believe that a sibling or their spouse may have struck the baby.

Dying Suddenly

Even after SIDS is diagnosed, it is natural for parents or other caregivers to wonder whether something was done wrong that could have prevented the death. Parents report being plagued with the thought that they should have tried to wake the baby from his nap sooner or that they should not have slept in that morning. We so desperately need to find a reason, a way to comprehend the incomprehensible.

No amount of foresight or care can totally prevent SIDS. Although SIDS happens most often at night, babies have been known to die in car seats and even while being held. You could not have prevented what happened. Nothing that you or anyone else did or didn't do caused your baby's death. Networks of parents who have experienced this loss do seem to help one another a great deal. If you have to endure this loss, be especially gentle with yourself and your spouse. Because this death is unexplainable, it will often cause real strains between a couple. Professional help is probably worth pursuing.

Some special issues: police, autopsy, and organ donation

In addition to the unexpected loss, sudden death often brings with it the need to deal with investigating authorities. Emergency workers, such as the fire department and the police, may have to ask questions. Although these people are only doing their jobs, it can be difficult for the family of a loved one who has died to understand and hard to cooperate. Sometimes the authorities will keep you away from the body of your loved one, either because an investigation is ongoing or because of the condition of the body. You will eventually get to be left alone and will be able to see the body, but no one may think to tell you so. Many police and emergency services are beginning to consider how to serve survivors better. You might ask if there is a chaplain or counselor who could accompany you, or you might insist on having a friend or family member along.

Sometimes there is confusion about what exactly did happen. There can be misunderstandings and miscommunications. At times like these, it is worthwhile to keep in mind that some questions may not be able to be answered accurately right away. It is hard to be patient, but it is better to have to wait for a correct answer than get a hurried answer that turns out to be false or misleading.

In cases of sudden death, the medical examiner will be notified and will decide whether an autopsy is required. An autopsy is a special examination of the body that often can determine a great deal about exactly what happened. The body is left looking normal and appropriate for family members to see. Nevertheless, people feel queasy about autopsy. In sudden deaths (except perhaps when serious chronic illness is the cause), the decision about autopsy is mostly out of your hands. If you have a strong religious objection, you should voice it, but the medical examiner is generally authorized to ignore your claim if there is any suspicion of foul play.

Sometimes members of the media want to ask questions. It is important to remember that you have a right to refuse to talk to reporters and to request to be left alone. If necessary, enlist the help of the authorities or friends or family members to ensure your privacy.

Among the people urgently wanting to talk to the bereaved family may be medical personnel who want a decision about organ donation. In the case of sudden death, particularly if the death itself takes place in the hospital setting, any undamaged organs of the patient are ideally suited for helping someone else. It can be very difficult in the midst of shock and loss to hear about someone else's needs. If your family member wrote out his or her wishes on a driver's license or an organ donor card, then you can be fairly comfortable in following those choices. If not, you need to know that any decision you make will be supported by the care team.

Many Americans believe that a sudden death is what they would want— preferably a sudden death in advanced old age. However, it is clear that a truly unexpected death is very hard on families and often deprives the dead person of the opportunity to complete his or her life, to say good-byes and to express hopes and wishes. Nevertheless, about one-tenth of all dying is truly unexpected, and our community must learn to help support those who are personally touched by sudden tragedy.

16
Enduring Loss

There is a sort of invisible blanket between the world and me. I find it hard to take in what anyone says.... Yet I want the others to be about me. I dread the moments when the house is empty. If only they would talk to one another and not to me.

C. S. LEWIS, from *A Grief Observed*

Grief is one of the most universal human emotions ... and one of the most isolating. All the world may love a lover, but few of us know how to honor grief, either how to be with a grieving person or how to handle our own grief. Sometimes grief is overwhelming; how can life possibly go on? Sometimes, though, grief is much less severe. Perhaps life has been so hard that survivors really feel death is a release. Perhaps faith in an afterlife helps. Perhaps the survivor has learned from a prior experience. Grieving is the mark of having been close to another person. The only way to avoid grieving is to avoid having loved.

Each person grieves in his or her own way, according to his own needs. There is no formula for grief, and no way around it. Like other emotions, grief is simply there, like love, joy, anger, or fear. As with other emotions, we cannot wish grief away, nor can we avoid it. Some of us may try to ignore grief or pretend it does not exist, but eventually we will feel it.

Grief, like death, is hard to discuss. Unlike other emotions that we have grown comfortable expressing or describing, we have no ready words for grief or bereavement. When we're happy, we can say we are on top of the world, flying high, on cloud nine. We can use clichés for anger, too, and say someone has had it up to here, sees red, or blows his top.

> Love, now all that is extinguished,
> the way joy is extinguished by grief,
> but grief is hardly lessened by joy,
> as a child's pain lessens with a kiss.
> How else to say this? There is no
> remedy. Silence moves
> in upon us
> like an infinite number line
> whose end is only farther away,
> no matter how I advance.
>
> JANICE LYNCH SCHUSTER
> from "When Numbers Breathe"

Grief has no such expression. But grief has a range of accompanying feelings: anger, loneliness, depression, guilt, relief, sorrow, fear, anxiety. In the midst of grief, we may swing from one emotion to the next, unprepared for the strength of our feelings and uncertain what to make of them.

Grief is a country we all must visit, and it helps to know what it's like there, how others have survived the journey, the maps they followed, the setbacks, and what they learned along the way. This chapter describes the grief that comes with dying. We talk about the changing nature of grief, and how grief can occur many times in the course of an illness, both before and after the death of someone you love. We offer suggestions on how to live through grief, ways to grieve with and for the dying person, and how to cope during difficult times, such as holidays, birthdays, and other anniversary dates. We describe problems that can occur when grief is overwhelming and where to turn when you need help.

Grieving your own dying

A life-ending illness can give you time to say good-bye to people you love and care about. You have time to make plans for how you want to be cared for at the end of your life and, perhaps, how you want to be remembered. You may, if you feel well enough, find time to do things you have always wanted to do, or you may wish to resolve old hurts and grievances.

If having a chance to say good-bye is a blessing, it can also be a curse. People who are sick and dying are often afraid and worried. Throughout the course of a life-ending illness, you must pass many milestones, and with each, experience some degree of loss.

Being very sick and coming to the end of your life, you face a series of changes. Each loss, such as the loss of independence, or dreams or abilities now gone, can give rise to grief.

Telling your story: why it is important

He wants to tell how his son was taken ill, how he suffered, what he said before he died, how he died..... He wants to describe the funeral, and how he went to the country.... And he wants to talk about her too.... Yes, he has plenty to talk about now. His listener ought to sigh and exclaim and lament.....

ANTON CHEKOV
from *Misery*

We are all storytellers. For most of our lives, we do just that—tell stories about our day, or something that happened last year, or when we got married or had our first child. Dying is the end of this life's story. People often find hope and comfort, and a sense of closure, by telling stories about their lives to others. You might ask a close family member, a trusted friend, a health care provider, or a counselor to listen to your story.

You might feel uncomfortable trying to tell the story of your life or encouraging a family member to hear it. Perhaps you grew up thinking it was important not to talk too much about yourself.

If you do not want to talk, or don't have someone to talk to, try writing things down. Just jotting down a few sentences each day can help you through this difficult time and might leave a powerful legacy as well. You might try borrowing or buying a recorder. If you feel comfortable in front of the camera, you could even ask someone to videotape parts of your story. Even though it might seem difficult, your story can be a gift to future generations, especially to very young children or grandchildren.

Your story can be short or long; you may not remember all of the details. It does not need to be great literature. It does not have to be told well.

Forget the rules you learned long ago in high school English. No matter what stories you tell, both you and your listeners are likely to benefit from the telling and to feel that living is meaningful because a relationship is strengthened.

People are often surprised to discover that other family members are usually quite interested in their life stories. Older people connect us to the past, to a family history that, left untold, will go unknown. Your story is a way for the people who will survive you to remain connected to you. Their memories can help them through the grief they will feel after your death.

Perhaps you can look at old photographs together and, if you feel like it, label them. If, like many people, you begin going through your possessions, you might ask someone else to help you. Along the way, you may have many stories to share.

Questions to Help you Tell your Life Story

Here are some questions to get you started:

1. Where were you born? Where did you grow up? What was school like when you were a child?
2. What did you like doing? What do you remember about your parents? If your parents were not born in this country, where did they come from? When did they arrive?
3. What are some of your earliest memories? Your happiest? Your saddest?
4. If you were in the military, where did you serve? What do you remember most?
5. If you worked, where was that? What did you do? Did you enjoy it? Do you wish you had done something else?
6. If you stayed home and raised children, what was that like? Do you have special memories?
7. When did you get married? Where? Did you take a wedding trip or honeymoon?
8. Did you travel? Where did you go?
9. Who were your best friends? What did you do together?
10. What are some of your favorite activities? Can you still do them? If you have a special skill, can you teach it to someone else?

Many community education programs, including hospice and other health centers, offer music and art therapy for people who are dying. Such therapy, which can range from painting or drawing to writing "life songs," can be very healing. Participation does not require any expertise other than a desire to express yourself. At one housing program for homeless people who are dying, residents often draw or paint; the paintings now decorate the home and are a way for the dying to be remembered and to comfort, in a way, those who follow them. Other residents work with a music therapist to compose "lullabies" of their lives. Such creative expression can have a profound and peaceful effect on one's life.

Understanding the cycle of grief

Several decades ago, Elisabeth Kübler-Ross described five stages people often experience when coming to terms with a terminal illness: denial, anger, depression, bargaining, and acceptance. Because these stages portrayed a common response so well, people began to think of the stages as the five stages of grief. Unfortunately, grief does not move along in an orderly fashion, according to a specific order or timeline. Some people may not go from one stage to another. Others find they cycle from anger to acceptance to depression again and again.

Counselors have noticed that people often follow a pattern of grieving:

- The loss and acceptance of it as being real
- Adjustment to loss
- Reinvestment in life

Grief is characterized by unexpected changes. People move from one point to another on the circle, then back again, depending on where they are in their lives and the events going on around them. New losses may trigger old grief. Unexpected moments may give rise to sadness. One man described bursting into tears on a busy street when a passerby tipped his hat, reminding him of his own late father.

When you are living with dying, you know how grief feels: lonely, cut off, isolated, sad, abandoned, angry, or lost. Grief can feel overwhelming, especially in the immediate aftermath of a death. It can begin to feel like a constant part of your life.

At some point, a survivor will find himself gradually reinvesting in life. That investment might be taking care of the survivor's interests, praying or finding meaning each day, or getting up and going to work. Somehow, people do find a way to survive, and eventually to thrive again.

How families and loved ones grieve

In taking care of a dying loved one, you may experience grief at many points throughout the illness. For instance, there is the grief of first learning about the person's illness, the grief as plans you shared are lost or as you realize you may be spending your final days together. People often think that they have

---

When you are Very Ill: Moments that Lead to Loss

- Being told you have a fatal illness
- Telling others you are dying
- Facing treatments
- Deciding to end treatments
- Coping when treatments fail
- Seeing people you care about
- Being hospitalized
- Going through possessions
- Making plans for the time of death and the time after

As I walk this last trail

And come to the last high pass

I step to the other side

Into the sunshine glow

Waiting there to greet me

Are all the ones I know

Love

Gordie

JULY 1991

"In loving memory of John Gordon Hamilton, 'Gordie.'"

grieved so much and that death will be a simple continuation of that familiar emotion.

Unfortunately, death usually brings a grief all its own. People are sometimes surprised to discover that mourning begins again, and grief appears anew. Often, in the immediate wake of death, we become numb just to survive funerals and memorial services or to take care of a person's estate and belongings. Then, as relatives and friends disperse, we are alone again with grief.

The things you decide to do (or not do) are usually perfectly good ways to deal with your own grief.

Common symptoms of grief

Grief, like other emotions, can make its presence known both in body and mind. You may:

- Lose your appetite
- Experience aches and pains
- Sleep too long or not enough
- Feel depressed, melancholy, hopeless
- Feel angry at the world, yourself, or your loved one
- Feel guilty for things left unsaid or undone
- Feel unable to concentrate

All of these feelings and sensations are grief's way of showing its force in your life. These reactions are the normal, human response to loss.

Ways to console yourself

Each person comes up with his or her own way to find comfort. For you, it might be:

- Participating in different forms of creative expression, such as art and music
- Keeping a journal
- Seeking spiritual or religious guidance and support
- Sharing your spiritual journey with loved ones.

Living after the loss of a loved one

Grief has its own timetable. In general, grief affects daily life for as long as a year. People often feel great sorrow from time to time for many years—but the time between surges usually lengthens as time goes on.

There are few, if any, ways to shorten the period of mourning. Instead, people learn to live with their loss and, in doing so, live through their grief.

Often, one way to cope with loss is to talk to others who have experienced similar losses. Many hospitals and hospices offer grief and bereavement support groups that meet periodically for several months. There you can share experiences, thoughts, and memories. Somehow, the process of talking to others, and sometimes just helping others with their grief, can have a healing effect.

Programs are often tailored to meet specific losses. For instance, people whose children have died will have concerns that are quite different from those whose spouses or parents have died. Check that the group you join is likely to be comfortable for you.

A recent Gallup poll showed that people are most likely to turn to friends and family for support, although one-third turn to members of the clergy. Specially trained members of the clergy, called pastoral counselors, may be able to help you with the spiritual and emotional issues that accompany grief. If you are active in a faith community, your religious leader should be able to give you the names of pastoral counselors in your community. Pastoral counselors generally offer services according to a sliding-fee scale.

Consolation

Here are a few ways to help survivors through this sad time of life.

SOLITUDE HELPS. You may need time to think about your loved one, to remember times you shared, to consider how your life will be now. You may be overwhelmed by your sorrow. You may want to stay in bed and cry or sleep, go for a walk, or sit in a chapel.

OTHER PEOPLE HELP. Friends and family members are likely to empathize with you. Even if they do not know what to say, just being with other people and talking can be supportive. Accept others' invitations to participate in activities, but leave if you feel you need to. Reach out to family or friends when the next hour or day seems unbearable.

ACCEPTING SUPPORT HELPS. Others may want to help by doing things for you. They may want to bring you food or talk on the phone or run errands. Accept these acts of kindness whenever you can.

REST AND SLEEP HELP. Caring for a dying person has been exhausting. You may need time alone simply to regain your physical energy, as well as your emotional and spiritual strength.

ROUTINES HELP. Even though your life may feel turned upside down, try to keep up a routine of healthy eating, occasional physical activity (even a ten-minute walk), and regular sleep.

TIME HELPS. Your life may never be the same again. Whatever your experience with death and dying, you will find that you see the world and your place in it differently. Time lessens some of grief's pain, but it does not diminish your loss or sadness.

DREAMS HELP. Many people dream of the dead person and feel that, in this way, they are with the person again.

NATURE HELPS. Take a walk and focus on something hopeful in what you see, such as the color of tree bark or the sound of the wind.

CREATIVITY HELPS. You might try writing about your feelings or creating a special area in your home to honor the memory of your loved one.

Other mental health counselors may be helpful, too, especially if you experience what is known as "complicated grief," a profound grief that continues for many months or years after the death of a loved one and that prevents you from enjoying and participating in life. Counseling may be especially important in cases of sudden and unexpected death.

POSTPONE MAJOR LIFE CHANGES. You may make decisions impulsively that will later prove not to be in your best interest. Impulse spending is only a temporary fix, and geographical changes (such as moving) will not leave grief behind. If you have to make a major life change, talk it over with people you trust and encourage them to counsel you about whether you are thinking clearly.

ASK FOR HELP. Other people may want to offer help but not know how. Ask! The process can be healing. If you are widowed and have children at home, you may need help with the practical issues of life, such as child care and survivor benefits.

TURN TO OTHERS. Tell others that you are grieving. There is no reason to hide your grief or sadness. Let others know how you are doing.

KEEP YOUR EXPECTATIONS WITHIN REASON. Grief is a major stress in anyone's life. Reduce other stresses, and try to keep your expectations of yourself reasonable. Lower your expectations if you need to.

AVOID THE "SHOULDS" AND "OUGHTS." Most mental health experts encourage grieving people to avoid the "shoulds" of life and focus on what unavoidably must be done and what one would like to do. Feeling that a good person "really should" do more is especially tough on the bereaved.

Music Can Comfort the Dying and the Grieving

For as long as there has been music, there has been music to help people through times of sadness. The origins of most Western music can be found in the Gregorian chants of medieval monks. Sometimes these were written for everyday prayers, but frequently they were written for funeral masses. From those beginnings, a tradition of funeral masses, or requiems, continued in classical music to the present.

Jazz music has long been played at New Orleans funerals. Sad songs are played at first, then happy songs celebrate the deceased and share the joy of his or her entering a better life. Show tunes, rock and roll, folk songs, and gospel hymns all deal with loved ones dying.

The songs and tunes we hear can serve as a unique companion. In offering comfort, music makes no demands on us at all. When singer and guitarist Eric

Enduring Loss

Clapton's son died, tragically and suddenly, he wrote a song to him called "Tears in Heaven." This beautiful song struck a chord with many people. For those who had lost a child, hearing someone else mourn a similar tragedy helped them to feel less alone in their grief.

No matter the reason, music helps us turn a flood of emotions into something more manageable. With or without lyrics, melodies communicate and interact with our emotions. That is why so many cultures use music, and why some songs cross many cultures with ease.

The music people use is as diverse as people can be—from electric guitars or trumpets to choirs; from slow and soft, as in Mozart's "Lacrimosa," to bright and crisp, as in "When the Saints Go Marchin' In." Often people choose to listen to something that was special to the person who has died. This is guaranteed to bring up memories that may be uncomfortable but may also be healing. There may also be special music which has helped before, in other times of struggle, and may help again now.

What Makes Music So Important to Those Who Grieve?

Perhaps listening to music gives us a special time just to think about the people we love. Often our minds are racing too fast, or not moving forward at all, in our initial moments of shock. Having music around gives us a rhythm, a structure around which we can reflect and grieve.

Like a metronome, or deep breathing, it gives a rhythm to our fragmented thoughts.

Music also has the powerful ability to draw out memories obscured by time or emotion. It seems to have a near-magical ability to penetrate through the present day to remind us of other occasions. Sometimes songs and melodies so accurately pinpoint an emotion that they transport the listener to another time and place. In times of grief, this magical quality can recall times and emotions long forgotten because of prolonged illness and strain.

Sometimes in our sadness and shock, we merely feel numb. Certainly this is a protective mechanism, a perfectly normal approach to grief, and not a reason to be ashamed. But sometimes music helps evoke welcome thoughts and feelings.

Ways to help a grieving loved one

Empathy is key to helping the bereaved. Sympathetic approaches or those that try to identify with the bereaved may miss the mark. Instead, try to understand the other person's experience without forcing meaning on it. If someone wants to share her stories with you, even stories that you have heard a million times, listening will be a great gift. You will bear witness to her life, to things that gave her pleasure, to her sorrows, fears, regrets. There are a few things to remember as you do this, but most especially:

- Listen.
- Do not judge the other person.
- Show compassion: offer a hug, if it's wanted, or a shoulder to cry on.
- Be supportive and offer comfort, even if this is simply by being silent.

Children's understanding of death: what to expect and how to help

If few of us know how to honor an adult's grief, or to handle our own losses, how much harder it is to help a child through the process! Children

> My life closed twice before its close;
> it yet remains to see
> If Immortality unveil
> A third event to me,
> So huge, so hopeless to conceive,
> As these that twice befell.
> Parting is all we know of heaven,
> And all we need of hell.
>
> EMILY DICKINSON

do grieve, deeply and over time. Their experience and expression of grief may be different from an adult's, but it will be no less painful or severe. Like adults, children benefit from attention and love. They may need solitude and companionship, someone to talk to, and someone to cry with. Sharing the reality of what is happening allows children to begin to understand, to cope with, and to integrate the experience of loss into their lives.

Within the first year of life, the infant is able to feel separation and a sense of loss. Creating a warm, safe environment, physical support, holding, hugging, rocking, and reassurances of personal safety ("We'll be here to take care of you") counteract the confusion and restore some security.

The preschool child, two to five years old, thinks death is temporary and reversible, something like a round trip. "Mommy is dead and will be coming home soon." Death (and illness) may be seen as contagious but also avoidable. Children imagine bogeymen, angels, skeletons, and devils that might take away bad people or those who are too old or too sick or too slow to outrun or outsmart death.

The school-age child observes death as the end of bodily life, final and universal. Even though older children and adolescents know it can happen to them, they believe it to be the remotest of possibilities and are prone to challenges and risk-taking behaviors. Children who "grow up with the loss" ordinarily reexamine and reintegrate that loss at each developmental level. When the loss is significant, the grown person will often still revisit his loss at significant milestones in life, such as marriage, graduations, births, and other deaths.

Maturity, of course, does not happen according to fixed age categories. Each child has her own timetable.

Very young children may not be able to talk about their grief. Instead, they may show it by acting out, reverting to more babyish behavior, clinging, or withdrawing. Because they have no way to make sense of death and dying, loss of someone close can be quite confusing.

Lynn, Harrold, Lynch Schuster

Comforting a grieving child

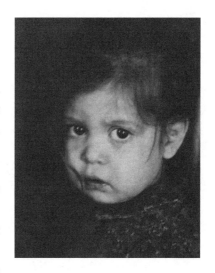

Speak in simple language the child can understand. Ask the child what he or she thinks, knows, and feels and respond specifically to those concerns. Don't overwhelm the child with excessive detail, and be sure to see how the child is putting it all together.

Be honest. Avoid half truths. Don't tell a child something you will need to correct later on. For example, when the child insists that "Mommy will be back in the spring ... like the flowers," don't, out of compassion, agree. Instead, say something like, "That would be nice, wouldn't it?"

Even the clumsiest statement is better than not discussing the loss at all. Children are quite aware when they are being shut out of a tragic event. They will judge correctly when a topic is taboo in a family setting and close off communication with adults. When this happens, angry outbursts, irritability, and changes in eating and sleeping habits will offer a clue that the child is suffering in his or her own private way. Remember that a child's imagination often creates more frightful images than reality ever could.

Expect expressions of anger: at God, at the lost loved one, at the surviving parent, at the doctors, at anyone in their sight. They can also turn the anger inward on themselves. Because children believe in magic, they sometimes believe that they caused the death because they were "mad" at the parent or other person who died.

Watch children at play. This will offer you valuable clues, particularly with a very young child. One of the many ways children can express their feelings when they cannot express them verbally is by acting them out with dolls or toys. Listen to the stories they make up, in words or in play. You can then encourage memories of the good times and also provide alternative ways of understanding the bad things they remember.

Don't be upset if, after a clear explanation of what happened, children appear to toss it off and go about their normal activities. It takes time for children to deeply internalize bad news.

Enduring Loss

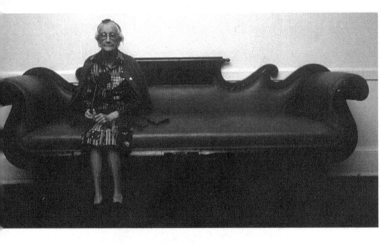

Expect the hard questions to come up eventually, perhaps many months later. Prepare yourself with answers because these questions will express the child's deepest fears. The four central questions are: "Did I cause Papa's (or Grandma's or Grandpa's) death?" "Will I die, too?" "Are you going to die, too?" "If you die, too, who will take care of me?"

Include grieving children in events that precede and follow a death. Help a child to say good-bye in the hospital, to attend the funeral service, and to participate in rituals with the family. They can cope with most situations, provided they are given appropriate choices, prepared for what to expect, given opportunities to talk it through, and supported emotionally. Simple ceremonies such as lighting a candle next to a photograph; placing a letter, picture, or special memento in a casket; or releasing a helium balloon with a message attached for the person who has died are effective leave-taking gestures.

Allow for the expression of emotions. The child may cry or may not. Adults can let their own tears flow, too. Children will find their own way, but they will look to adults, too, for some examples to follow.

Older children, especially adolescents, may need help to express their grief, especially over the loss of a parent. Adolescence is a difficult enough passage, and grief adds layers of complexity and emotion. Address a teenager's needs early and often, and ask your child's school for help or guidance.

Use books, TV, and movies, too. Many wonderful after-school specials and prime-time programs deal with the death of a parent, grandparent, sibling, or pet: *The Yearling*, *All the Way Home*, and *Death Be Not Proud* are available for rent. Among the many wonderful books written for children is *Badger's Parting Gifts* by Susan Varley. Old Badger dies, leaving a note for his friends: "Gone down the Long Tunnel. Bye Bye, Badger." His friends,

Mole, Fox, and Rabbit, talk about the things each learned from Badger, realizing that he has left them many good memories and abilities. This book can help you talk to a child about an older relative who is dying or about anyone in the child's life who has died. Many communities offer special grief programs to provide support for children who are dying or whose parents or siblings have died. Such programs are frequently coordinated through local hospices, religious institutions, and Internet support groups. Some focus on losses through violence, AIDS, or other particular illnesses.

Reinvesting in life after the loss of someone you love

Eventually, those who live on will find ways to become engaged in life again and, like old Badger's friends, will remember good aspects of the time before the illness or even during the illness. At various points, a survivor will often feel ready to reinvest in life. Someone living without a spouse, for example, might find a new job or hobby. Someone involved in a bereavement or support group might feel ready to share experiences with others. People do discover new loves, interests, and habits. People experience the immediate effects of the loss, but they may also experience long-term changes as well, changes in how they see the world and how they see themselves. They may discover new meaning and purpose in their own lives or pursue new passions and dreams. For the most part, people are remarkably resilient and adapt to the changes brought about by a loved one's death.

> I wake to spring rain in mid-winter
> from a dream about my mother.
> It's as if I've just been with her
> in the bright square of our kitchen.
> Scene from a thousand schooldays—
> I'm sitting, she's standing,
> busy at the counter, cutting up an orange:
> a conjured image sharp as longing.
>
> JODY BOLZ
> from "I Wake to Spring Rain in Mid-Winter"

Survivors often devise their own ways to remember and honor the person who died. Some people create special areas in a home where they arrange items that belonged to their loved one, such as toys, collections, books, photographs, or trinkets that serve as glad reminders. Perhaps they ask members of their worship community to remember the family at special times.

Enduring Loss

241

A Story of Comfort: *The Sweater*

Donna Peratino's eighty-year-old father was dying of pancreatic cancer. Thin after radiation and chemotherapy, he became very cold and began to wear a sweater. This is Donna's story:

I asked my father about the sweater one day, noting that it belonged to his brother, George, who had died of cancer just over a year before. My father had gotten the sweater from his sister-in-law, who had asked if there was anything he had wanted to remind him of George. Although my father did not need a physical object, he accepted the sweater as a gesture of courtesy to my aunt. George had worn the sweater throughout his own illness and dying.

I asked my father how he felt while wearing the sweater. He said that it made him feel that he was "next in line." I nodded and, after a few moments of quiet, asked if there was a different path for him to choose. I then asked him if, given a choice, what color sweater he would like and what characteristics it would need to have to comfort him and keep him warm.

That afternoon, I returned with a deep blue, cable-knit cardigan that lit up my father's eyes and evoked a sigh when the shopping bag was opened. He tried it on and the new, smaller sweater fit perfectly. His delight and appreciation for this seemingly small act of kindness radiated and touched my soul.

After a few moments, we agreed there was one step left. We had agreed that the new sweater would replace the old one. After my father had reached up to the closet shelf and brought down the carefully folded green sweater, I held it with him as he passed it to me. We paused and I asked him to think of all that his brother had been to him and all they had shared. While my father appreciated the sweater and how it had served George, he was going to let it go. My father and I locked eyes for an all-too-quick instant, and then he raised his open palm, kissed his fingers to his lips, and brought the kiss to the sweater.

This shared moment has brought me great comfort in knowing there were many small, important ways that I contributed to my father's long-term battle, in which he outlived his doctor's prognosis by one year. Throughout this time, he wore the blue sweater as a symbol of his commitment to continue as long as he could and to move on when it was his time.

After my father's death, my mother hurriedly disposed of his clothes as a way of coping with the reminders of all she had lost. Slacks, shirts, ties, and tuxedo were all gathered and donated to charity—except one piece that found its way to the third drawer of my dresser.

Family may visit the graveyard, feeling there a place to talk to the person's spirit. Some plant a tree or garden, install a special stone somewhere, or make donations to a charity. One woman, to honor her late aunt, donated books to a school library with special bookplates in her aunt's name. Some say prayers on behalf of a loved one or talk to him or her. There are as many ways to remember those who have died as there are people to remember them.

It can be very hard to cope with loss during holidays that encourage family togetherness or on anniversary dates, such as the person's birthday or the anniversary of the death. Again, people often develop rituals or prayers to honor the dead on special days.

As a survivor reinvests in life, he or she may feel pangs of guilt that somehow, by finding pleasure in life, the loved one who died is being forgotten. Try to honor your memories by letting joy enter your life. One mother, writing about the loss of her teenage daughter, states it most eloquently: "The memory does not go away when you start to heal, and living a full life does not deny the emptiness left by loss."

17

Resources

Don't assume that it's too late to get involved.
MORRIE SCHWARTZ from Tuesdays with Morrie

This book contains a wide array of information to help you as you face serious illness. Although it answers many of your questions and helps you work through some difficult times, you may well need more questions answered or perhaps a person to talk to. Many voluntary and governmental organizations distribute very useful information in multiple ways: a simple brochure, a phone conversation, or a Web page. The amount of information can be overwhelming, but with a little guidance, this sea of information can readily be navigated.

This chapter has been broken up as shown in the chapter's Table of Contents on page 247. You will find books and references throughout the chapter. Keep in mind that the descriptions here are sometimes general. The organization may offer information or services that are not mentioned. Don't hold back from exploring a little. If you find a good resource that we didn't mention or if you are disappointed with one of these, please let us know by e-mail: info@medicaring.org.

When contacting an organization, be as clear as possible about the needs you have. It is appropriate and reasonable that you ask questions and request written materials or references from organizations that claim to focus on your issue. Look through this chapter and highlight a few resources you think will be helpful. Organizations are listed because of their aim to educate and support people during this often difficult period. Contact these groups and see what they can do for you. Many national organizations have local chapters. There are also many local organizations that are not affiliates of national organizations and are not listed here. So take a look in your phone book or check with your Area Agency on Aging (in the United States). You may be surprised by the amount of information that you will find there. Also, talk with your doctor, nurse, social worker, and religious leader. Your local library is another excellent resource. Librarians can assist you in finding the resources that are right for you. Many libraries have audio or talking books, large print materials, and Braille resources available. Not only will they be able to help you find other good reference materials and listings of local information and support groups, but they may help you with the Internet if this is new to you.

Some of these resources will be more helpful than others. One of the best Internet sites we have found is Growth House (http://www.growthhouse.org). This site has a comprehensive collection of information on topics such as hospice and home care, palliative care and pain management, death with dignity, depression, anxiety, and grief. The search capabilities of Growth House are gradually expanding to give you one-stop access to an array of Web resources.

Locally compiled resource guides can be quite helpful in locating local organizations that will be able to help you deal with issues such as nutrition, legal services, recreation, home care, and other supportive services. In the

> Dead
> This is where I died
> This is where I hide
> This is my only place
> This is like a vase
> It is like a vase,
> A person case,
> Holding a flower
> Until its last hour.
>
> NICHOLAS GUY LYNN
> Child of seven, undergoing chemotherapy (when asked to explain, the author printed, "It's like a vase because a coffin holds a person like a vase holds a flower").

United States, you can contact your local Area Agency on Aging or check the yellow pages under headings such as Senior Services, Health Care Management, or Home Health Services.

Call or e-mail your local Agencies on Aging

Throughout the United States, Area Agencies on Aging provide information and referral and help to match you with services such as meals at senior centers, Meals on Wheels, transportation, financial help, telephone reassurance, grocery shopping assistance, income tax assistance, or any other special need you might have. You may also qualify for financial assistance through this office. If you do not know how to contact your local Area Agency on Aging, call the national toll-free hotline at 1-800-677-1116. Or visit their website (www.eldercare.gov) to search by city, state, and zip code for programs available in your area. You can download or order many useful fact sheets and booklets, including information on planning for a crisis with an older family member, making home safety modifications, and dealing with transportation issues.

Table 17.1 Medicare and Medicaid Coverage for Services

Service	Medicare	Medicaid
Hospital care	yes	yes
Emergency ambulance	yes	yes
Subacute (after hospital care)	often covers most	part
Nursing home	very little	usually yes
Medications	usually yes	yes
Home health nurses	usually yes	usually yes
Home health aides	usually not	usually yes

How do I pay for end-of-life services?

Knowing and understanding how each kind of end-of-life health care service is paid for is not simple. Here is a brief guide of what is covered in the United States by traditional Medicare and Medicaid. As always, these services and how they are paid for vary depending on where you live and on recent changes in coverage. If you have private insurance, talk to your insurance case manager. If the coverage is provided by your employer, talk to a benefits manager in the Human Resources department. Ask your doctor, nurse, social worker, or case manager to guide you as well.

Table of Contents for Chapter 17

Resources

Pain and Symptom Management
Spiritual Concerns and Complementary Care

II. CONDITIONS AND DISEASES
Alzheimer's and Other Dementias
Cancer
Chronic Heart or Lung Disease
Diabetes
Frailty of Old Age
HIV/AIDS
Kidney Disease
Liver Disease
Neuromuscular Disease
Parkinson's Disease
Stroke

III. GENERAL INFORMATION AND RESOURCES FOR REFORM

I. Issue-specific

Advance Directives, Treatment Decisions, and Law

Aging with Dignity: Creator of the Five Wishes advance directive, now valid in most U.S. states. Download a copy, for a fee, from its website.
http://www.agingwithdignity.org

Compassion and Choices: Provides a toll-free number for patients and families seeking support or information about pain management, advance directives, and local referrals. Advocacy component focused on aid in dying (physician-assisted dying).
http://www.compassionandchoices.org/learn

Doukas, David John and William Reichel. *Planning for Uncertainty: Living Wills and Other Advance Directives for You and Your Family.* Baltimore, MD: Johns Hopkins Press Health Book, 2007.

Go Wish Cards. A card game to help people communicate their preferences and priorities.
http://www.codaalliance.org/gowishcards.html

Lynn, Harrold, Lynch Schuster

Harwell, Amy. *Ready to Live, Prepared to Die—A Provocative Guide to the Rest of Your Life.* Wheaton, IL: Shaw Publications, 2000.

Kaplan, Karen Orloff and Christopher Lukas. *Staying in Charge: Practical Plans for the End of Your Life.* Hoboken, NJ: Wiley, 2004.

MedicAlert: A nonprofit organization offering access to online health records, medical information jewelry, and Lifeline, a twenty-four-hour emergency response center for subscribers.
http://www.medicalert.org/home/Homegradient.aspx

National Academy of Elder Law Attorneys: A professional association for attorneys who serve older people or those with special needs. Website helps users locate elder law attorneys nationwide.
http://www.naela.org

National Healthcare Decisions Day: Website for an annual event, with useful links to state-level resources and an array of Web-based free resources.
http://www.nationalhealthcaredecisionsday.org

Your Life, Your Choices: Planning for Future Medical Decisions: How to Make a Personalized Living Will.
http://www.rihlp.org/pubs/Your_life_your_choices.pdf

Aging

AARP: Membership organization for people age 50 and older, offering services, information, and advocacy, with information for family caregivers.
http://www.aarp.org

Aging in the Know: Created by the American Geriatrics Society with information about common conditions that affect older adults and includes tips on how best to communicate with health care providers.
http://www.healthinaging.org/agingintheknow/

U.S. Administration on Aging: Part of this federal website provides older adults and family caregivers with resources about aging issues, including elder rights, family caregiving, and how to find help, along with links to state area agencies on aging.
http://www.aoa.gov/AoARoot/AoA_Programs/OAA/How_to_find/Agencies/find_agencies.aspx

U.S. National Institute on Aging: Agency leads federal research efforts on an array of topics related to aging, including caregiving; chronic conditions, especially dementia; and advance care planning and end of life care.
http://www.nia.nih.gov

Bereavement

Berger, Susan A. *The 5 Ways We Grieve: Finding Your Personal Path to Healing after the Loss of a Loved One.* Boston: Trumpeter, 2009.

Bouvard, Marguerite, and Evelyn Gladu. *The Path through Grief: A Compassionate Guide.* New York: Prometheus Books, 1998.

Compassionate Friends: Offers bereavement support to families who have experienced the death of a child.
http://www.compassionatefriends.org

Frigo, Victoria, Diane Fisher, and Mary Lou Cook. *You Can Help Someone Who's Grieving: A How-to Healing Book.* AuthorHouse, 2000.

GriefNet: Online support, including discussion groups and other resources, for people dealing with grief and loss, with special programs for veterans and their families.
http://www.griefnet.org

GrowthHouse.org: Extensive information about coping with different kinds of grief, ranging from the death of an infant to suicide, with tips on how to find local resources for grief support and links to healing music.
http://www.growthhouse.org/death.html

Rainbows: An organization founded to help children deal with grief due to death, divorce, or separation; offers programs in five thousand communities nationwide, with special programs for preschoolers and adolescents.
http://www.rainbows.org

SympathyTree: A commercial site with useful resources on what to do after someone dies, with step-by-step information on planning a funeral or memorial service, dealing with paperwork, and creating an online memorial.

Zonnebelt-Smeenge, Susan J., and Robert C. De Vries. *Getting to the Other Side of Grief: Overcoming the Loss of a Spouse.* Ada, MI: Baker Books, 1998.

Care Management, Resource and Benefit Coordination

Benefits CheckUp: A service of the National Council on Aging to help people over fifty-five find and enroll in government and private benefits programs for health and social support services.

http://benefitscheckup.org

Medicare Rights Center: Offers counseling and educational programs about Medicare, including an interactive online feature and a hotline for questions about Medicare benefits and coverage.

http://www.medicarerights.org

National Association of Professional Geriatric Care Managers: Professional association of health and human services specialists who help families care for older relatives by offering support and guidance ranging from health assessment to long-term care selection. Offers online care manager locator.

http://www.caremanager.org

Next Step in Care: Sponsored by the United Hospital Fund, this site helps patients and caregivers organize transitions between care settings.

http://www.nextstepincare.org

U.S. Department of Veterans Affairs: Information about benefits and programs available to veterans and their families, including hospice and home health services.

http://www1.va.gov/health/index.asp

Caregiving

Alzheimer's Foundation of America: Website includes resources and tips for family caregivers.

http://www.alzfdn.org

ARCH National Respite Network and Resource Center: A national database that includes a respite locator program and an information clearinghouse.

http://chtop.org/ARCH.html

Caring Bridge: A nonprofit that offers families and friends a Web-based way to stay in touch during a loved one's illness, with a guestbook to share messages.

http://www.caringbridge.org

Carter, Rosalynn and Susan Galont. *Helping Yourself Help Others: A Book for Caregivers.* Three Rivers Press, 1995.

Children of Aging Parents: A nonprofit organization offering information, referrals, and support, including online support groups in several states.

http://www.caps4caregivers.org

Eldercare Locator: Sponsored by the U.S. Administration on Aging, this site offers local referrals and resources for older adults nationwide.

http://www.eldercare.gov/Eldercare.NET/Public/Home.aspx

Family Caregiver Alliance: Services, programs, and publications for family caregivers.

http://www.caregiver.org/caregiver/jsp/home.jsp

Fourteen Friends. *The Fourteen Friends' Guide to Eldercaring: Practical Advice, Inspiration, Shared Experiences, Space for Your Thoughts.* Broadway, 2000.

Meyer, Maria M., with Paula Derr, RN. *The Comfort of Home: An Illustrated Step-by-Step Guide for Caregivers.* CareTrust Publications LLC, 1998.

National Alliance for Caregiving: A coalition of organizations focused on family caregiving, with resources and publications designed for family caregivers.

http://www.caregiving.org/pubs

National Center on Elder Abuse: Promotes understanding and action to prevent and end elder abuse, neglect, and exploitation.

http://www.ncea.org

Net of Care: Information and Resources for Caregivers: Sponsored by the Beth Israel Medical Center, offers resources, facts, and advice about caring for your loved one and yourself.

http://www.netofcare.org

Next Step in Care: Offers checklists, resources, and information for professionals and family caregivers dealing with transitions between health care settings.

http://www.nextstepincare.org

U.S. National Institute on Aging, *So Far Away: Twenty Questions for Long-Distance Caregivers.* Bethesda, MD: 2006.

http://www.nia.nih.gov/HealthInformation/Publications/LongDistance Caregiving

Children

American SIDS (Sudden Infant Death Syndrome) Institute: Focuses on research and education to understand and prevent SIDS, including a memorial page for families.

http://www.sids.org

Blueblond-Langner, Myra. *The Private Worlds of Dying Children.* Princeton, NJ: Princeton University Press, 1980.

Brain Tumor Foundation for Children, Inc.: Offers financial assistance, education, and emotional support for families whose children have brain or spinal tumors.

http://www.braintumorkids.org/web/aboutus.asp

Candlelighters Childhood Cancer Foundation: Provides information and education for children and adolescents, and their families, living with childhood cancer.

http://www.candlelighters.org

GoodGrief.org: Developed by a health care professional for people grieving many kinds of loss; includes links to other grief resources.

http://www.goodgrief.org

KidsAid.com: Online support sponsored by GriefNet.org, focused on helping children cope with grief and loss through online groups and by posting original artwork.

http://www.kidsaid.com

Kroen, William C., and Pamela Espeland. *Helping Children Cope with the Loss of a Loved One: A Guide for Grown-Ups.* Free Spirit Publishing, 1996.

McClellan-Mariano, Julie. *We Love Each Other: A Healing Journal for Grieving Children.* Trafford Publishing, 2005. For children 9 and over.

Mundy, Michaelene. *Sad Isn't Bad: A Good Grief Guidebook for Kids Dealing with Loss.* Abby Press, 1998. For children ages 4 to 8.

Schaefer, Dan, and Christine Lyons. *How Do We Tell the Children? A Step-by-Step Guide for Helping Children Two to Teen Cope When Someone Dies.* New York: Newmarket Press, 1993.

Varley, Susan. *Badger's Parting Gifts.* Lothrop, Lee & Shepard, 1984.

Counseling and Support

American Association for Geriatric Psychiatry: Membership organization for psychiatrists who specialize in working with older adults; website links to resources for patients and families. Links to its foundation, the Geriatric Mental Health Foundation, which includes an online tool to find a specialist.
http://www.aagpgpa.org
http://www.gmhfonline.org/gmhf

Billing, Nathan. *Growing Older and Wiser: Coping with Expectations, Challenges, and Change in the Later Years.* Lexington Books, 1993.

Medicare and Your Mental Health Benefits: An online booklet detailing mental health benefits for Medicare beneficiaries.
http://www.medicare.gov/publications/pubs/pdf/10184.pdf

Mental Health America: An organization devoted to advocacy and education, with online resources on coping with anxiety and depression and tools for finding support groups.
http://www.mentalhealthamerica.net

National Alliance on Mental Illness: An advocacy and education organization for people with mental illnesses, along with resources and information for people seeking help for problems with depression and anxiety.
http://www.nami.org

Dying—General Resources

End of Life: Helping with Comfort and Care, a sixty-eight-page booklet for patients and caregivers from the National Institute on Aging; order up to ten free copies or read it online.

http://www.nia.nih.gov

GrowthHouse: One of the Web's most comprehensive sites for information about death and dying, hospice and palliative care, and bereavement support, with useful reviews of resources ranging from music to books.

http://www.growthhouse.org

Brody, Jane. *Jane Brody's Guide to the Great Beyond: A Practical Primer to Help You and Your Loved Ones Prepare Medically, Legally, and Emotionally for the End of Life.* New York: Random House, 2009.

Buchwald, Art. *Too Soon to Say Goodbye.* New York: Random House, 2006.

Byock, Ira. *The Four Things that Matter Most: A Book about Living.* Free Press, 2004.

Fershleiser, Rachel and Larry Smith. *Not Quite What I Was Planning: Six-Word Memoirs by Writers Famous and Obscure.* New York: Harper Perennial, 2008.

Pausch, Randy and Jeffrey Zaslow. *The Last Lecture.* New York: Hyperion, 2008.

Funerals and Memorials

Department of Veterans Affairs: Offers information about burials and headstones for which eligible veterans may apply.

http://www.cem.va.gov/bbene/bbene.asp

Funeral Consumers Alliance: A nonprofit organization dedicated to helping consumers make informed choices to ensure a meaningful, dignified, and affordable funeral, with online and print resources.

http://www.funerals.org

FuneralPlan.com: Free online site sponsored by a casket company, with resources ranging from how to plan a funeral to how to donate a body for research.

http://www.funeralplan.com

National Funeral Directors Association: Membership organization for funeral directors; website includes links to consumer resources, including a toll-free help line for people in the midst of funeral planning.

http://www.nfda.org

National Caregivers Library: A nonprofit site created by the founder of CarMax to provide an integrated, comprehensive library of information and resources for family caregivers, including a funeral planning worksheet.

http://www.caregiverslibrary.org/Default.aspx?tabid=70#FCL6

Many private organizations and companies, including funeral homes, now offer opportunities to post online memorials about loved ones. Be sure to find out details of such a service, including privacy protections and costs, before posting tributes.

Home Health Services and Nursing Home Care

American Association of Homes and Services for the Aging: Has tips and advice on choosing a provider and locating a service.

http://www.aahsa.org

Assisted Senior Living: Comprehensive database on senior living options nationwide, including hospice care.

http://www.assistedseniorliving.net

Nursing Home Compare: Detailed information from the federal government about every nursing home in the country certified by Medicare and Medicaid.

http://www.medicare.gov/NHCompare/Include/DataSection/Questions/SearchCriteriaNEW.asp?

Hospice and Palliative Care

American Academy of Hospice and Palliative Medicine: A membership organization for physicians, with a section of the website devoted to providing information about palliative care to patients.

http://www.aahpm.org/education/patienteducation.html

Caring Connections: Sponsored by the National Hospice and Palliative Care Organization, offers information about advance care planning, caregiving, bereavement, and hospice services.

http://www.caringinfo.org/Home.htm

Dying Well: Developed by a palliative care physician, the site offers resources and links for patients, families, and professional caregivers.

http://www.dyingwell.org

Hospice Foundation of America: Includes resources to locate hospice care, along with a caregiver corner with information and ideas.

http://www.hospicefoundation.org

Hospice Net: Offers information about hospice for patients and caregivers, with an extensive question-and-answer section.

http://www.hospicenet.org

National Hospice and Palliative Care Organization: Membership organization for thousands of hospices, with links and referrals aimed at patients and families.

http://www.nhpco.org

Organ Donation

OrganDonor.gov: Website sponsored by the U.S. government with information on how to become an organ donor with basic information on what it means to be an organ donor.

http://www.organdonor.gov

Organ Procurement and Transplantation Network: Another federal website with information for people interested in becoming organ donors.

http://www.optn.transplant.hrsa.gov

Resources

Pain and Symptom Management

American Academy of Pain Medicine: The medical specialty society for pain management doctors with a link for patients to find certified physicians.
http://www.painmed.org

American Pain Foundation: An advocacy organization that features education, information, and resources on improving pain management, along with resources for patients and families.
http://www.painfoundation.org

Beth Israel Medical Center, Department of Pain Medicine and Palliative Care: An online resource from a leading medical center with resources for patients and caregivers, including special links on palliative medicine and pain management.
http://www.stoppain.org

National Pain Foundation: An organization that seeks to improve the quality of life for people living with pain, with links to resources on living with different kinds of pain.
http://www.nationalpainfoundation.org/index.php

Spiritual Concerns and Complementary Care

Albom, Mitch. *Tuesdays with Morrie.* New York: Random House, 2002.

American Self-Help Group Clearinghouse: An online searchable database of more than one thousand self-group groups, including those that help with loss and bereavement.
http://www.mentalhelp.net/selfhelp

Benson-Henry Institute for Mind-Body Health: A leader in the world of mind-body medicine, with information for outpatient services and links to a national affiliate network. Site offers resources about the "relaxation response" and tips on stress reduction and management.
http://www.massgeneral.org/bhi/about

Bullens, Cindy. *Somewhere Between Heaven and Earth.* Insightful and inspiring music from Grammy-nominated singer-songwriter Cindy Bullens, this CD is a memorial to her daughter, Jessie, who died from cancer at the age of eleven.

Kushner, Harold. *When Bad Things Happen to Good People.* New York: Schocken Books, 1981.

Remen, Naomi Rachel, M.D. *Kitchen Table Wisdom—Stories that Heal.* New York: Riverhead Books, 1996.

Schaller, James, and Sound Covenant. *The Blessings of Music:* A two-CD collection featuring Celtic harp and solo acoustic guitar, meant for compassionate listening in visits with sick loved ones. Includes a booklet with advice on how to use.
http://www.cdbaby.com

U.S. National Cancer Institute. Spirituality in Cancer Care: PDQ: An overview of the role of spirituality in the care and treatment of cancer patients.
http://www.cancer.gov/cancertopics/pdq/supportivecare/spirituality/Patient

Voces Novae. *Meditations on Life-Death:* A 2001 two-CD collection from an amateur chamber choir meant to bring comfort to the bedside.
http://www.cdbaby.com

II. Conditions and diseases

Alzheimer's and Other Dementias

Alzheimer's Association: A national voluntary organization that focuses on education, information, referral, and support for patients and their families, with local chapters that offer support groups and special services.
http://www.alz.org

Alzheimer's Disease Education and Referral Center: Sponsored by the federal government with information about the disease for patients and families, including links to resources for caregivers.
http://www.nia.nih.gov/Alzheimers

Mace, Nancy L. and Peter V. Rabins. *The 36-Hour Day: A Guide to Caring for Persons with Alzheimer's Disease, Related Dementing Illnesses and Memory*

Loss in Later Years, 4th edition. Baltimore: Johns Hopkins University Press, 2006.

Radin, Lisa and Gary Radin, eds. *What If It's Not Alzheimer's: A Caregiver's Guide to Dementia*. Prometheus Books, 2003.

Cancer

American Brain Tumor Association: National organization that offers help and support to patients and families.
http://www.abta.org

American Cancer Society: A national voluntary organization that focuses on research, education, advocacy, and service, with local chapters available to patients and families nationwide. Also supports the Cancer Survivors Network.
http://www.cancer.org

CancerBackup and Macmillan Cancer Support: Organization based in the United Kingdom that provides pratical, medical, emotional, and financial support to people living with cancer.
http://www.macmillan.org.uk/Home.aspx

Cancer Care, Inc.: A national organization that services patients and families through counseling, support groups, and educational programs, including online support groups.
http://www.cancercare.org

Cancer Information Service: Sponsored by the National Cancer Institute to provide patients and families with the latest and most accurate cancer information, including a toll-free helpline and live chat for online support. Also offers links to regional information centers.
http://www.cancer.gov/aboutnci/cis

Livestrong: The Lance Armstrong Foundation: An international resource for people living with and affected by cancer, including an online treatment decision tool. Also supports The Wellness Community, a network of community-based programs that provide support, education, and hope for patients and families after cancer treatment.
http://www.livestrong.org

Chronic Heart or Lung Disease

American Heart Association: Information and resources about heart disease for patients and families; also includes extensive information for patients and families coping with stroke.

   http://www.heart.org/HEARTORG

American Lung Association: Information, resources, and support for people living with lung disease, along with an online memorial wall for tributes to those who have died.

   http://www.lungusa.org

Center to Improve Care of the Dying. *Living with Congestive Heart Failure and Living with Chronic Obstructive Pulmonary Disease.* Two online manuals with details on how best to cope with issues specific to each of these diseases.

   http://www.mywhatever.com/cifwriter/library/chfcopd/index.html

Stanford Self-Management Programs: Workshops in English and Spanish on self-management for a variety of chronic diseases, with an online tool to find programs by state.

   http://patienteducation.stanford.edu/organ/cdsites.html

Diabetes

American Diabetes Association: This organization, with its local chapters, provides educational materials, support services, information, and referral aimed at improving the lives of persons with diabetes.

   http://www.diabetes.org

Frailty of Old Age

Meals on Wheels Council, Inc.: A volunteer program that provides one hot meal and a light supper once each day, five days a week, to the homebound. Weekend delivery is available in some locations. Fees vary; contact your local agency (check the listing in your local Yellow Pages) for more information or for meals to serve the frail elderly.

Resources

261

Volunteers of America: A community-based organization that offers a variety of client services for those most in need.

http://www.voa.org

HIV/AIDS

HIV-AIDS Treatment Information Service. Information resource on federally approved treatments for HIV infection. Distributes treatment-related publications.

http://www.hivatis.org

National Association of People with AIDS: This organization serves as a national information and resource base.

http://www.napwa.org

The Body: A Multimedia AIDS And HIV Information Resource: An Internet site that allows you to connect with others, find where to get help, and obtain useful information about HIV and AIDS.

http://www.thebody.com

Kidney Disease

National Kidney Foundation: Among its many goals, the foundation strives to improve the health and well-being of individuals affected by kidney diseases and to educate the public.

http://www.kidney.org

National Kidney and Urologic Diseases Information Clearinghouse: The clearinghouse provides information about diseases of the kidney and urologic system.

http://www.niddk.nih.gov

Liver Disease

American Liver Foundation: At a small cost, pamphlets and information can be mailed to you. Their Website has information, as well as links to other sites with liver information.

http://www.liverfoundation.org

Neuromuscular Disease

The Amyotrophic Lateral Sclerosis Association (Lou Gehrig's Disease): A national voluntary organization focused on patient support, education, and information dissemination.

http://www.alsa.org

The Muscular Dystrophy Association National Headquarters: The Association provides support services, an information hotline, and educational materials.

http://www.mdausa.org

The National Multiple Sclerosis Society: The organization provides information and referral, counseling and self-help groups, special activities and programs, and written materials.

http://www.nmss.org

Parkinson's Disease

American Parkinson's Disease Association: A voluntary organization that provides patient education, support services, and written materials.

http://www.apdaparkinson.com

Duvoisin, Roger C. *Parkinson's Disease: A Guide for Patient and Family.* New York: Raven Press, 1996.

United Parkinson Foundation: An international organization that provides extensive information and referral service, patient and family education materials and programs, and support services.

upf_itf@msn.com

Stroke

National Stroke Association: This national organization is dedicated to prevention, treatment, research, and rehabilitation and provides a variety of services for stroke survivors and their families.

http://www.stroke.org

Stroke Connection of the American Heart Association: Offers information packages ranging from prevention to caregiving. Also maintains a list of more than one thousand stroke support groups around the country for referral to stroke survivors, their families, caregivers, and interested professionals. Also publishes Stroke Connection magazine, a forum for stroke survivors and their families to share information about coping with stroke.

http://www.heart.org/HEARTORG

III. General information and resources for reform

AARP: A consumer organization that provides a number of services and information with a focus on improving the quality of life for older persons. Services include counseling groups, advocacy, educational materials, information, and assistance to the homebound.

http://www.aarp.org

Assisted Living Federation of America: This organization provides a listing of member-assisted living organizations.

http://www.alfa.org

Compassion in Dying: This organization and its affiliates offer information and emotional support for all end-of-life options, including intensive pain management comfort or hospice care, and humane, effective aid in dying for those who are in the final stages of illness and whose suffering has become intolerable.

http://www.CompassionInDying.org

Growth House: An award-winning website providing resources on life-threatening illness and end-of-life issues ranging from hospice care and pain management to grief and bereavement. Their own online search engine offers quick access to a comprehensive collection of information and issue-specific Internet links. Also available are a chat room and an online bookstore.

http://www.growthhouse.org

Healthfinder: A health and human services information website. Can guide you to online publications, clearinghouses, databases, other websites, and support and self-help groups. Government agencies and not-for-profit organizations that have been found to provide reliable information are also listed in this website.

http://www.healthfinder.gov

The End of Life: Exploring Death in America: National Public Radio program.

http://www.npr.org/programs/death/readings/essays/gartan.html

Albom, Mitch. *Tuesdays with Morrie: An Old Man, a Young Man, and the Last Great Lesson.* New York: Doubleday, 1997.

Byock, Ira. *Dying Well: A Prospect for Growth at the End of Life.* New York: Riverhead Books, 1997.

Doka, Kenneth J. *Living with Life-Threatening Illness: A Guide for Patients, Their Families, and Caregivers.* Lexington Books, April 1993.

Lynn, Joanne. *Sick to Death and Not Going to Take it Anymore!.* Berkeley: University of California Press, 2004. A guide for policy reform for those who know how the care system could be better.

Miller, James E. *When You Know You're Dying: Twelve Thoughts to Guide You Through the Days Ahead.* Willowgreen Publishing, 1997.

Nuland, Sherwin B. *How We Die: Reflections on Life's Final Chapter.* New York: Knopf, 1994. The author has used his experience and knowledge to explore the meaning of death. His approach is straightforward and personalized. Included are the author's insights and recommendations.

Quill, Timothy, M.D. *A Midwife through the Dying Process.* Baltimore: John Hopkins University Press, 1996. Dr. Timothy Quill examines the partnership and the complex end-of-life issues that surround physician-assisted death, demonstrating the tension inherent between the fight for life and the mandate to relieve suffering.

The Task Force to Improve the Care of Terminally-Ill Oregonians. *The Oregon Death with Dignity Act: A Guidebook for Health Care Providers.* Portland, OR: OHSU Center for Ethics in Health Care, 1998. For an order form, write to:

OHSU Center for Ethics in Health Care
3181 SW Sam Jackson Park Road
Portland, OR 97201

Seakwood, John (Producer/Director). *Walk Me to the Water: Three People in Their Time of Dying.* (Video.) An award-winning program that portrays

Resources

265

the special needs and insights of the dying and their families. For additional information contact:

"Walk Me to the Water"
100 Bird Road
PO Box 55
Lebanon, NY 12125
518-794-8081

Acknowledgments

Introduction

Carol Guzy, *The Washington Post*, Getty Images, p. xv.

By William Carlos Williams, from *The Collected Poems: Volume II, 1939–1962*, copyright ©1944 by William Carlos Williams. Reprinted by permission of New Directions Publishing Corp, p. xvi.

Walt Whitman, from *Whitman: Leaves of Grass*. New York: First Vintage Books, 1992, p. xvii.

Art Buchwald. "Having a High Time Where You'd Least Expect It." *The Washington Post*. 7 March 2006, p. xviii.

Dana Jennings. "Time Is a Trickster When Cancer Runs the Clock." *The New York Times*. 9 March 2009, p. xviii.

Raul Mustelier, cancer patient a few months before his death, p. xix.

Chapter 1

Photo by Joan Harrold (Hospice of Northern Virginia), p. 2 and 13.

Benjamin Spock and Michael B. Rothenberg. *Dr. Spock's Baby and Child Care*. New York: Simon and Schuster Inc., 1992, p. 3.

Sarah L. Delany with Amy Hearth, *On My Own at 107: Reflections on Life without Bessie*. New York: Harper Collins Publishers, 1997, p. 4.

Adapted from *Dying Well: The Prospect for Growth at the End of Life*, by Ira Byock. New York: Riverhead Books, 1997, p. 6.

Photo by Barry Lynn, p. 7.

Patient with a serious illness, Hospice of Northern Virginia; Joan Harrold, MD, p. 8

Hospice patient who died one hour later; Richard J. Smith, MD, p. 10.

Used with permission by On Lok Senior Health Services, San Francisco, CA, p. 10.

Henry David Thoreau, p. 11.

Elizabeth Alexander, "Praise Song for the Day," from *Crave Radiance*. Minneapolis: Graywolf Press, 2010. Used with permission, p. 12.

Chapter 2

Photo by Joan M. Teno. Used with permission, p. 15 and 26.

Thomas Mann. *The Magic Mountain*. New York: Alfred A. Knopf, Inc., 1955, p. 16.

Photo courtesy of shutterstock.com, p. 17.

Photo by Rob Crandall (Arlington, VA). Used with permission, p. 19.

"Mother and Daughter." Photo by Sandra Bertman. Palliative Care Project, National Center for Death Education/159 Ward Street Studio, Newton, MA. Used with permission, p. 20.

Rebecca Brown. *The Gifts of the Body*. New York: Harper Perennial Library, 1995, p. 19.

Grateful acknowledgment is made to Mayapple Press for use of the poem "Surgery," which appeared in *Harmless* in 2010, copyright Myra Sklarew, p. 19.

Alan Marks, as quoted in *The Washington Post*, "The Life of the Party: Dying Stockbroker Alan Marks Is Guest of Honor at His Wake." February 16, 1998: D1, p. 25.

Mitch Albom. *Tuesdays with Morrie: An Old Man, a Young Man, and Life's Greatest Lesson*. New York: Doubleday, 1997, p. 27.

Chapter 3

Photo courtesy of istockphoto.com, p. 28 and 39.

Steven A. Schmidt. "When You Come Into My Room." *Journal of the American Medical Association* 1996; 276: 512. Copyright © 1996, American Medical Association. All rights reserved. Used with permission, p. 28.

Used with permission of Gara LaMarche, Director of the U.S. Programs of the Open Society Institute, New York, NY, p. 29.

Photo courtesy of shutterstock.com, p. 30

Used with permission of Rabbi Kenneth L. Cohen, Bethesda, MD, p. 31.

Mother Julian of Norwich, in *Dying: A Book of Comfort*, Pat McNees, editor. New York: Grand Central Publishing, 1998, p. 32.

Reverend Patrick McCoy, Director of Chaplaincy, Dartmouth-Hitchcock Medical Center, Lebanon, NH. Dr. Thomas Smith, Executive Director, National Institute for Healthcare Research, Rockville, MD, p. 36–37.

Ellen Glasgow. *Barren Ground*. New York: Houghton Mifflin Harcourt, 1985, p. 37.

Anonymous. Beth Baker, "The Faith Factor." *Common Boundary Magazine*, July/August 1997, p. 20–26, p. 40.

Chapter 4

"Meredith Rose helps her great-grandmother Mary walk across the yard." Photo by Janice Lynch Schuster, p. 42 and 53.

Robert J. Samuelson, "Death With Common Sense." *Washington Post*, Wednesday, July 19, 1995; pg. A21, p. 42.

Denise Brown from www.caregiving.com, p. 43–44.

"Daughter of a Cancer Patient, Video Vignette Trigger Tapes." Palliative Care Project, National Center for Death Education/159 Ward Street Studio, Newton, MA. Used with permission, p. 45.

Wallace Stegner. *Crossing to Safety*. New York: Random House; 1987, p. 46.

Photo by Elizabeth Menkin, MD. Used with permission, p. 48.

Photo by Joanne Lynn at the Washington Home, p. 50.

Rosalynn Carter & Susan K. Golant. *Helping Yourself Help Others: A Book for Caregivers*. New York: Times Books, 1996, p. 51.

Thomas Ponton, "A Lesson Before Dying, From Mother to Son." *Washington Post*, Sunday, May 10, 2009, p. 52.

Chapter 5

Photo by Thomas Treuter, used with permission from Hospice of Michigan, p. 54 and 65.

Robert Stinson, from *The Long Dying of Baby Andrew* by Robert & Peggy Stinson. Boston: Little, Brown and Company, 1983, p. 54.

Photo by Joanne Lynn at the Washington Home, p. 55.

Photo courtesy of the Program of Medical Humanities, UMASS Medical Center, Worcester, MA. Used with permission, p. 59.

Sherwin B. Nuland. *How We Die: Reflections on Life's Final Chapter*. New York: Alfred A. Knopf, Inc., 1994, p. 62.

Used with permission by On Lok Senior Health Services, San Francisco, CA, p. 64.

Chapter 6

Photo Courtesy of the DANA Project, Bertman Archives, 159 Ward Street Studio, Newton, MA. Used with permission, p. 69 and 78.

"Found," by Jamie Brown. Used with permission, p. 70.

Photo courtesy of Altarum Institute, p. 71.

National Institute on Aging. *Talking with your Doctor: A Guide for Older People*. December 1994, p. 74.

Photo Courtesy of the Bertman Archives, 159 Ward Street Studio, Newton, MA. Used with permission, p. 78.

Photo courtesy of Altarum Institute, p. 79.

Photo courtesy of shutterstock.com, p. 81.

Photo by Sandra L. Bertman, from *Facing Death: Images, Insights, and Interventions*. Bristol, PA: Taylor & Francis 1991, p. 83.

"Patient and Doctor." Photo courtesy of the Bertman Archives, 159 Ward Street Studio, Newton, MA. Used with permission, p. 84.

Chapter 7

Photo by Joanne Lynn at the Washington Home, p. 87 and 98.

By William Carlos Williams, from *The Collected Poems: Volume 1, 1909–1939*, copyright ©1938 by New Directions Publishing Corp. Reprinted by permission of New Directions Publishing Corp, p. 87.

A. Jacox, D.B. Carr, R. Payne, et al. *Management of Cancer Pain. Clinical Practice Guideline* No. 9. AHCPR Publication No. 94-0592. Rockville, MD. Agency for Health Care Research and Quality, U.S. Department of Health and Human Services, Public Health Service, March 1994, p. 88.

Reynolds Price. *A Whole New Life: An Illness and a Healing*. New York: Atheneum, 1994, p. 97.

Charles Frazier. *Cold Mountain*. New York: Atlantic Monthly Press, 1997, p. 99.

Photo by Joanne Lynn at the Washington Home, p. 102.

Paul Wilkes, "Dying Well is the Best Revenge." *The New York Times Magazine*, July 6, 1997; pp. 32–38, p. 103.

Archie Cochrane. One Man's Medicine: An Autobiography of Professor Archie Cochrane. *British Medical Journal*, 1989, p. 105.

Photo by George Gryzenia, used with permission of Hospice of Michigan, p. 107.

Chapter 8

Photo by Joanne Lynn, p. 109 and 118.

Helen Keller, p. 109.

Tim Brookes. *Catching my Breath: An Asthmatic Explores His Illness*. New York: Vintage Books, 1995, p. 110.

Photo by Sandra L. Bertman, from *Facing Death: Images, Insights, and Interventions*. Bristol, PA: Taylor & Francis 1991, p. 111.

A Handbook for Hospice Families: When Comfort is the Focus. Hospice of Lancaster County, p. 113.

Photo courtesy of Altarum Institute, p. 120.

Chapter 9

Photo by Joanne Lynn at the Washington Home, p. 121 and 125.

Dody Shall, 7 year breast cancer survivor, Texas. From Shirley M. Gullo's *Silver Linings: The Other Side of Cancer*. Pittsburgh, PA: Oncology Nursing Press, Inc., 1997, p. 121.

Bob Greene, "Commentary: A Mother's Day we didn't expect." http://articles.cnn.com/2009-05-10/living/greene.mothers.day_1_extratime-mother-s-day-reading-new-books?_s=PM:LIVING . May 10, 2009, p. 121.

Peter Siegenthaler (ed). *Emily Dickinson: Collected Poems*. Philadelphia: Courage Books, 1991, p. 124.

Janice Lynch Schuster, "My Father Breathes." Published in *Poet Lore*, April 2011. Used with permission, p. 128.

Photo courtesy of Margaret Campbell, Detroit, MI, p. 129.

William Shakespeare, *King Richard II*; Act ii Sc. 1, p. 129.

Bob Greene, "Commentary: A Mother's Day we didn't expect." http://articles.cnn.com/2009-05-10/living/greene.mothers.day_1_extratime-mother-s-day-reading-new-books?_s=PM:LIVING . May 10, 2009, p. 129.

Photo courtesy of shutterstock.com, p. 132.

Photo courtesy of shutterstock.com, p. 133.

S. Haywood, from Mark Rosenberg's *Patients: The Experience of Illness*. Copyright W.B. Saunders Publishing (Elsevier), 1980, p. 134.

Photo courtesy of Margaret Campbell, Detroit, MI, p. 136.

Photo Courtesy of the Bertman Archives, 159 Ward Street Studio, Newton, MA. Used with permission, p. 137.

R. Bergin. *Anthony Perkins: A Haunted Life*. London: Little Brown & Co., 1995, p. 139.

Photo courtesy of shutterstock.com, p. 139.

Photo courtesy of T.J. Keay, MD, MA-Th. Photograph by Anita S. Frankenberg, p. 143.

James and Hilde Lindemann Nelson. *Alzheimer's: Answers to Hard Questions for Families*. New York: Doubleday, 1996, p. 144.

Photo by Michael Geissinger. Used with permission, p. 145.

Thomas Jefferson, from a letter to John Adams, July 5, 1814, p. 147.

Chapter 10

Photo by Joan M. Teno. Used with permission, p. 150 and 159.

Jane Kenyon, excerpt from "Otherwise" from *Collected Poems*. Copyright © 2005 by The Estate of Jane Kenyon. Reprinted with the permission of Graywolf Press, Minneapolis, Minnesota, www.graywolfpress.org, p. 150.

Photo Courtesy of shuttershock.com, p. 151.

"Resident." Photo by Sandra Bertman. Used with permission of Riverside Health Care Center, Missoula, MT, p. 152.

The Community Conversations on Compassionate Care: An Advance Care Planning Program, developed by the Community-wide End-of-Life/ Palliative Care Initiative and Excellus Blue Cross Blue Shield, p. 153.

Vermont Ethics Network. *Taking Steps: To Plan for Critical Health Care Decisions*. Montpelier, VT: Leahy Press, 1995, p. 154.

The Community Conversations on Compassionate Care: An Advance Care Planning Program, developed by the Community-wide End-of-Life/ Palliative Care Initiative and Excellus Blue Cross Blue Shield, p. 157.

Photo courtesy of shutterstock.com, p. 159.

Photo courtesy of shutterstock.com, p. 163.

Chapter 11

Photo by Joanne Lynn at the Washington Home, p. 167 and 169.

"My Death", from *Where Water Comes Together with Other Water* by Raymond Carver, copyright © 1984, 1985 by Raymond Carver. Used by permission of Random House, Inc, p. 167.

Michael Vitez. *Final Choices: Seeking the Good Death*. Philadelphia: Camino Books, Inc. 1998, p. 168.

Peggy Stinson, from *The Long Dying of Baby Andrew* by Robert & Peggy Stinson. Boston: Little, Brown and Company, 1983, p. 174.

William Shakespeare, *Julius Caesar*, p. 175.

"David N. Borkum: The Dignity is the Choice." Photo by Sandra Bertman. Palliative Care Project, National Center for Death Education/159 Ward Street Studio, Newton, MA. Used with permission, p. 177.

Chapter 12

Photo by David Terbush, p. 179 and 184.

Rand Richards Cooper. The Dignity of Helplessness. *Commonweal* 1996; 123: 12–14, p. 179.

"My Death", from *Where Water Comes Together with Other Water* by Raymond Carver, copyright © 1984, 1985 by Raymond Carver. Used by permission of Random House, Inc, p. 184.

Photo courtesy of the Program of Medical Humanities, UMASS Medical Center, Worcester, MA. Used with permission, p. 185.

Joanne Lynn. "Travel in the Valley of the Shadow." *Empathy and Practice of Medicine*. (Howard Curnen, Enid Peschel and Deborah St. James, eds). New Haven: Yale University Press, 1993, p. 188.

Chapter 13

Photo by Sandra L. Bertman, from *Facing Death: Images, Insights, and Interventions*. Bristol, PA: Taylor & Francis 1991, p. 190 and 203.

Peter Siegenthaler (ed). *Emily Dickinson: Collected Poems*. Philadelphia: Courage Books, 1991, p. 190.

Helen Chen, "Reflections in the Dusk." Translated by her husband, Myles Chen. Used with permission, p. 191.

"The Death of a Good Old Man," from *The Grave* by Robert Blair. Used with permission of the Clendening History of Medicine Library, Department of History and Philosophy of Medicine, University of Kansas School of Medicine, p. 193.

"Go Gentle". Copyright © 1975 by Linda Pastan, from *Carnival Evening: New and Selected Pomes 1968-1988 by Linda Pastan*. Used by permission of W.W. Norton & Company, Inc, p. 192.

Nathaniel Hawthorne. *The American Notebooks*. Claude M. Simpson, (ed), Ohio State University Press, 1972, p. 194.

Sarah L. Delany with Amy Hill Hearth. *On My Own at 107: Reflections on Life Without Bessie*. New York: HarperCollins Publishers, 1997, p. 195.

Leo Tolstoy. *The Death of Ivan Ilyich*. New York: Bantam Books, 1987, p. 194.

"Helping Children Cope." Project on Loss and Grief/Charitable Trust, Bertman Archives, 159 Ward Street Studio, Newton, MA. Used with permission, p. 200.

Photo Courtesy of the Bertman Archives, 159 Ward Street Studio, Newton, MA. Used with permission, p. 201.

Peter Siegenthaler (ed). *Emily Dickinson: Collected Poems*. Philadelphia: Courage Books, 1991, p. 199 and 202.

Chapter 14

Photo by Thomas Treuter, used with permission from Hospice of Michigan, p. 205 and 214.

Peggy Stinson, from *The Long Dying of Baby Andrew* by Robert & Peggy Stinson. Boston: Little, Brown and Company, 1983, p. 205.

Dr. Seuss. *Horton Hears a Who*. New York: Random House, 1956, p. 206.

Henry David Thoreau, from a letter to Ralph Waldo Emerson, March 11, 1842, in Harding and Bode's *The Correspondence of Henry David Thoreau*. New York: New York University Press, 1958, p. 207.

Photo by Richard J. Smith, MD, p. 209.

Photo by Brenda Eng, from Sandra Bertman (ed). *Grief and the Healing Arts: Creativity as Therapy*. Courtesy of Baywood Publishing Co., Amityville, NY, 1998, p. 211.

Photo by Chuck Kidd. Barre Rd. Gilbertville, MA. UMASS Medical Center, Program of Medical Humanities, p. 212.

"Children, Families and Death." Project/Charitable Trust. Photo Courtesy of the Bertman Archives, 159 Ward Street Studio, Newton, MA. Used with permission, p. 214.

Chapter 15

Photo courtesy of istockphoto.com, p. 217 and 221.

Madeleine L'Engle. *A Severed Wasp*. New York: Farrar, Straus, Giroux, 1982, p. 217.

Dr. Billy Graham. Prayer Service, Oklahoma City. In: *Requiem for the Heartland: The Oklahoma City Bombing*. San Francisco: Collins Publishers, 1995, p. 218.

Photo courtesy of istockphoto.com, p. 219

Chapter 16

Photo by Joanne Lynn at the Washington Home, p. 226 and 240.

C.S. Lewis, *A Grief Observed*. San Francisco: Harper & Row, Publishers, 1961, p. 226.

Janice Lynch Schuster from "When Numbers Breathe," p. 227.

Anton Chekhov. *Misery*. Copyright 1972 by Macmillan Company, p. 228.

Photo by Joan M. Teno. Used with permission, p. 230.

"In loving memory of John Gordon Hamilton, 'Gordie,'" written by Gordon Hamilton for his funeral mass, p. 232.

Photo courtesy of Kathy Vargas: *San Antonio AIDS Foundation: Sharon and Robert Rupp in Their Garden, 1995*. Used with permission, p. 236.

Peter Siegenthaler (ed). *Emily Dickinson: Collected Poems*. Philadelphia: Courage Books, 1991, p. 238.

"Louisa." Photo by Sandra Bertman. Bertman Archives, 159 Ward Street Studio, Newton, MA. Used with permission, p. 239.

Photo by Joanne Lynn, p. 240.

Used with permission of Jody Bolz, p. 241.

"The Sweater." Written by Donna Peratino, in memory of her father, p. 242.

Chapter 17

Photo courtesy of Altarum Institute, p. 244 and 247.

Mitch Albom. *Tuesdays with Morrie: An Old Man, a Young Man, and Life's Greatest Lesson*. New York: Doubleday, 1997, p. 244.

"Dead," by Nicholas Guy Lynn, p. 245.

Index

Guilt, 9, 19, 46, 102, 141, 181, 183, 210,
219, 221, 222, 227, 232, 243
over suicide, 221

Hallucinations, in kidney failure, 135
Hastening death, 179–89. *See also*
Death; Dying
Hawthorne, Nathaniel, 194, 275
Haywood, S., 134, 272
Health care proxy, 151–56. *See also*
Advance directives
definition, 156
Health care system, 54–56, 58, 61–67
Healthfinder, 122, 264
Heart disease, 17, 105, 111, 147, 222
dying from, 124–27
resources about chronic, 261
Heat, as pain relief, 106. *See also* Pain
Heel protectors, 117
Help(s)
accepting support, 234
for caregivers, 50
creativity, 234
dreams, 234
in home, 57–58
how to find, 55–56
nature, 234
other people, 234
rest and sleep, 234
routines, 234
solitude, 234
time, 234
Hemodialysis. *See* Dialysis
History of dying, 8–9
HIV/AIDS, 138–41
and adult day care, 66
bereavement for, 140
caregivers, and universal precautions,
139–40

death certificates for, 140
resources about, 262
treatment for, 140–41
Home health services, 64–65, 246
in lung disease 131
resources about, 256
Hope
redefinition, 62
Hospice, 62–63, 180, 194,
195, 230
and caregivers, 51
and bereavement, 233
for children, 213
for heart disease, 126
for kidney failure, 136
for lung disease, 133, 134
resources about, 257
Hospital(s/ization), 61
for children, 215
decisions on, 6
in dementia, 144
in liver failure, 138
Hotline, Medicare, 251
Hydromorphone, 93, 97, 110
Hypercapnia, 131
Hypertension, 147, 148, 181
Hypnosis, and pain relief, 106.
See also Pain
Hypoxia, 131, 173. *See also* Shortness of
breath

Ibuprofen, 92, 93, 98
Imagery *See* Guided imagery
Implanted defibrillator (ICD), 127
Incident pain, 91. *See also* Pain
medication for, 100.
Independence, 47, 228
maintaining, 145
Infants, seriously ill, 206–8

Nonsteroidal anti-inflammatory drugs (NSAIDs), 93. *See also* Pain; Medications
Norma's story, 15, 17, 19, 20, 26
Notes, on doctor's visit, 73, 75, 77
Nuland, Sherwin B., 62, 265, 270
Nurse, as "primary doctor," 71
Nurse practitioner, as "primary doctor," 71
Nursing home(s)
    as care setting, 63–64
    need for, 48
Nursing home care
    resources about, 256

Obituary
    information in, 199–200
    in newspapers, 198
Obstructive lung disease. *See* Chronic obstructive pulmonary disease (COPD)
One Man's Medicine (Cochrane), 105, 271
Opioids
    common, 93
    continuing near death, 191–92
    doses of, 98–99
    for pain control, not assisted suicide, 185
    safety of, 94, 101–2
    schedule of, 97
    and shortness of breath, 110–11, 113, 134
    side effects of, 104
Oral medications for pain, 96. *See also* Pain
Oregon, physician-assisted suicide in, 184, 185–86
Organ donation, 199, 225
    resources about, 257

Osteoarthritis, 148
Osteoporosis, 148
"Otherwise" (Kenyon), 150, 273
Over-the-counter medicine(s), for pain, 92, 93–94. See also Medications; Pain medicine
Oxycodone, 93, 97, 101, 110. *See also* Pain; Opioids
Oxygen therapy
    in lung disease, 131. *See also* Chronic obstructive pulmonary disease (COPD)
    for shortness of breath, 131, 135. *See also* Shortness of breath

Pain
    alternative ways of relieving, 106
    breakthrough, 91, 97, 98, 100
    in cancer, 128
    controlling, 87–108
    description of, 91–92
    and disease activity, 99–100
    duration of, 89
    incident, 91, 100
    internal, 90
    location of, 90
    in lung disease, 131–32
    neuropathic, 90, 105, 107
    pattern of, 91
    physical, 90
    psychological, 90
    resources about, 258
    rules about management, 100–2
    severity of, 91
    types of, 89–92
    words for, 90
Pain medicine
    choosing right, 92–96
    doses of, 98–100